PTC

Social inclusion and young people: breaking down the barriers

Edited by:
Helen Colley, Philipp Boetzelen, Bryony Hoskins
and Teodora Parveva

Council of Europe Publishing

Directorate of Youth and Sport
European Youth Centre
Council of Europe
F-67075 Strasbourg Cedex

Tel: +33 (0) 3 88 41 23 00
Fax: +33 (0) 3 88 41 27 77

e-mail: youth@youth.coe.int
www.coe.int/youth

Cover design: DTP Unit, Council of Europe
Layout by the Documents and Publications Production Department (DPPD), Council of Europe

Council of Europe Publishing
F-67075 Strasbourg Cedex
http://book.coe.int

ISBN 978-92-871-6100-0

Printed at the Council of Europe

About this publication

This publication is an edited collection of articles from the research seminar on social inclusion organised in the framework of the Partnership on Youth between the Council of Europe and the European Commission. The seminar was held in Budapest in October/November 2005. A comprehensive report on this event can be found on the European Knowledge Centre for Youth Policy at www.youth-knowledge.net.

About the partnership publications on youth research:

A series of research books are produced in the framework of the partnership between the Council of Europe and the European Commission in the field of youth. These publications are the outcome of research seminars on priority topics of the partnership in the field of youth policy. The research seminars and publications aim to bring together research knowledge about the situation, needs and lifestyles of young people in Europe today in order to inform European youth policy and educational practice.

Within this context the following titles have been published by Council of Europe Publishing:

- *Resituating culture*, ISBN: 978-92-871-5396-8
- *Revisiting youth political participation*, ISBN: 978-92-871-5654-9
- *Trading up: potential and performance in non-formal learning*, ISBN: 978-92-871-5765-2
- *Charting the landscape of European youth voluntary activities*, ISBN: 978-92-871-5826-0

Planned for the year 2007:

Diversity, human rights and participation

Co-ordination Partnership on Youth:

Hans Joachim Schild

Partnership research team:

Marta Medlinska
Philipp Boetzelen

Contact details:

Council of Europe
Partnership Secretariat
NGEN
1, quai Jacoutot
F-67075 Strasbourg Cedex
France
Tel: +33 (0)3 88 41 23 00
Fax: +33 (0)3 88 41 27 77
www.coe.int/youth
www.youth-partnership.net

European Commission
Directorate General for Education
and Culture
rue de la Loi 200
B-049 Brussels
Belgium
Tel: +32 (0)2 296 20 09
Fax: +32 (0)2 299 40 38
http://ec.europa.eu/youth/index_en.html
http://europa.eu/youth/

Contents

Foreword

A few months ago I talked to a 23-year-old man in an Estonian prison. He had been in prison for five years and had another ten to go, maybe eight if he is lucky. He told me the story of the life that brought him to this place, among 1 600 other men in nine blocks.

Coming from a violent family, he started to drink vodka when he was 8, which was also the age that he started to be involved in petty crime. As he got older, he started using all kinds of drugs, and the stealing went on and became worse. School was not his thing and he dropped out. It all ended badly when one drunken night he killed a taxi driver. He was just not lucky. Born into the wrong family, in the wrong neighbourhood. Nobody took care of him. So, fifteen years in prison.

When he gets out of prison he wants to be a youth worker, and at the moment he is applying for possibilities to study in prison. However, the chance that he will keep up this motivation for the coming eight to 10 years under these living conditions is small.

Around the same time I had a talk with a young Dutch student – a motivated 19-year-old studying to be a social worker. He got kicked out of school the week before. His results were above average, but he crossed the limit of 20% absence. The reason for being absent at school was that he is the drummer in quite a successful band, and sometimes he just does not manage to come home until four in the morning from performing at a concert and then be present for the first lesson at nine. But still, by working hard and planning his time well, he manages to get good marks. Teachers recognise him as one of the most motivated and involved students at that school. Still, his absence reached 26% in recent months. When he brought his good results into the discussion, the director of the school told him that rules should be kept and exceptions cannot be made.

"Systems" do not like to question themselves. When somebody does not fit in, he or she is seen as the problem and should leave the system or change his or her behaviour according to the system. A question that Estonian society, or so many other civilizations, could have asked themselves is this: How on earth is it possible that a young kid grew up like this in our country? Where have we gone wrong when an 18-year-old boy ends up in prison for fifteen years? Why could we not include him in our society? The Dutch school could have wondered why their rules do not allow a good and motivated student to finish his studies.

Societies striving to be more inclusive need to have the courage to reflect critically on themselves. They need to be ready to replace "the fear" of those who act differently with the search for and recognition of the potential of these fellow citizens.

The contributions of researchers from all over Europe in this book explore the possibilities and challenges of becoming an inclusive Europe.

I wish you inspiring reading.

Paul Kloosterman

May 2006, Melito di Porto Salvo, Italy

1. Social inclusion and young people: breaking down the barriers

Helen Colley, Bryony Hoskins, Teodora Parveva and Philipp Boetzelen

Introduction

This book presents the key findings from a seminar organised by the European Youth Research Partnership on the theme of Social Inclusion and Young People, which took place at the European Youth Centre in Budapest in October/November 2005. The seminar brought together researchers from across Europe, with youth activists and policy representatives, in order to develop a better understanding of social exclusion for young people, and to help provide evidence about the progress of strategies to promote social inclusion. We are only able to present a selection of the papers in this book, but others focused on a wide range of topics, from the "digital divide", to living with HIV/Aids, and civic engagement around environmental issues. The full report, with recommendations from the seminar (Colley et al., 2005) and all the original papers presented there are available at the European Knowledge Centre for Youth Policy. The summary report and recommendations can be found in Appendices I and II of this book.

During the very days that the seminar was taking place, youth protests were exploding first on the streets of Paris, and then across France. In tragic scenes, young people from disadvantaged neighbourhoods protested violently night after night against their exclusion from decent education and training, decent housing, decent jobs. Only a few months earlier, similar protests had also taken place in the English Midlands. Evidence presented in the seminar – especially on the problems facing minority ethnic youth – suggests that conditions in many other communities across Europe might lead to further such unrest. A few months after the seminar, widescale protests organised among students and other youth swept through France in response to laws proposed to restrict contracts for newly hired young workers. And as this book goes to press, Hungary has also witnessed large street protests, sparked by perceptions that public information has been manipulated by politicians. All of these instances reflect a deep-seated malaise among European youth about their inclusion in society, from employment to democratic processes, which demands understanding, attention and evidence-informed responses.

In the seminar itself, concerns were raised that policies to combat social exclusion for young people have too often "hit the target, but missed the point", as Professor

Howard Williamson put it in his keynote address. In 1995, the EC's White Paper "Teaching and learning – Towards the learning society" emphasised that "social exclusion has reached such intolerable proportions that the rift between those who have knowledge and those who do not has to be narrowed" (EC, 1995, p. 30). But the recent protests – as well as considerable research evidence – indicate that there is much still to do. In particular, the youth sector, with its commitment to non-formal education and to fostering democratic participation and active citizenship, faces new opportunities and challenges, especially those presented by the Youth Pact within the Lisbon Strategy for growth and employment.

The Youth Pact initiative (CEU, 2005; EC, 2005a) is certainly the most high-profile European youth policy development to date, though it is still too early to measure its full impact. For the first time, it places priority on a "concerted, cohesive and cross-cutting policy focused on young people" (CEU, 2005, p. 3), with an emphasis on measures to integrate more young people into the labour market, including through entrepreneurship, an appeal to employers for social responsibility in supporting this goal, and recognition of other factors, such as a balance between working and family life, to promote social cohesion.

In order to address this significant shift in youth policy, this book has a rather unusual focus within the series published by the Youth Research Partnership, which has until now located much of its work in the non-formal sector. Many of the chapters here focus on more formal educational settings and, in particular, on vocational education and training (VET). But this does not mean that the book is any less relevant to youth workers, youth work trainers, or youth policy makers across Europe. On the contrary, readers from that audience may be surprised to see how strongly the research presented here draws on concepts and practices familiar to them. In particular, we want to draw attention to the way in which these studies are informed by more recent theories of learning that foreground the informal aspects of learning even within formal settings. They emphasise the importance of young people's democratic participation, and of their sense of belonging and identity, in the "communities of practice" constituted by VET programmes and workplaces, as well as other settings. There is also strong continuity with other books in the Youth Research Partnership series, in the attention paid to questions of social equity and justice, particularly with regard to gender, ethnicity, disability, and their intersection with social class. Before introducing the content of individual chapters in more detail, we first outline the policy context that forms the backdrop for their findings.

Social inclusion: the current political context

Social inclusion is one of the central goals stated in European policies, especially in relation to employment, lifelong learning and vocational guidance.

Council of Europe

In the Council of Europe, debates around social inclusion are framed by a concern to promote social cohesion. A strategy was developed by the European Committee for Social Cohesion in 2000, and was revised and adopted by the Committee of Ministers in 2004. This defined social cohesion as:

"the capacity of a society to ensure the welfare of all its members, minimising disparities and avoiding polarisation. A cohesive society is a mutually supportive com-

munity of free individuals pursuing these common goals by democratic means" (European Committee for Social Cohesion, 2004, p. 2).

This strategy draws on the European Convention on Human Rights and the revised European Social Charter, and focuses on the need for social policy to ensure access to rights. Combating social exclusion and poverty are seen as key tasks. The strategy acknowledges that this requires building a sense of solidarity and co-operation within society; and that certain groups – such as young people – are particularly vulnerable, and therefore need greater support. The responsibility for social cohesion is placed jointly on co-operation between the state, business, civil society, family and the individual. Within the youth sector, the Council of Europe has organised training courses to promote learning about human rights and the empowerment of vulnerable groups.

European Commission

The European Commission also embraces these goals, and places them increasingly in the economic context of global competitiveness. The European Council which took place in Lisbon in 2000 set a ten-year agenda to create a Europe that is:

"the most dynamic and competitive, sustainable knowledge based economy in the world capable of sustaining economic growth with more and better jobs and greater social cohesion" (CEU, 2000, p. 2).

Its goals were revised in December 2002, at the Employment, Social Policy, Heath and Consumer Affairs Council, to emphasise the need to reduce the risk of poverty, and to ensure that women and immigrants were targeted by inclusion policies. In 2005 the Lisbon Strategy itself was relaunched (EC, 2005b), with a greater emphasis placed on growth and jobs. With high employment and economic difficulties in many of the countries in Europe, employment is considered the crucial element to tackling social exclusion. Common objectives already adopted in pursuit of these goals at the European Council in Nice in December 2000 focused on:

- employment;
- access to resources, rights, goods and services;
- preventing risk of exclusion;
- helping the most vulnerable;
- the mobilisation of relevant bodies.

In response to National Action Plans to implement these common objectives, the European Commission produced a joint report on social inclusion adopted in 2004 (CEU, 2004). This formulated six key policy priorities:

- promoting investment in and tailoring of active labour market measures to meet the needs of those who have the greatest difficulties in accessing employment;
- ensuring that social protection schemes are adequate and accessible for all and that they provide effective work incentives for those who can work;
- increasing the access of the most vulnerable and those most at risk of social exclusion to decent housing, quality health and lifelong learning opportunities;
- implementing a concerted effort to prevent early school leaving and to promote smooth transitions from school to work;
- developing a focus on eliminating poverty and social exclusion among children and facilitating access to new technology;

- making a drive to reduce poverty and social exclusion of immigrants and ethnic minorities.

These national action plans were reviewed during 2005. In addition, the European Commission's White Paper "A new impetus for European youth" (EC, 2001) – the first White Paper to focus on young people – has many references to combating social exclusion in different forms, ranging from employment, education and training, and quality services, to racism and xenophobia, and the inaccessibility of new technology.

Employment, young people and social inclusion

For the Council of Europe, employment is a key issue for the social inclusion of young people, since they face particular difficulties in entering the labour market and accessing sustainable employment and social protection. These are considered important aspects of creating a socially cohesive society, so the social cohesion strategy emphasises decent employment opportunities, rather than short-term contracts or poor quality training that lead to further social exclusion. It also highlights the need to invest in human resources, and create participatory forms of social protection that lead towards employment.

On the part of the European Commission, adoption of the European Youth Pact by the European Council in March 2005 (CEU, 2005b) made young people a key part of the renewed Lisbon partnership for growth and jobs and proposed taking action for young people in the fields of employment, integration and social advancement, education and training, mobility, and reconciling family and work life. As a follow-up to the pact, the European Commission Communication on "European policies concerning youth" (CEU, 2005a) proposes concrete action, in particular with regard to employment and social inclusion: the Commission and member states should improve the situation of the most vulnerable young people by using the Social Inclusion Strategy.

Amongst other factors, strategies in the youth field link social inclusion to young people's needs for a flexible guidance and counselling system to support ongoing access to lifelong and life-wide learning, including "second-chance" opportunities. For young people in particular, guidance is supposed to help reduce non-completion rates in education and training, promote closer matches between individual and labour market needs, and expand individuals' awareness of civic and leisure opportunities as well as learning and work.

Young people, participation and social inclusion

Participation in civil society is another important factor for social cohesion. Both the Council of Europe and the European Commission youth sectors focus on active participation in civil society. This aspect of the Council of Europe's strategy focuses on participation in NGOs, voluntary work and other aspects of civil society that help bind society together and create a collective sense of belonging. The European Commission, as a follow-up to the White Paper on youth published in 2001, has set up, together with member states, a framework of European co-operation in the youth field focusing, on the one hand, on promoting young people's active citizenship and, on the other hand, on integrating young people in social and professional life.

Within the "active citizenship" strand of their co-operation, the Commission and member states focus amongst other things, on participation of all young people in democratic life and in voluntary activities. An open method of co-ordination was set up to help member states work towards common objectives on these issues. The political co-operation and policy developments in the youth field are supported by the YOUTH programme and the future YOUTH in action programme which prioritises inclusion of young people, in particular through assisting young people with fewer opportunities in participating in the European Voluntary Service (EVS) and other actions proposed by the programme.

Some questions about policy on young people and social inclusion

The role of government and European institutions in educational policy making at different levels (European, national and local) for the development and continuation of civil society, and in particular for developing individuals' competence to be active citizens, has become a point of contention in all of this. From a general perspective, there are questions as to whether the European Commission should continue to focus support on the development of civil society or rather concentrate more upon growth and jobs, leaving civil society to renew and develop by itself? If it is agreed that the civil society needs institutional support, then we need to ask: to what extent can European policy and research support and evaluate this progress? And how can this be done?

In order to understand why the above questions are important in the context of youth policy, it is necessary to reflect on the recent developments outlined above, and their impact on youth work practice. Up until 2005 and the introduction of the Youth Pact, the youth sector has focused almost exclusively on the development and continuation of civil society, with priorities across the European Commission and the Council of Europe reflecting the need for greater youth participation, more young volunteers and greater intercultural understanding. This can be seen in the European Commission's open method of co-ordination and support for the development of European-wide common objectives on topics such as participation and voluntary activities.

One of the first signs of a need for a change to this policy approach came from young people themselves, demanding better recognition of participation in non-formal learning activities for employment and education purposes. In a parallel process, youth workers and youth trainers argued for better recognition of their profession. These changes have been gradual, and often not well accepted by the established European youth community, who felt that activism and volunteering needed to remain the focus for their work rather than assisting people into employment.

However, on this occasion, the push to maintain the change in focus was from the bottom up, in particular from disadvantaged young people. These young people wanted youth work to support them to find decent jobs. What the established youth work community found difficult to realise was that, unless you come from a privileged background, it is not possible to undertake full-time voluntary work or activism without pay. Volunteers, non-governmental organisation (NGO) workers and activists have to eat, live in a home, be able to afford transport, and may need to support a family (children, partners and/or elderly parents). In order to function as an active citizen today, you need to be part of the community, and to be included in today's community, you need a job which also allows you the economic resources, time and energy to participate in these other roles. Identity – who you are in today's society – is often reflected by what occupation you have. To be unemployed has a low social status and often creates low self-esteem. In today's increasingly individualised world, it is young people themselves who tend to be blamed for unsuccessful transitions to the labour market. The need for reasonable and sustainable employment is clear, so why not simply focus now on employability?

This poses a further question, though (discussed in more detail by Helen Colley in Chapter 6): to what extent is full and sustainable employment across the whole of Europe for all young people really possible? It is unlikely that such solutions will be found quickly – there is no "magic wand". In the meantime, young people need purposeful activities and learning opportunities that do not solely focus on work as an outcome (see Howard Williamson's Chapter 2). As Beatrix Niemeyer and Andreas Walther both mention in their chapters (7 and 8), vocational education and training should offer life skills and citizenship skills along with skills related to practical work.

- Work itself is tied into civil society with issues of equality and human rights. Equal opportunities for work, sustainable contracts and number of hours and days worked are all bound to active citizenship such as membership and active participation in unions.
- One consequence of a complete switch to focus exclusively on employment ignores the importance of the work that has been carried out in the youth sector and the reasons behind it.
- If all of Europe's attention focuses on the economy and jobs who will care about our human rights and the continuation of European values? The European project, its historical development and focus on values is not simply a job creation scheme but is about European integration and peace.

This, then, is the complex policy background to the research presented in this book, and we move on now to introduce a brief overview of each chapter.

Research for a better understanding of young people and social inclusion

A key purpose of the Youth Research Partnership is to promote a better understanding of key issues facing young people and the practitioners and policy makers working to support them. This need for greater knowledge of the situation and experiences of young people in Europe was specifically highlighted in the Youth Pact. The chapters in this book contribute to this goal in a number of ways, by:

- identifying key issues about social inclusion for youth;
- presenting important empirical evidence about how social exclusion is experienced by young people;
- reporting on initiatives to promote social inclusion through training and employment, formal education, non-formal learning and multi-agency strategies;
- and offering constructive critiques of the current situation, especially in relation to groups who remain highly marginalised because of "blind spots" or unintended consequences of policy.

In Chapter 2, Howard Williamson offers a powerful overview of crucial issues, both pragmatic and theoretical, that must be addressed in confronting the much-debated topic of social exclusion. He presents a constructive framework for understanding social exclusion and developing appropriate strategies to combat it

across a wide range of different circumstances. The strength of his model is that it does not rely on a single, prescribed definition of "social exclusion", but serves to ground our understanding of it in the real experiences of young people. His questions start from the metaphor of social exclusion as a "box" in which young people are trapped, and prompt us to think about the scale of the box, differentiation within it, and the causes and consequences of entering it. Importantly, he also asks how we can build barriers to keep more young people out of the "box", and construct bridges that allow them to move beyond it. Above all, Williamson writes passionately about the human cost of social exclusion to disadvantaged young people and their communities, and warns us of the danger of social inclusion policies that may "hit the target, but miss the point".

The chapters which follow, by Siyka Kovacheva and Axel Pohl, Eldin Fahmy, and Daniel Blanch, speak directly to questions about the experience of social exclusion posed by Williamson. Each of these chapters uses a different methodology and scale of research to investigate different aspects of that experience, contributing to a fuller understanding of young people's lives.

In Chapter 3, Kovacheva and Pohl report on a thematic study of disadvantage in school-to-work transitions across 13 European countries. They present a detailed picture of the diverse ways in which the individualisation and uncertainties of youth transitions are being played out in different parts of Europe. Their findings, based on national reports, Eurostat survey data and examples of good practice in policy interventions, revealed significant problems for young people in most of these nations. Their discussion focuses on the clustering of key problems in "constellations of disadvantage" in young people's transitions from education to employment; and on the match, mismatch, or dilemmas of current policies in relation to these problems. They conclude that key factors for success involve starting from the biographical perspectives and potential for agency of young people themselves; decentralised, flexible and realistic policies to ensure access to opportunities and reduce systemic barriers to inclusion; the reflexivity of institutions dealing with young people, with attention to balanced power relations between and within them; and flexibility not just of employment conditions, but also of policy measures, to avoid the "revolving door" syndrome of repeated exclusion for young people.

Eldin Fahmy, in Chapter 4, addresses the issue of youth poverty, which he argues is often neglected in policies that focus on the disaffection and alienation of "problem" youth. He offers an innovative analysis of large-scale survey data from the European Communities Household Panel, to reveal the extent and duration of income poverty and deprivation among young Europeans. Fahmy argues that social inclusion policies and welfare regimes are too often based on assumptions from an earlier era that young people are less vulnerable to poverty than other groups, while the opposite is now true. In particular, domestic and labour market transitions represent a major factor in shaping young people's vulnerability, notwithstanding national variations. This chapter presents some other challenging findings. Fahmy's analysis of poverty as a relative (rather than absolute) measure suggests that even in more favourable contexts, such as the social democratic welfare regimes of Scandinavia, young people can find themselves in difficult circumstances of deprivation that are not adequately addressed by policy. Moreover, despite the policy focus on reducing numbers outside education, training and employment, the evidence indicates that significant numbers of students and young workers are living in poverty – a problem that remains largely unaddressed.

Chapter 5, by Daniel Blanch, presents findings from a very different type of research. Smaller scale but in-depth and fine grained, his qualitative study of social exclusion risks for young people in Galicia (a region of north-western Spain) provides a vital perspective on their experiences, perceptions and responses in the face of complex pressures. These coalesce around the tensions between living in a postmodern world of uncertainty and a local context steeped in traditional structures, in the region's distinctive political autonomy and in differentiation from the dominant Spanish culture. The resulting "negative social capital" restricts rather than enhances young people's opportunities. His research reveals the sense of powerlessness facing young people who have to rely on their families for protection in the face of unemployment, while they feel constrained by families' traditional values and beliefs that they do not share. These young people also speak of their disillusionment with conventional political participation. This evidence suggests that it is a mistake to define social exclusion too narrowly, or to see employment as the main solution, since social structures and practices also contribute to young people's marginalisation. Blanch concludes that the emancipation of young people should also be considered as a serious goal for social inclusion policies.

Having presented these rich and complementary analyses of social exclusion for young people, the rest of the book moves on to look at the effectiveness of various strategies for social inclusion, with important lessons for policy and practice. Chapter 6, by Helen Colley, offers a critical context to these chapters, by reviewing recent research that interrogates European social inclusion policies over the last fifteen years. Her chapter begins by analysing continuity and change in policies on social inclusion and young people since the early 1990s, and goes on to discuss key research findings that challenge the direction policy has taken. These pose serious questions about how the concept of "social exclusion" shapes the way we think about society; about posing employment as the primary route to social inclusion, when the labour market is riddled with inequalities; about the feasibility of the Lisbon Strategy's promise of "more and better jobs"; and about "employability" as the link between social and economic goals. Colley argues that, whilst it is often essential for researchers and practitioners to work pragmatically within the policy context (the *realpolitik*, as Williamson puts it), this too can represent a "box" in which our thinking about social inclusion can become trapped – and that we also need research which thinks "outside the box" if more substantial progress towards social justice is to be achieved. Importantly, attention needs to be devoted to the way in which education systems and businesses should be reformed to create bridges to social inclusion for young people, rather than focusing predominantly on reforming young people themselves.

Beatrix Niemeyer's chapter (7) on socially inclusive pedagogies brings this latter point to vivid life. Based on her keynote address to the Budapest seminar, she highlights the potential application of some cutting-edge learning theories for developing more effective pedagogies and more inclusive forms of vocational education and training (VET) for disadvantaged young people. By thinking about learning, even in formal contexts, as an often informal process of social participation in a learning community centred on practice, Niemeyer asks us to think about young people's sense of identity and belonging as a vital aspect of their engagement and inclusion. She analyses different models of school-to-work transition and systems of VET across Europe, and points to the strengths and weaknesses of each. Drawing on practical research to identify good practice in VET for socially excluded young people in a number of European countries, she notes that all too often policies for VET and policies for social inclusion are not coherent enough to create

much-needed synergies in practice between these two spheres. Yet the model she presents for a more socially inclusive VET should be feasible if greater coherence and synergy can be promoted, and if employers can be encouraged – particularly through the use of policy and resources at the European level – to play their part in creating opportunities to do so. Viewed in the light of previous research presented to the Youth Research Partnership on non-formal learning, Niemeyer's work presents exciting new opportunities for the youth sector. It suggests that those committed to informal and non-formal learning approaches could make a major contribution to improving VET in ways that support disadvantaged young people's engagement with it, and that such approaches should be a priority for further research and development.

Chapter 8, by Andreas Walther, continues this theme by looking at some of the contradictions between labour market integration and active citizenship that exist in current support arrangements for young people's transitions to work. The chapter presents evidence from an EU-funded study of the potentials of participation and informal learning for young people's transitions to the labour market in nine European countries. Drawing on young people's own biographical narratives, the chapter reflects on the relationship between young people's motivation, social inclusion and citizenship. It then presents case studies of exemplar projects that addressed youth transitions through participatory approaches, noting that some have had significant success, only to see this undermined by the loss of short-term funding. Walther's conclusions emphasise those made elsewhere in this book: that policy makers need to do more to involve target groups in interpreting their own needs and developing effective responses to them, in order to avoid further individualising risk and exclusion through the imposition of bureaucratic norms. Once again, the weakness of one-sided labour market activation policies, focused on remedying young people's deficits, appears to be a central problem in creating sustainable measures for social inclusion.

Bryony Hoskins, in Chapter 9, describes the early stages of an important European initiative to bring questions of active citizenship centre stage in policy development. Although not concerned solely with young people, her research project, supported by the EC in co-operation with the Council of Europe, aims to propose indicators on education and training for active citizenship, and on active citizenship in practice. Hoskins outlines why governments across Europe are increasingly interested in active citizenship; she explains why such indicators are important for the monitoring of policy at national and European levels, as well as for broader public debate on policy; and she discusses the need for sensitivity both in the specification of indicators and in the interpretation of results measured against them.

She considers particular issues about how to define active citizenship, especially in a global context where the threat of terrorism has risen to critical levels. Hoskins shows that the construction of indicators for active citizenship is therefore a complex process, but argues that, if successful, they can provide a tool for citizens themselves to monitor policy and exercise political leverage for improvement.

Throughout the seminar on social inclusion, a recurring theme was the importance of personal testimony as a form of evidence for research on disadvantage and oppression. Amineh Kakabaveh's Chapter 10 is an excellent example of such witness-bearing as a means to access lived experiences of exclusion. As a Kurdish refugee in Sweden, a social worker in migrant communities there and a campaigner for women's rights, Kakabaveh exposes the ways in which women's experiences of

exclusion are all too often overlooked when policy and practice treat particular migrant communities as undifferentiated groups. She sensitively explores the contradictions of living in a "host country" which has a very supportive welfare system, while at the same time experiencing the intensified pressures of conservative traditionalism and patriarchal social relations in a "home country" community that is in exile. The chapter also renders vivid the ways in which domestic violence against Kurdish women – a problem for native-born Swedish women also – is sensationalised by the media in ways that foster racism against this community, while at the same time presenting female victims themselves as helpless and inadequate. Most importantly, the chapter shows how Kurdish women have taken a major and successful initiative by setting up their own radio station to discuss, debate and educate themselves about key issues in their lives as a basis for asserting their citizenship and integrating into democratic society.

In Chapter 11, Anna Kende also focuses on young people's success stories rather than deficits, as a way of identifying factors which support resilience to social exclusion. She uses life-history methods of research to understand how university students from the Roma ethnic minority in Hungary have overcome serious problems of discrimination and segregation within the Hungarian school system to access higher education. Family background, experiences of prejudice and discrimination (including in education), and identity appear to be key influences on the career trajectories of Roma youth. Their strategies are complicated by those previously adopted by successful Roma in their parents' generation, who tended either to assimilate into Hungarian society by denying their Roma identity, or by accepting pressures to define themselves as a Roma elite. Kende's findings show that external interventions, either by non-governmental organisations (NGOs) or by individual teachers who were supportive, were often crucial to successful transitions in higher education. This prompts us to ask how exclusionary practices in schooling can be eliminated, and how supportive interventions can be made more accessible. These are, of course, questions that might apply to the situation of all minority ethnic youth across Europe, not only to the case of Roma youth in Hungary.

Chapter 12, by Lorna Roberts, explores issues of social inclusion and exclusion related to racist discrimination in formal schooling, and measures by the UK Government to address this by trying to increase the number of teachers from Black and minority ethnic backgrounds. She goes on to present and discuss evidence from her longitudinal study of trainee teachers making the transition to qualified teacher status. Here, as in Kende's chapter, there are tensions and dilemmas the trainees face in respect of their identities and their perceptions that they are racialised as "Other" by majority ethnic pupils, parents and colleagues. Like Kakabaveh, Roberts shows how class, race and gender intersect to multiply the sources of exclusion and position Black and minority ethnic teachers as marginal. The data she presents, analysed through the application of critical race theory, also reveals powerfully the pressures these teachers feel to "make a difference" to the degree of inclusivity in their schools, and the additional burden that the responsibility of being a role model places on their shoulders. This chapter ends by discussing the complexity of dealing with racism that is deeply ingrained in our society. Roberts argues that perhaps the focus should not be so much on expecting individual members of Black and minority ethnic communities to act as the primary agents of change, but on the "problem of whiteness", and the systems and practices which create exclusion and discrimination.

Rachel Gorman, in Chapter 13, considers problems caused by policies made without the full participation of those who are targeted by them. Her powerful analysis of the testimony of disabled artists and activists in Canada offers important lessons for practice too. These stories present a sobering picture of the ways in which well-intentioned legislation (for example, to improve disabled access to buildings) can result in counterproductive situations that marginalise and exclude disabled people further still. Her use of Marxist-feminist theory to conduct her analysis is both challenging and illuminating. Like Roberts on racism in schooling, she shows that the way we name a problem affects how we address it. Gorman offers a radically different way of conceptualising "social exclusion", arguing that it is more appropriate to think of disabled people's experiences in terms of oppression, objectification and alienation – processes which dehumanise those whom our society marginalises, as well as those who provide services for them. However, she also presents a very optimistic view, echoing that of Kakabaveh. The barriers which constitute Williamson's "box", she argues, are not inevitable or immutable obstacles for young people. They are constructed by particular practices, and shaped by relations of ruling and the interests of dominant groupings: as such, they can be dismantled, primarily by the self-organisation and activism of those who suffer oppression.

Chapter 14, by Kate Philip and colleagues, zooms out from the three previous chapters' micro-level accounts of lived experiences, to discuss the strategic effectiveness of a large and long-term project (Healthy Respect) in Scotland, using a multi-agency approach to promote social inclusion. It explores the importance of teenage sexual health as an aspect of social inclusion, and the location of these issues within a complex set of cultural and gendered practices in which young people's power to negotiate – with each other and with those who act as gatekeepers to health care – is often limited. Rigorous evaluation of initiatives to promote young people's sexual health is lacking, but the authors review the potential benefits and challenges of multi-agency partnership strategies, and go on to show how such an approach was developed within Healthy Respect. The findings of this evaluation show promise for such partnerships in facilitating professionals to share expertise, and for public agencies to work together in tandem with the voluntary sector and with local communities. However, they also reveal real tensions in multi-agency working, where established practices and values can clash, especially when a project brings taboo subjects, such as teenage sexual practices, into public policy and debate. As in Amineh Kakabaveh's account (Chapter 10), the role of the media in intervening into these debates is of some concern, as are the difficulties in ensuring that professionals actively engage young people in developing social inclusion initiatives, rather than imposing such initiatives on them.

Christiane Weis, in the final chapter (15), also presents a large-scale study, this time focusing on language issues in education that are particularly complex in Luxembourg, but which are highly relevant across Europe, given both the scale of migration and policies to promote mobility. The first part of her chapter describes the diverse composition of the population that lives and works in Luxembourg. The second section analyses how the school system copes with plurilingualism and the problems it generates, while the final part of the chapter identify strategies for sustainable improvement to the education system, in particular through the development of a language education policy agenda that furthers the social inclusion of young people. Weis' analysis is important, since it shows how multilingual contexts can provide rich opportunities for some, while (resonating with Blanch's reference to "negative social capital" in Chapter 5) for others it can trigger a "negative

career", causing some young people to find themselves inside school, but outside learning. In Luxembourg today, there are positive economic pressures to resolve these questions in order to ensure an adequately qualified workforce to compete in global markets, but school curricula have not yet adjusted to these needs. As Weis points out in her conclusion, language skills are essential for active citizenship, and commitment to their promotion for all should be an aspect of democratic policies and values.

Three key themes

While each of these chapters presents very different types of research on young people and social inclusion, from a wide variety of contexts, three key themes emerge from the collection as a whole. First, there is much that signals the need to avoid overly narrow definitions of social exclusion or social inclusion. In particular, the social and psychological aspects of exclusion should be foregrounded at least as much as the economic and employment-related aspects. This demands research, policy and practice which begin with young people's experiences and perspectives, and which ground responses to social exclusion in those experiences and perspectives. Second, it is important to have large-scale quantitative data which tell us about trends in social inclusion, but it is also essential to complement this with smaller-scale qualitative research that enable us to differentiate between diverse groups, rather than treating "the socially excluded" as a homogeneous group and assuming that, by and large, they share the same needs. All too often this erases the special vulnerability of young people. In particular, it also risks further marginalising women, ethnic minorities, and other groups who suffer multiple disadvantage. Third, attention must be paid to breaking down structural and systemic barriers to social inclusion, especially in relation to education at all levels, and to the labour market. The research presented here, as well as the actions of youth on the streets across Europe, warn of the dangers when we focus too predominantly on fixing the deficits of young people rather than challenging and changing the exclusionary practices of others, which marginalise them.

Researching with young people on issues of social inclusion

Unfortunately, the resources of a single book cannot enable us to present all of the important research that was reported at the Youth Research Partnership seminar, and we have prioritised in this collection research topics that have not been discussed previously in this series. However, we want to pay tribute here to all those researchers who work with young people to investigate social exclusion, its consequences and strategies for social inclusion. While researchers enjoy, it is true, a privileged status in comparison with these young people, they do work that confronts them, day in and day out, with the realities of disadvantage that have a deep emotional impact. Researchers in this field tend to be passionately committed to social justice, and at the seminar, there were times when frustration with the slow pace of change was palpable. This led us to reflect very soberly on the need to equip researchers to engage effectively in dialogue with policy makers, and vice versa.

It also leads us to express our thanks here to our kind host for the seminar, Antje Rothemund, Director of the European Youth Centre in Budapest, and all the team who work there. Antje welcomed the participants to the seminar, and offered us a very beautiful and peaceful environment in which to conduct our discussions, which contributed greatly to the sense of positive engagement and collaboration that predominated. Hans-Joachim Schild, of the Council of Europe Directorate of

Youth and Sport, was also very supportive in the preparation of the seminar and throughout the event, bringing to these tasks his many years of experience in this field and great encouragement to our work. And as the lead editor, Helen Colley expresses her thanks to Bryony Hoskins, Philipp Boetzelen and Teodora Parveva for their support in editing this collection, and to Bryony and Philipp also for their unflagging help in organising the seminar.

Our hope is that this book will contribute to ongoing dialogue and action about and (most importantly) with young people in Europe, in ways that tangibly break down the barriers to social inclusion.

References

Colley, H., Hoskins, B., Parveva, T. and Boetzelen, P. (2005), "Social inclusion and young people: report of a research seminar 31 October-2 November" (online). Strasbourg: Council of Europe and European Commission Youth Research Partnership (accessed 2 October). Available at:
www.youth-knowedge.net/system/galleries/download/research_reports/2005_social_inclusion_report.pdf.

Council of the European Union (CEU) (2000), "Presidency conclusions, Lisbon, 23 and 24 March" (online). Brussels: Council of the European Union (accessed 14 June 2006). Available at:
www.bologna-berlin2003.de/pdf/PRESIDENCY_CONCLUSIONS_Lissabon.pdf.

CEU (2004), "Joint report by the Commission and the Council on social inclusion" (online). Brussels: Council of the European Union (accessed 14 June 2006). Available at:
http://ec.europa.eu/employment_social/soc-prot/soc-incl/final_joint_inclusion_report_2003_en.pdf.

CEU (2005a), "Council conclusions on youth in the framework of the mid-term review of the Lisbon Strategy". Brussels: Council of the European Union (accessed 14 June 2006). Available at:
http://ec.europa.eu/youth/whitepaper/download/st06609-re01_en.pdf.

European Commission (EC) (1995), "Teaching and learning – Towards the learning society", COM (95) 590 final (online). Brussels: Commission of the European Communities (accessed 26 September 2006). Available at:
http://aei.pitt.edu/1132/01/education_train_wp_COM_95_590.pdf.

EC (2001), "A new impetus for European youth". Brussels: Commission of the European Communities.

EC (2005a), "Working together for growth and jobs: a new start for the Lisbon Strategy". Brussels: Commission of the European Communities.

EC (2005b), "Communication from the Commission to the Council on European policies concerning youth: addressing the concerns of young people in Europe – Implementing the European Youth Pact and promoting active citizenship". Brussels: Commission of the European Communities (accessed 14 June 2006). Available at:
http://ec.europa.eu/youth/whitepaper/post-launch/com_206_en.pdf.

European Committee for Social Cohesion (2004), "Revised Strategy for Social Cohesion" (online). Strasbourg: Council of Europe (accessed 26 September 2006). Available at:
www.coe.int/T/E/social_cohesion/social_policies/Revised_Strategy.pdf.

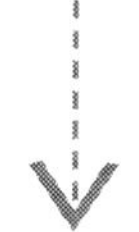

2. Social exclusion and young people: some introductory remarks

Howard Williamson

Preface

> "Throughout the world today, metropolitan areas are filled with people who match the profile of the rebels in France: poor, jobless, socially marginalised and defined as 'different' – and therefore angry. If they are teenagers they have the energy to rebel, and lack even the minimal family responsibilities that might restrain them. Furthermore, the anger is reciprocated. Those in the more comfortable majority fear these young people precisely for the characteristics they have. The better-off feel that the poor youths tend to be lawless and, well, 'different'. So many of the better-off (but perhaps not all) tend to endorse strong measures to contain these rebellions, including total exclusion from the society, even from the country" (Wallerstein, 2005).

These words were written almost one month after the Budapest seminar and they reflect the "harder" edge of the softer debate that had hitherto informed discussion of social and political concerns about the social exclusion of young people. A reactionary and punitive response, juxtaposed against more visible and active "rebellion" by excluded young people (not just in France, but also recently in the English Midlands), lies just below the surface of a reasoned, more liberal and progressive approach to addressing such concerns. Indeed, in the English press, Shaun Bailey (see Bailey, 2005) – a young black graduate and community activist from the "wrong side of the tracks" – was apparently confirming the need to accept the existence of a distinctive "underclass", first mooted well over a decade ago by the American sociologist Charles Murray (1984, 1990), and to respond accordingly. That response, Bailey maintains, must be more hard-hitting, for liberal, sympathetic approaches have been largely unproductive with "the poor". Murray himself has recently been the advocate of "custodial democracy", suggesting the need for more robust measures to contain and control those who have developed a way of life outside of the "normal" parameters of legitimate employment and family responsibilities.

What is not in doubt, then, is the need for a forthright and wide-ranging discussion about the increasingly polarised life chances of different sub-populations of young people and the extent to which public policy may address different manifestations of "poverty" and "social exclusion". This short paper briefly scans the various

concepts that theoretically inform the debate and suggests a framework within which the issues may be weighed, analysed and tackled.

introduction

It may be that we have become too comfortable, perhaps comforted, by the somewhat vague and generic concept of "social exclusion". Poverty may remain a more apt term, for there is little doubt, within youth transition theory, that the broadening of opportunity for the majority of young people has been matched with corresponding risks, to which a significant minority of young people have been particularly vulnerable. This has been manifested in growing levels of early drop-out from learning, non-participation in vocational preparation and subsequently marginalisation from the labour market or engagement only with low-level, always low-paid, and often casual and short-term employment. Making a life in young adulthood on this basis is a hit and miss affair, as I first suggested over twenty years ago (Williamson, 1985). I argued then that the absence of stable occupational pathways produced a knock-on effect in terms of unstable housing transitions and more precarious personal relationships – the very stuff that is now central to the debate about "vulnerable" youth transitions and the character of "social exclusion".

I have always maintained, however, that any fixed depiction of a distinctive population of "socially excluded" young people is somewhat premature. Whether or not some young people, at particular times, display a number of the facets of what remains a rather loosely defined concept, there is little doubt that most aspire to ordinary, mainstream lifecourse trajectories – they are not (yet) locked into some alternative way of living. Some may, on the other hand, have become trapped – possibly with some permanency – within contexts of significant structural disadvantage and others may have developed a cultural response to the circumstances they face, presenting lifestyle "choices" that apparently consign them – in other people's minds at least – to a "socially excluded" position. However, I still favour the idea invoked by Dahrendorf (1987) of "permeable boundaries", when we are discussing both the "underclass" and the concept of "social exclusion". There is a fluidity between the mainstream and the marginal which public policy – given the political will, suitable resources and appropriate understanding – can address, both through supporting more vulnerable young people and ensuring bridges for the re-integration of those who have slid, temporarily, to the edge. It is to those empirical and practical questions that this paper is primarily concerned. First, however, I will turn briefly to the broader theoretical context in which such attention needs to be embedded.

The theoretical context

This section draws unashamedly, and with due acknowledgement, on the recent work of MacDonald and Marsh (2005), who have captured the issues in an exemplary way. They point out that there is a long tradition of debating the existence of an "underclass". Indeed, one can go back so far as the anthropological work of Oscar Lewis (1966) and consideration of the poor in Victorian London (Stedman-Jones, 1971). The transmutation of the debate from "underclass" to "social exclusion" has not dramatically altered the nature or tone of that debate. It remains locked into analyses within the dichotomies of personal agency versus social structure, structure versus culture, and within and beyond questions of income poverty, unemployment, cultural detachment and relative deprivation – which, in one form or another, produce the likelihood of exclusion from normative participation in society.

MacDonald and Marsh discuss these issues at some length, pointing to much confusion about concepts such as "social exclusion" before identifying some areas of consensus. That consensus has six components. First, social exclusion is more than just income poverty: beyond economic marginality, there are political and cultural dimensions. Second, social exclusion is manifested through a combination of linked problems: it is the accumulation of interrelated difficulties that typifies the condition and experience. Third, social exclusion is not characterised by random distribution across individuals or households but concentrated spatially – a product of increased social polarisation between neighbourhoods. Fourth, social exclusion is a consequence of a political economy by which some groups secure privilege and power at the expense of others. Fifth, social exclusion is a dynamic process that takes place over time. And sixth, social exclusion carries the risk of producing inter-generational effects, as cumulative disadvantage is passed on from one generation to the next.

Implicit within this apparent "consensus" are some very different theoretical and philosophical underpinnings. The political economy argument fits squarely with proponents of more "radical" structural underclass theory, whereas the inter-generational transmission thesis has parallels with more "conservative" cultural underclass positions. This sustains the contested nature of the debate and generates little agreement about what could, should or might be done to alleviate the effects of social exclusion or to prevent its occurrence in the first place. The discourse swings painfully between one of "social integration" and that of "remoralisation", or entrenches stubbornly on one side or the other. Thus "solutions" range from radical social intervention based on the redistribution of wealth and opportunity to more punitive, individualised, "correctional" interventions culminating in, as noted above, Murray's advocacy of the need for "custodial democracy".

Such theoretical analysis can appear to be light years away from the grounded position of the daily lives of young people who are faced with the prospect of social exclusion – young people excluded or self-excluded from learning and the labour market, involved in criminal offending, engaged in the drugs culture or growing up in divided families. In other respects, the analysis is dramatically close, for it informs the nature of the response, if any, to those – and other – circumstances. The "warm" debate about young people and participation and citizenship has, on the other side of the coin, a "cold" debate about "feral yobs" who require regulation and control. Yet, notwithstanding the argument as to whether or not young people are characterised by moral decay rather than the "respectable fears" of the older generation (cf. Pearson, 1983), they have to live a life. As my own long-term study of the "Milltown Boys" – a group of young men who have been unequivocally "socially excluded" for most of their lives – shows quite clearly, they have endeavoured to "get by" one way or another (Williamson, 2004). Some have failed in this aspiration and followed a life course that might have been predicted for young people with no qualifications and criminal records. Others, perhaps surprisingly, have displayed remarkable resilience and commitment, and have "come through", against the odds, on both sides of legitimate enterprise. Getting by, however, on the wrong side of the tracks – in positions that others would depict as "socially excluded" – is rarely easy; there is risk and vulnerability both for the individual concerned and those around them. How we may pre-empt and protect young people from such futures is therefore both a moral and political challenge, raising a host of

questions about the timing, nature and scale of policy interventions. What follows is a framework that offers few specific answers, but raise the key questions that demand attention if any effective strategy to "combat" social exclusion is to be developed.

An empirical strategy

The strength of the model presented below lies in the fact that it can be applied on any issue, with any group, at any level. It does not require an a priori definition of "social exclusion" but instead demands that those involved "work up" their own definition, based either on one single, strongly indicative, criterion (for example, secondary school age children excluded from learning) or on some combination of more than one indicator. It may be used to explore the "social condition" of particular subgroups of young people (for example, those from ethnic minorities or those from lone-parent families) or of young people in a particular neighbourhood. And it may be invoked for the purposes of producing a national strategy or one more tailored to regional or local needs. The questions to be asked are simple, though essential. Their answers are, inevitably, rather more complex, but the nature of the answers will be critical if effective action is to be delivered.

Six key questions

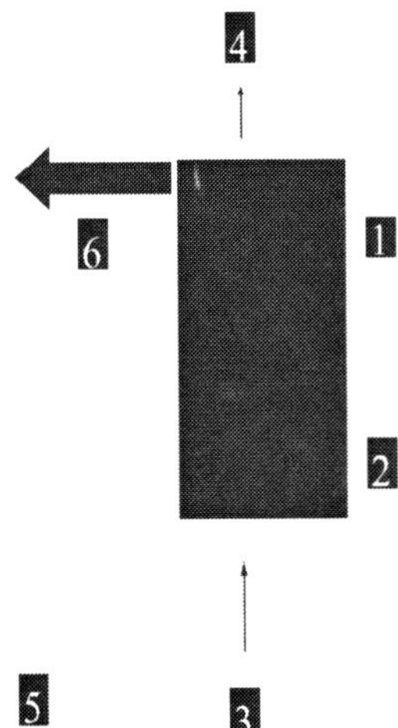

The first four questions are essentially research questions, though the capacity to answer them may be elusive. The final two questions are policy questions, the first to do with preventing the possibility of "social exclusion" (however defined), the second to support the re-inclusion of those who have already become "excluded".

Question 1 is concerned with the scale of the "problem". In short, "how big is the box"? It is a quantitative exercise in achieving the best possible estimate of the numbers of young people who have become "excluded" – whether this refers to educational exclusion, teenage pregnancy, youth offending, substance misuse or something else. Drawing the definitional parameters within which to frame the question is often the most difficult task. Once drawn, however, one needs to establish whether or not the scale of the "problem" represents a "significant policy challenge" or a "residual policy problem", as a House of Commons Education Select Committee once put it (Education Committee, 1998). Does the scale of the problem suggest that these are "public issues" rather than "private troubles" (Wright Mills, 1971). Data can be notoriously unreliable, in that double counting has to be avoided; estimates will invariably be crude, but they will nevertheless serve as a guide to the "volume" of the task.

Question 2 seeks to calibrate and differentiate within the box. Not all the young people identified as possessing particular characteristics will possess them for the same reasons. Some young women, for example, will have become purposefully and constructively young mothers, while others will regret and resent the wider (negative) consequences of their pregnancy, such as the curtailment of their education and reduced opportunities in the labour market. Question 2, therefore, is a qualitative exercise, seeking to unravel the different attitudes, experiences and circumstances of those who find themselves collectively in currently the same predicament. My own calibration, developed some years ago, was to distinguish three subgroups within a population of 16 and 17 years who were now outside of education, training and employment (those I referred to as "status zero" youth). There were those (probably a majority) who were essentially confused, somewhat at a loss as to why they had reached this position and not fundamentally opposed to returning to learning or training. There were those who were temporarily sidetracked, who currently had more significant priorities in their lives (such as caring responsibilities or addressing a drugs problem) but were also not essentially "disaffected" from participation in education and legitimate employment. And there were those who were deeply alienated, who had often already found alternative "ways of living", which subdivided roughly into purposeless and purposeful lifestyles: the former characterised by drug and alcohol use, the latter by instrumental offending behaviour. Policies, projects and programmes would need to take heed of such calibration if their intentions were to be effective.

Question 3 is concerned with the causes of the particular predicament of these young people. To what extent has their specific form of exclusion derived from individual choice and circumstance, from family situations, their schooling or neighbourhood contexts, or from wider social and economic infrastructures. The answer is invariably a combination of all of these, yet some factors within these different elements are often more pronounced than others. Are we able to isolate particular contributory factors to their "exclusion" in order to give them particular policy attention?

Question 4 seeks to explore the consequences of their exclusion. Will young people "get through" it or "grow out" of it? In terms of youth crime, for example, there was once strong advocacy of a position of radical or judicious "non-intervention", on the grounds that the prevalence of youth offending tapered as young people reached adulthood and "settled" into secure relationships and employment. The argument is still often advanced, yet the counter-point is that, especially now that secure employment is less accessible (especially for the more disadvantaged), young people most prone to youthful offending no longer "naturally" grow out of crime. What was perhaps once "benign neglect" is now, arguably, "malign indifference" in the face of complex and challenging youth transitions, particularly for more vulnerable and "at risk" young people. Certainly there is evidence, from longitudinal studies in the UK, that positions of social exclusion in youth (such as non-participation in learning) produce greater marginality and exclusion well into young

adulthood, with abject consequences not just for the individual but also for the state (in terms of the costs of imprisonment, unemployment benefits, support for broken families and so on). If this is so, then the case for policy intervention is strengthened. If it is not so, and young people do, somehow, generally "escape" from youthful positions of exclusion through their own devices, then the case for policy action (certainly at the "re-integration" end of the spectrum) is clearly more questionable.

Question 5 is a policy question about building the necessary barriers to preventing social exclusion in the first place. Should these be positive or punitive, deterrent or developmental? Should they focus on the character and behaviour of the individual, or engage with their wider context – of families, peers and communities? Should policy be general and universal, or targeted and selective? These are old social policy debates, though the mantra of "evidence-based" policy making has led to an increasing focus on targeted and constructive interventions that produce "measurable" outcomes. Where young people and their families do not appear receptive to constructive and voluntary action, more coercive and regulated intervention is deemed to be appropriate. Views about effective preventative intervention remain as much ideologically as evidence derived and the jury remains out on what exactly makes a difference. My view is that different things make a difference with different young people at different times. The critical feature of most preventative interventions is the relationship forged between young people and the professional practitioner, and the motivation of young people to change the direction of their lives, which is itself contingent on their belief in the credibility and relevance of what is on offer instead. Thus a broad menu of possibility and opportunity is required, renewed at regular intervals, but that is inevitably tempered by the constraints of resources and political will. From educational awareness programmes (around, for example, the importance of qualifications, the consequences of crime, the risks of unprotected sex, or the dangers of substance misuse), through mentoring and personal support strategies, to practical measures such as alternative curricula or needle exchanges, prevention needs to operate on a broad front if the risks of social exclusion are to be diminished.

Question 6 tackles similar ground, though it is more concerned with building bridges back to participation in mainstream pathways of transition to adulthood. Winning the hearts and minds of young people who have already become excluded in one way or another also requires a broad church of policy and practice, in order to take account of the very different attitudes, experiences and circumstances of those who are excluded. Just as Question 5 is integrally linked to the analysis derived from Question 3, so the ideas emanating from Question 6 have to be connected closely to the conclusions drawn from Question 2. In contrast, Question 1 sets out the general need for policy action, while Question 4 demonstrates the personal and social consequences if nothing is done and therefore the case for action. As somebody once noted wisely, it is better (and cheaper) to build fences at the top of the cliff than to provide ambulances and police vans at the bottom.

Conclusion

This, then, is the terrain on which the *realpolitik* concerning the social exclusion and inclusion of young people needs to be conducted. There will be different presenting issues in different places. Numerous definitional challenges (of, for example, "social exclusion", "young people", "mainstream transition pathways") will constantly undermine and usurp attempts at analysis and action. Purist academics will throw spanners into the works by questioning whether, in this post-modernist world, it is possible to delineate the mainstream from the marginal. After all, are not at least some "excluded" young people quite "conduct normative" within their own cultures and communities, even if they are considered "conduct disordered" outside of those contexts? What right do we (or does anybody) have to attempt some therapeutic correction of what we (or at least the powers that be) consider to be deviant, unacceptable or "disaffected" behaviour?

I conclude then, not as a researcher or a policy adviser, but as a youth work practitioner. I have worked, too much and too often, with young people rejected from schooling, at the sharp end of serious substance misuse, and brutalised by uncaring and sometimes violent families. I have visited too many young people institutionalised for their selfish and often nasty criminal behaviour. I have witnessed the absence of "positive" career pathways in education and training, or the poor quality of vocational provision which takes young people absolutely nowhere. I have seen too much policy intervention, both directly by the state and by voluntary organisations (NGOs), that excels at "hitting the targets" but simultaneously "misses the point". The point is that young people who are "socially excluded", for all kinds of reasons, are obstructed from fulfilling their own potential and, at the same time, are often damaging the quality of other people's lives. They are sometimes troublesome, but invariably troubled. They need calibrated, individualised attention, built on commitment and patience. Too often, public policy demands "outcomes" too quickly, which simply results in programmes indulging in the "perverse behaviour" of cherry-picking those it is easiest to work with, and missing the most socially excluded altogether.

Youth research (cf. Furlong and Cartmel, 1997) points unequivocally to the complexities of youth transition and heightened levels of risk and vulnerability, particularly for more disadvantaged young people. Charles Murray has a point when he talks up his case for "custodial democracy". There are significant populations, which include significant populations of young people, who are living (and having to live) life at the margins of mainstream society – who are perhaps "making a living" through some combination of benefit dependency, and informal and illegal economic activity. However, the costs and risks to them are significant (seven of the Milltown Boys were dead before the age of 40), just as the economic costs of Murray's proposal for dramatically increasing the prison population are phenomenal. An opportunity-focused youth policy across Europe is the alternative. Framed at local, regional, national and European levels, it is not only economically more sensible, but more morally and socially defensible. But in order to secure the social inclusion of young people, political courage and the strategic investment of financial and human resources, based on both a quantitative and qualitative analysis of the causes and consequences of "social exclusion", will be required. The chapters in this book represent important contributions to that task.

References

Bailey, S. (2005), "No man's land: how Britain's inner city young are being failed". London: Centre for Policy Studies.

Dahrendorf, R. (1987), "The underclass and the future of Britain". Windsor: 10th Annual Lecture.

Education Committee (1998), *Disaffected children*. London: The Stationery Office.

Furlong, A. and Cartmel, F. (1997), *Young people and social change: individualisation and risk in late modernity*. Buckingham: Open University Press.

Lewis, O. (1966), *La Vida*. New York: Random House.

MacDonald, R. and Marsh, J. (2005), *Disconnected youth? Growing up in Britain's poor neighbourhoods*. London: PalgraveMacmillan.

Murray, C. (1984), *Losing ground*. New York: Basic Books.

Murray, C. (1990), "The emerging British underclass". London: Institute for Economic Affairs.

Pearson, G. (1983), *Hooligan: a history of respectable fears*. London: Macmillan.

Stedman-Jones, G. (1971), *Outcast London*. London: Oxford University Press.

Wallerstein, I. (2005), "The inequalities that blazed in France will soon scorch the world". The *Guardian*, 3 December.

Williamson, H. (1985), "Struggling beyond youth". *Youth in Society*, 98, pp. 11-12.

Williamson, H. (2004), *The Milltown boys revisited*. Oxford: Berg.

Wright Mills, C. (1971), *The sociological imagination*. Harmondsworth: Penguin.

3. Disadvantage in youth transitions: constellations and policy dilemmas

Siyka Kovacheva and Axel Pohl

Over the past few decades, young people's transitions from education to work have become increasingly de-standardised and have been made an important focus of policy and research. While these changes have had an effect on all young people, it is clear that some young people are more vulnerable than others to risks of social exclusion such as unemployment, precarious employment and early school leaving. The European Commission's joint report on social inclusion published in May 2004 (European Commission (EC), 2005a) has identified disadvantaged youth as a strategic target group, and defined both increasing labour market participation and tackling disadvantages in education and training as two of the seven key policy priorities. The European Youth Pact adopted in spring 2005 as part of the revised Lisbon Strategy (EC, 2005b) ascertains the social integration of young people as a means for sustainable and inclusive growth in Europe. It builds upon the first cycle of implementation of the White Paper "A new impetus for European youth" (EC, 2001) which launched numerous initiatives for enhancing young people's participation and active citizenship. In order to move forward it is necessary to achieve consistency between the various policies and activities targeting young people through a new level of co-operation between social partners, most notably youth organisations and regional and local authorities (EC, 2005c).

This chapter draws on the results of a thematic study the DG Employment and Social Affairs commissioned in 2004 (see Walther and Pohl, 2005). This study aimed at enhancing the understanding of disadvantage in young people's transitions from school to work, and the policy approaches developed, applied and evaluated within the enlarged EU context. It provided comparative analysis of risks in youth transitions and policy interventions for social inclusion in 13 countries. From the countries involved, Bulgaria, Finland, Greece, Italy, Poland, Portugal, Romania, Slovakia, Spain and the UK display noticeable problems with the inclusion of either unemployed youth or early school-leavers; while Austria, Denmark and Slovenia are referred to as contrasting countries with a better performance. The study made use of three main sources: national reports produced by national experts according to a standardised questionnaire and discussed at seminars with representatives from the academic community, policy makers and stake holders in each country; Eurostat data mainly from the Labour Force Survey in 2004; and descriptions of policies presenting good practices according to a common structure. A wealth of comparative and contextualised information was gathered about the multiple

forms of barriers blocking the social integration of young people. Over 30 models of policy interventions were evaluated as good practice and analysed in more detail by the national experts from the 13 countries participating in the study.

The thematic study first identified and clustered key problem constellations in the countries involved; second, it assessed current policies and their (mis-)match with problems in each of the countries; third, it analysed factors in the success or failure of policies for disadvantaged youth; and, finally, it developed recommendations for how the processes of decision making and policy implementation may profit from "good practice" while considering context-bound specificities. This chapter focuses on two issues: the constellations of disadvantage in youth transitions from education to employment; and the policy dilemmas faced by the strategy for social inclusion in different European countries and regions.

Challenges to employability and social inclusion of young people

De-standardisation of youth transitions

Social research (Furlong and Cartmel, 1997; Walther et al., 2002; López Blasco et al., 2003; Catan, 2004) has established that youth transitions in the member countries of the EU are becoming prolonged, more complex and individualised, without clear-cut trajectories. Even more dramatic has been the shift from the orderly and strictly controlled pathways typical for large groups of young people living under the communist regimes in central and eastern Europe into the flexible and diversified routes in the developing market societies (Ule and Rener, 1998; Machacek, 2001; Kovacheva, 2001). Young people in present-day European societies face more choices and greater risks under the influence of globalisation, which destroys the clear markers of the past and creates insecurity and changeability. In this situation of uncertainty and growing individualisation, young people can no longer rely on collective patterns of progression, and need counselling and advice that take into consideration the complexity of (post)modern life.

Instead of following a linear sequence of transitions steps – finishing education, getting a job, establishing an independent housing and forming a family – young people today are experiencing simultaneous and often reversible combinations of doing paid jobs and studying, and a pluralisation of relationship forms and housing situations (Wallace and Kovatcheva, 1998; Ule and Kuhar, 2003; Kovacheva and Matev, 2005). Individualisation and de-standardisation take different forms and affect different numbers of young people in particular countries, but are present in all of them as significant social trends. While these trends do not replace structural factors of exclusion like social inequality, gender or ethnicity, the study found an increasing number of young people outside the classical target groups of inclusion policies having difficulties in finding stable entry into the labour market. Their transitions often become "yo-yo" trajectories of oscillating between autonomy and dependency, and between different forms of education, training and employment (Walther et al., 2002; du Bois-Reymond and López Blasco, 2003). For example, Jung (2005) speaks about the trend in Poland, whereby leaving formal education is followed by zigzagging between employment and unemployment, eventually with short-term vocational training or re-training. Working for non-governmental organisations (NGOs) in the voluntary sector has become an increasingly important way to gain work experience for young people in Poland in the context of the high unemployment rate there. This de-standardising and intertwining of major life transitions forces young people to make complex decisions in an attempt to achieve autonomy

in work, family and wider life. Thus staying longer in the parental home – a widespread strategy among youth in south and south-east Europe – might solve the problem of rising housing costs for the young, but it limits their work prospects to the jobs available in the local labour markets (see Daniel Blanch's chapter in this book for detailed insights into this problem). Temporary emigration abroad is an option preferred to unemployment by many young people in eastern Europe, but it often means doing precarious low-skilled jobs which do not increase their desired career prospects. The individualisation of the growing-up process multiplies the number and extent of risk decisions and lifecourses for all young people. As lifecourses are becoming more fragmented, young people cannot find a system of adequate information, advice and guidance provided by the state, employers or civil society.

Forming constellations of disadvantage

Stressing the diversification and individualisation of youth transitions does not mean a rejection of the structural links between origins, routes and destinations. On the contrary, de-standardisation itself creates further structures of inequalities among youth, allowing some to profit from the new opportunities, while others remain caught in a downward spiral of stagnation and exclusion.

Disadvantage is conceptualised in the study as a result of the interplay of socio-economic structures, institutional measures and individual strategies. The analysis of the national reports in the present study reveals that problems leading to disadvantage arise at various points in youth transitions. These include problems at school; leaving compulsory schooling early or without qualifications; meeting with a lack of access to training or a mismatch between qualifications and labour demand; lack of entry routes into the labour market; falling into poverty; losing housing security; partnerships breaking up; and as a result, limited citizenship. All these barriers to social inclusion are produced and reproduced by individual, structural and institutional deficits. Disability and type of motivation feature most prominently among individual factors. Socio-economic inequality, poverty rates, the labour market situation and economic development more generally, rates of unemployment and long-term unemployment, gender and ethnic inequalities, and migration status are all structural factors that affect the social integration of young people. Institutions such as school and training systems, employment offices and social security systems themselves can create barriers or enforce misleading trajectories (Walther et al., 2002).

In the study, we found that those factors act in complex interrelationships, creating different patterns in different countries. Depending on the national context, there are different constellations of disadvantage with regard to early school leaving and unemployment. We used Eurostat definitions according to which "early school-leavers" means 18-24-year-olds without upper secondary qualifications, while "youth unemployment" refers to young people out of work who are actively seeking a job (whether registered or not). The "youth unemployment rate" denotes the share of unemployed among the 15-24-year-old labour force, while the "youth unemployment ratio" refers to the 15-24 -year-old population as a whole. Thus early school leaving is low (less than 10% of the relevant age group) in the Nordic countries and central Europe, including Slovenia, Poland and Slovakia from the new member states (see Figure 1). It is medium (in the range of 10-20%) in the UK and Greece, and is high (over 20%) in south Europe (countries such as Portugal, Spain, Italy), and in the south-east (Romania and Bulgaria). The low rates in the Nordic

countries and in Slovenia are linked to low social inequality as measured by the Gini coefficient (a commonly used measure of income inequality varying from 0 to 1), but to medium inequality in Austria, Poland and Slovakia. Additionally, in Austria the school system is selective, training is based on apprenticeships in real work settings and access to higher education is low. The low rate of early school leaving in Poland and Slovakia, although close to that in Austria, is linked to a comprehensive school system, training that is mainly school-based, a mismatch between qualifications and jobs, and general lack of jobs in the tight labour markets.

Figure 1 – Early school leaving and youth unemployment in 2004 (Eurostat, LFS)

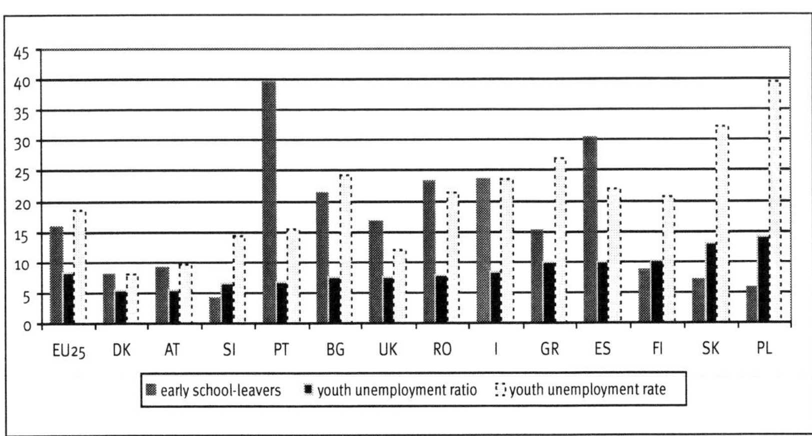

Different groupings of countries appear when we analyse disadvantage in terms of unemployment among youth. The highest youth unemployment rates are in Poland and Slovakia (over 30%), which also have the highest youth unemployment ratio. In the other southern and eastern European countries, the high unemployment rates (between 20% and 30%) are combined with low activity rates and a low unemployment ratio. In the south and east of Europe, unemployment is higher among young women, while in the north of Europe and particularly the UK, there is higher male youth unemployment. Long-term unemployment of one year and more is high (over 50% of the young unemployed) in the new member and accession countries, as well as in Italy and Greece. However, in the other two south European countries – Portugal and Spain – as well as Austria it is medium (30-50%), and in the Nordic countries and the UK it is low: below 30%. In the northern and central European countries and Bulgaria, those with lower qualifications meet higher risks of becoming unemployed, while those with post-secondary education have lower risks. On the contrary, in the southern European countries, in Poland and in Romania, all groups according to educational level have average chances of unemployment.

Social disadvantage is not limited to early school leaving or unemployment. Various forms of non-standard work can serve to extend disadvantage after labour market entry and into later stages of the lifecourse. The Labour Force Survey (LFS) established high precariousness of youth employment, although in different patterns in different countries. Risky employment among youth takes the form of temporary contracts in Spain, Poland, Finland and Slovenia; of part-time work in Denmark; and of undeclared work in Greece, Italy and the two accession countries. The dominant patterns of non-standard work are not related in any linear way to the poverty rate among youth in each country, which is low in the Nordic countries and

Slovenia, medium in Austria, Bulgaria and Poland, and high in the rest of the countries in the study. The study shows that disadvantage increasingly includes young people who are working, when they also encounter restricted access to social security, which in turn causes precariousness in the later stages of the lifecourse. The deregulation of the labour market does not automatically mean increasing chances of social integration if it is not linked to quality employment.

The study identified one group at particular risk of social exclusion in most European countries. It is formed by young people not in education, training or employment and not registered as unemployed in the labour offices, often referred to as the "status zero" group (Williamson, 1997). Potential factors are limited access to benefit entitlements, low trust in the effectiveness and integrity of the public employment service, experience of bad treatment by institutional actors, and alternative options such as informal work. There is no reliable data about this group in many of the countries, and one of the recommendations of the "Disadvantaged Youth" study is the creation of a joint data set at European level about the status of young people, including inactivity and non-registered work.

Patterns of social inclusion policies

Policy dilemmas

Given the harsh situation of accumulated youth disadvantages in Europe, the national strategies devised to create employment pathways for the young face two main policy dilemmas:

- individualised versus structure-related approaches – those aiming to adapt individuals to the demands of education, training and labour market, or those oriented toward making structural opportunities more accessible and relevant to young people's motivation;
- preventive versus compensatory measures – those addressing risk factors which create disadvantage, or those trying to alleviate accumulated problems.

From the national reports in the "Disadvantaged Youth" study, it became clear that most countries apply different combinations of both approaches. Examples of structure-related and preventive solutions to the problem of early school leaving are educational reforms directed toward extending compulsory education, making schools and universities more accessible, and developing national qualification frameworks, as in the UK and Slovenia; introducing educational allowances to reduce the impact of social inequality and prevent dropping out (in Bulgaria, Romania and Slovakia these are directed toward the most disadvantaged groups such as the Roma, while in Denmark they are universal); and counselling directed at early identification of problems and young people's educational decisions, such as the total counselling network in Slovenia. Examples of individualised and compensatory policies include "second chance" schools, both formal and informal, providing qualifications for early school-leavers (thus in Greece 6% of the population aged 14-24 study in evening courses); and prevocational measures which focus on personal competences, such as "Getting connected" in the UK and "Production schools" in Denmark.

In the field of strategies for combating unemployment, preventive measures are known as "active labour market policies" while compensatory measures are mostly associated with welfare benefits. In some countries unemployment benefits are universal, in others they are linked only to previous employment period with paid social security benefits, while excluding first-job seekers and those who have worked in the informal economy. Among the most common measures in active labour market policies are the deregulation of labour market entry, reducing the costs of hiring young people, and vocational education and training. The first measure, leading to increased flexibility of labour, has been accompanied by social rights and expansion of training in countries such as Slovenia and Denmark; while in southern Europe, it has led to a growth of precariousness and poverty among the young. Expanding vocational education and training also takes different forms in different countries: in Austria, the apprenticeship system successfully facilitates a smooth transition to skilled employment for a significant proportion of youth; in countries such as Italy, Portugal, Poland and the UK, apprenticeship programmes have been introduced as an alternative to the school-based vocational education and training (VET); and in other countries, company-based training is mostly directed to young people who are registered unemployed (Bulgaria, Romania, Slovakia, Greece, Spain). Other measures of active labour market policy include offering subsidies for employers to hire young people without work experience, which are particularly found in central eastern and south-east Europe; and job creation and self-employment schemes, which target the skilled unemployed (in countries such as Greece, Italy and Poland) or young people with disabilities (in Austria and Denmark). Anti-discrimination policies are also a form of preventive and structure-related approach. They aim at lifting barriers for ethnic minority and immigrant youth, young women and people with disabilities. Measures directed at the inclusion of Roma youth are of particular relevance in central eastern and south-east Europe.

The choice of policy approaches to early school leaving and youth unemployment is obviously dependent on funding among other factors. An effective preventive policy requires more resources than remedial measures. The countries in the study differ in their levels of investment in education and active labour market policies (ALMP) even when these are measured by national expenditures for the two policies as percentages of the gross domestic product (GDP) (see Table 1). Countries where both types of expenditures are low are Greece (4% for education and 0.22% for ALMP) and Romania (3.53% for education and 0.17% for ALMP), while Denmark is at the opposite pole with 8.5% of GDP spent on education and 1.6% on ALMP. While these indicators cannot be compared directly, given the large differences in the GDP levels, still they provide information about the resources allocated and the significance placed on these policy objectives.

Table 1 – Expenditures on education and ALMP in 2002 as % of GDP (Eurostat, OECD)

Education / ALMP	Low (‹ 5%)	Medium (5-6%)	High (› 6%)
Low (‹ 0.5%)	Greece, Romania, Slovakia	Austria, Poland, Portugal, United Kingdom	Slovenia
Medium (0.5-1%)	Bulgaria, Spain, Italy	Finland	
High (› 1%)			Denmark

The trend toward activation policies

However, the policy mixes that appear from the combination of different policy solutions in the different national contexts have one common trend – toward activation of young people, that is, mobilising individuals to engage more actively in the process of their own labour market integration and wider social inclusion. A key mechanism of activation policies are individual action plans (IAP). The national approaches to IAP can be broadly placed on a continuum between:

- limiting activation to labour market integration based on restricted choices, and reliance on negative incentives and extrinsic motivation;
- broadening activation to social inclusion based on offering a wide range of educational and training options and individual counselling, and reliance on positive incentives and intrinsic motivation.

The first approach is applied most often in central eastern Europe, Austria, Portugal and Spain, where restricted benefit entitlements and removal from the register are directed at preventing long-term unemployment. In Bulgaria and Romania, for example, IAPs are centred on employment only and they do not have full coverage. The second perspective is most clearly represented in Denmark, Finland and Slovenia among the countries included in our study. In Denmark, IAPs are devised, implemented and co-ordinated between a wide range of actors – schools, vocational guidance centres, employment services, local authorities and communities. Starting from the individual's needs and expectations, the plans include steps toward educational, career and personal development from a cross-sectoral perspective.

Clearly, activation policies might have unintended "side effects" of pushing young people into inactivity. Demotivation and disengagement occur more often in countries relying on limited benefits and negative sanctions, especially where the spread of informal and undeclared work is significant. Limiting activation to job placements and measuring its success by the increase in the numbers of young unemployed gaining employment without taking into account income, duration and personal satisfaction does not facilitate social inclusion. Activation has been more successful in countries where it is matched with adequate funding for education and active labour market policies, such as Finland, Denmark and Slovenia. By contrast, its effect has been insignificant in Italy and Greece, where investments in these two spheres have been minor. Activation policies can foster social integration best when ensuring the reconciliation of subjective and systemic perspectives.

The trend toward co-ordinated and integrated policies

The study clearly showed that policy measures for disadvantaged youth can have the desired lasting effect on youth transitions when they form part of a co-ordinated and integrated youth policy. The necessity of such policies arises from the destandardisation and individualisation of youth transitions that force young people to make complex decisions; and from the constellations of disadvantage in each country and in Europe as a whole, which cannot be tackled with a narrowly focused policy. A policy addressing these challenges needs a holistic approach to understand and support young people's efforts to achieve autonomy in work, family and wider life.

The trend toward co-ordination and integration of policies in support of disadvantaged youth was clearly shown in the examples of good practice collected during the study. The analysis of expert descriptions showed several essential elements of such policies. Projects such as the Joint Service Centres in Finland, the guidance and counselling reform in Denmark and the Total Counselling programme in Slovenia, all started with defining holistic objectives for youth programmes and measures; then proceeded with creating networks for co-operation among partners; and were realised through the integration of activities.

The first element – holistic objectives – is in recognition of the complexity of problems, the "constellations of disadvantage", that the young unemployed or early school-leavers face. Therefore many of the above policies widened their goals beyond a narrowly understood notion of employability, to include the development of young people's skills for life management (as formulated in the Finnish report), or social, personal and physical skills as part of young people's life competency (Danish report). Attaining social skills and life competences is not just a requisite for labour market integration, but for a wider and sustainable social integration of young people. Stimulating a process of life learning is an objective in itself, and should be perceived as an investment, especially in difficult economic contexts. As objectives are broadened, so is the scope of institutions, agencies and groups involved in the implementation of the programme.

The second element of an integrated approach of policies is the involvement of different types of actors (from the state, market and civil society), at different levels (central, regional and local) and in different policy sectors (not only education and employment, but also social protection, health, leisure, housing and family policy). The most successful of the projects have ensured the participation of young people in the design, implementation and evaluation of the measures. This is done both on an individual basis in the individual action plans which are being developed in all countries, and at the level of youth associations. Here it is important to consider as partners not only established organisations, but also more informal youth networks and groups (Kovacheva, 2000). In many countries the young person's parents are also involved in the implementation of the measures – most notably in southern Europe but also in Finland in the Joint Service Centres. This is in recognition of the important role that families play in support of youth transitions in modern societies (see Biggart and Cairns, 2004).

The integration of activities as the third element of co-ordinated policies is a prerequisite when pursuing holistic objectives through the association of a wide range of actors (the chapter in this book by Kate Philip et al., discusses this issue in greater detail). United actions are required at all stages of developing a policy – setting the objectives, providing the resources, including funding, implementing programmes, evaluating results and initiating an expansion or reshaping the strategy. Negotiation, networking and mediation are key mechanisms for a workable co-ordination. Many projects analysed in the study represent integrated models of servicing the individual and meeting their needs in education, work, leisure and wider life. The Danish guidance and counselling reform uses a high-tech device for the integration of activities – the national guidance portal (www.ug.dk), where information about education, training, labour market issues, professions and possibilities abroad are given. Another means of integration is the national dialogue forum providing means for a cross-sectoral dialogue and development of a new quality-control system. National qualification systems, together with a systematic approach to recognise informal and non-formal learning like the one introduced in Slovenia, can help to build bridges between different strands of the education system and the labour market for young people with "yo-yo" careers.

Conclusions

The "Disadvantaged Youth" study has identified a wide range of success factors for policies in support of disadvantaged young people. Based on an overview of the trends in youth transitions and policy dilemmas, this paper concludes by focusing upon four of them: biographical perspective, accessibility, institutional reflexivity and flexibility of measures.

The present study has clearly shown that a key factor for the success of policies is defining policy objectives in a way that starts from the individual's life perspective and needs, not from the institutional perspective or narrow institutional considerations. Acknowledging the structural barriers that face youth integration, programmes and measures in support of disadvantaged youth should build upon the biographical perspective of the young person and their subjective orientations, values and skills, and allow them to take a role as key actors in their own transitions, their own social integration. (Beatrix Niemeyer examines in detail how such an approach might transform the provision of VET across Europe in her chapter in this book.) Individual motivation to participate in or drop out of counselling, education, training or employment determines the sustainability of policy initiatives. Such a focus on the individual does not mean placing the blame for failures upon the young person, but employing the resources of the individual in the changeable and de-standardised process of growing up and achieving autonomy. When setting objectives and assessing the implementation of measures, it is important that possible "side effects" are taken into consideration, and that policies across sectors are co-ordinated. A sustainable labour market and social integration of an individual both require individual support measures such as psychological stabilisation, health-related interventions, solutions to housing problems and others besides – and often these are needed prior to the stage of job search. A highly effective tool for such an individualised approach is face-to-face counselling, acknowledging the perspective of the individual in coping with transition problems not only in the transition from school to work, but also in wider life. Successful social inclusion implies not only fulfilling institutional targets for placing individuals into training or jobs, but also giving access to a subjectively meaningful life.

Inclusion and active labour market policies are only effective if they actually reach their target groups. In particular, both immigrant and ethnic minority youth as well as young women are often under-represented in such measures – or they profit less in terms of meaningful outcomes. Accessibility depends first on the coverage of measures, which itself is dependent on funding. Second, it also requires the decentralised distribution of measures that allows for low-threshold access. Third, access requires reliable communication networks between institutions as well as between young people and institutions. Fourth, access depends on the conditions of attendance: flexible or unconditional access helps to ensure that individuals do not remain excluded from meaningful support due to bureaucratic rules. Fifth, anti-discrimination policies may be a tool to provide improved access (and supply) for immigrant and minority youth, as well as according to gender and age. Finally, the persistence of the phenomenon of "status zero" suggests that limitations are not only structural and administrative, but are also related to potential participants' perceptions that such measures lack value in their eyes.

A requirement for the success of policy interventions in dealing with de-standardised and flexible youth transitions is the reflexivity of institutions: their ability to shape and re-shape measures in a flexible way. It is necessary for policy makers and practitioners to reflect upon objectives, structures, processes in the implementation

of programmes and their assessment. For all policies, and particularly for a co-ordinated policy for disadvantaged youth, the organisational ability to reflect upon activities and redesign them when necessary is of key significance. Institutional reflexivity is effective when built upon a balance of power. All actors have to be able to participate in the shaping and monitoring of policies on an equal footing. Forced partnerships – for example, when funding is conditional on partnership structures – devalues the potential of a co-ordinated policy and stimulates only the extrinsic motivation of actors (see also Chapter 14 by Kate Philip et al.). The balance of power is secured by respective rules, and it allows for co-ordination to be applied for the sake of quality delivery of services, and not for other reasons. The power balance includes symmetric relationships not only between different types of institutions, but also between institutional and individual actors. All successful projects in our study have made efforts to provide avenues for young people to participate in all stages of delivery, including direct feedback on the subjective relevance of measures.

While increased flexibility of employment has been widely promoted as a remedy for economic difficulties (see EC, 2005c), the need for flexibility in policy measures is often neglected. Making employment more flexible in terms of working time and schedules, working place and functions, and contractual conditions will operate in favour of young people's social integration when matched with open and adaptable policies. In the successful projects in our study, modularisation of tasks and step-by-step approaches have been applied to fit better with the "yo-yo" transitions of young people. Policy measures have to be open and flexible in their criteria for access, content and duration, and allow switching between trajectories, instead of pushing young people into misleading trajectories (du Bois-Reymond and López Blasco, 2003) with a "revolving doors" effect that makes them feel stuck in "scheme careers". As others argue elsewhere in this book (see, for example, the chapters by Howard Williamson, Helen Colley and Daniel Blanch), it is necessary to underline the importance of integrating economic and youth policies if the latter are to have a sustainable effect on youth social inclusion. Just as policies for disadvantaged youth have been geared to economic outcomes, social inclusion now has to become a "hard" criterion for economic policies at European, national, regional and local levels.

References

Biggart, A. and Cairns, D. (eds.) (2004), "Families and transitions in Europe: comparative report". Belfast: University of Ulster.

Catan, L. (2004), *Becoming adult: changing youth transitions in the 21st century.* Brighton: Trust for the Study of Adolescence.

Du Bois-Reymond, M. and Lopez Blasco, A. (2003), "Yo-yo transitions and misleading trajectories: towards integrated transition policies for young adults in Europe", in Lopez Blasco, A., McNeish, W. and Walther, A. (eds.), *Young people and contradictions of inclusion. towards integrated transition policies in Europe.* Bristol: Policy Press.

EC (2001), "New impetus for European youth", White Paper, COM(2001)681. Luxembourg: Office for Official Publications of the European Communities (accessed 23 June 2006). Available at: http://ec.europa.eu/youth/whitepaper/index_en.html.

EC (European Commission) (2005a), "Joint report on social protection and social inclusion", COM(2005)14. Luxembourg: Office for Official Publications of the

European Communities (accessed 23 June 2006). Available at: http://ec.europa.eu/employment_social/emplweb/publications/2005_en.cfm.

EC (2005b), "Annex 1 of Presidency Conclusions of the European Council, Brussels, 22 and 23 March 2005" (7619/05). Luxembourg: Office for Official Publications of the European Communities (accessed 23 June 2006). Available at: www.consilium.europa.eu/ueDocs/cms_Data/docs/pressdata/en/ec/84335.pdf.

EC (2005c), "Communication from the Commission to the Council on European policies concerning youth", COM(2005)206. Luxembourg: Office for Official Publications of the European Communities (accessed 23 June 2006). Available at: http://eurlex.europa.eu/smartapi/cgi/sga_doc?smartapi!celexplus!prod!DocNumber&lg=en&type_doc=COMfinal&an_doc=2005&nu_doc=206.

EC (2005d), "Draft joint employment report", COM(2005)13 final. Luxembourg: Office for Official Publications of the European Communities (accessed 23 June 2006). Available at: http://ec.europa.eu/employment_social/emplweb/publications/2005_en.cfm.

Jung, B. (2005), "National report for the disadvantaged youth study – Poland", in Walther, A. and Pohl, A., *Thematic study on policy measures concerning disadvantaged youth*, Volume 2, Tübingen: IRIS (accessed 23 June 2006). Available at: http://ec.europa.eu/employment_social/social_inclusion/docs/youth_study_annex_en.pdf.

Kovacheva, S. (2000), *Keys to youth participation in eastern Europe*. Strasbourg: Council of Europe.

Kovacheva, S. (2001), "Flexibilisation of youth transitions in central and eastern Europe", *Young*, 9 (1), pp. 41-60.

Kovacheva, S. and Matev, A. (2005), "Analysis of biographical interviews. Transitions national report Bulgaria", Plovdiv: University of Plovdiv.

López Blasco, A., McNeish, W. and Walther, A. (eds.) (2003), *Young people and contradictions of inclusion. Towards integrated transition policies in Europe*. Bristol: Policy Press.

Machacek, L. (2001), "Youth and creation of civil society", in Helve, H. and Wallace, C. (eds.), *Youth, citizenship and empowerment*. Aldershot: Ashgate.

Ule, M. and Kuhar, M. (2003), "Young adults and a new orientation towards family formation", paper presented at the European Sociological Association Conference, Murcia, September 2003.

Ule, M. and Rener, T. (eds.) (1998), *Youth in Slovenia. New perspectives from the nineties*. Ljubljana: Youth Department.

Wallace, C. and Kovatcheva, S. (1998), *Youth in society. The construction and deconstruction of youth in east and west Europe*. London: Macmillan and New York: St Martin's Press.

Walther, A. and Pohl, A. (2005), "Thematic study on policy measures concerning disadvantaged youth. Final report to the European Commission". Tübingen: IRIS (accessed 23 June 2006). Available at: http://ec.europa.eu/employment_social/social_inclusion/docs/youth_study_en.pdf.

Walther, A., Stauber, B., Biggart, A., Du Bois-Reymond, M., Furlong, A., Lopez Blasco, A., Morch, S. and Machado Pais, J. (eds.) (2002), *Misleading trajectories – Integration policies for young adults in Europe?* Opladen: Leske+Budrich.

Williamson, H. (1997), "Status zero youth and the 'underclass': some considerations", in Macdonald, R. (ed.), *Youth, the "underclass" and social exclusion.* London: Routledge.

4. Poverty and youth transitions in Europe: an analysis of the European Communities Household Panel

Eldin Fahmy

Despite the high profile of life-cycle approaches in understanding poverty, few studies have focused on the income and living conditions of young Europeans, and youth poverty has received comparatively little attention from policy makers. Although official statistics reveal higher rates of income poverty amongst young people than across the European population as a whole (for example, Dennis and Guio, 2004), youth policy, as outlined for example in the European youth White Paper (CEC, 2001), has tended to concentrate on encouraging youth participation and challenging processes of exclusion and discrimination. By focusing only upon the most extreme forms of social marginalisation, this approach risks obscuring the extent of poverty and inequality amongst Europe's young people. Tackling the apparent disaffection and alienation of "problem" groups is not a substitute for policies which address underlying structural processes of marginalisation and recognise the widespread nature of poverty amongst young people. This chapter addresses such wider objectives by examining the extent and duration of income poverty and deprivation amongst young Europeans, and the ways in which vulnerability varies across Europe depending upon young people's domestic and labour market transitions.[1]

Youth, poverty and the life cycle

Pioneers of poverty research in the early 20th century, such as Seebohm Rowntree (1901/2000), demonstrated a cyclical pattern of vulnerability to poverty over the lifecourse. The risk of poverty was highest in childhood; in the early middle years of adult life (for adults with dependent children); and in later life; and with corresponding troughs in vulnerability to poverty for working age adults without dependents. In that era, the very concept of "youth" as a life stage was virtually

1. This research research was funded by CEPS/INSTEAD (Luxembourg). The author is grateful for their financial support, and for the support of colleagues at the ESRI, Dublin, especially Dorothy Watson. I am also indebted to Bernard Maitre (ESRI, Dublin) and the ECHP Users Network for access to the income and deprivation poverty thresholds syntax used here. This paper summarises work presented at the European Youth Research Partnership Seminar on Social Inclusion and Young People. Readers interested in the more technical aspects of the methodology and results presented here are referred to the full conference paper available via the European Knowledge Centre for Youth Policy (http://www.youth-knowledge.net).

meaningless. However, headline rates today suggest that the relative risk of poverty across the lifecourse has changed substantially since then. Table 1 (below) plots poverty rates across the lifecourse in the EU15 member states based upon the EU's preferred definition – the proportion of individuals living in households with incomes less than 60% of the national equivilised median. It is clear from these data that Rowntree's model of poverty across the lifecourse no longer fits the social situation of young Europeans at the beginning of the 21st century. In many cases, vulnerability to poverty either increases substantially in the transition from childhood to youth (Sweden, Finland, Denmark, the Netherlands), or continues at similarly high levels (Germany, Greece, France, Italy, the UK). Only in Ireland are rates of income poverty amongst 16-24-year-olds lower than those found amongst the rest of the working age population.

Table 1 – At-risk-of-poverty rate across the life cycle by age, 2001

	0-15	**16-24**	**25-49**	**50-64**	**60+**	**All**
Ireland	26	12	17	16	44	21
Greece	18	19	14	21	33	20
Portugal	27	18	15	16	30	20
Italy	25	25	18	16	17	19
Spain	26	20	15	17	22	19
UK	24	20	12	11	24	17
France	18	21	12	13	19	15
Belgium	12	12	10	12	26	13
Luxembourg	18	20	11	9	7	12
Austria	13	11	8	9	24	12
Finland	6	23	7	9	23	11
Netherlands	16	22	10	7	4	11
Germany	14	16	9	10	12	11
Denmark	7	21	7	5	24	10
Sweden	7	18	7	5	16	9
EU15	19	19	12	12	19	15

Source: Eurostat New CRONOS database (accessed 16 September 2005).

It is also well known that income measures tend to underestimate the extent of poverty amongst young people, because they take no account of the additional "start-up costs" incurred by young people to attain the same standards of living enjoyed by their elders (for example, deposits on housing, buying furnishings, household goods, clothing for special occasions, educational fees). Thus relatively high levels of disposable income may not equate to similarly high standards of living for young people, whose unavoidable outgoings are atypically high. Equally, income approaches tend to neglect the impact of withdrawals from savings and the accumulation of assets over the lifecourse in cushioning the impact of declining income in later life. Thus for elderly households, relatively low income levels can obscure disproportionately high standards of living.

One obvious starting point in explaining these changes in vulnerability to poverty across the lifecourse is the impact of socio-economic change in recent decades. Youth transitions today are more protracted, more complex, and more precarious than for previous generations, and this is reflected in their re-conceptualisation in terms of risk, individualisation and multi-dimensionality (Catan, 2004). This transformation raises basic questions about the adequacy of existing social policies in addressing the changing needs and circumstances of young Europeans, since policies and institutions are still oriented towards a linear transition from youth into adulthood, and focus primarily upon labour market insertion (Biggart et al., 2004). As Sikya Kovacheva argues in this volume, the fact that young people undergo various interdependent and bi-directional labour market, domestic and housing transitions makes it imperative that policy makers consider this complexity addressing youth poverty; and that they design services "from the bottom up", based on young people's needs and perspectives.

Similarly difficult questions arise regarding the adequacy of existing welfare arrangements in meeting the needs of European youth in these changed circumstances. The goal of social welfare provision can be viewed in terms of the equalisation of risk across the lifecourse. For example, the British welfare state was formulated with the express goal of tackling poverty and deprivation amongst vulnerable groups, including children and the elderly. However, as we have already noted, at the time of its inception in the 1940s, the very concept of "youth" as a social category hardly existed. Welfare provision was therefore originally designed without specific acknowledgement of the vulnerability of young people to poverty and disadvantage, and has failed to take account of subsequent changes in the nature of youth transitions. Indeed, in the UK, as in many other European countries, young people's eligibility for welfare payments has been increasingly restricted as a result of the "residualisation" of welfare in which state welfare is increasingly constructed as providing only a minimal safety net for the most disadvantaged rather than a universal system of public provision (Mizen, 2003).

At the same time, these factors are likely to vary in their impact upon young people's well being, depending upon both the welfare mix within particular countries and individual-level variations in young people's transition profiles. The increasingly protracted nature of youth transitions means that many more young citizens are vulnerable to relative low income and insecure employment than may have typically been the case in the immediate post-1945 period. However, those most at risk of poverty are likely to be those young people making early labour market and domestic transitions, for example as a result of low pay, job insecurity and inflated rents.

The remainder of this chapter explores the extent and dynamics of low income and deprivation amongst European youth, based upon analysis of the European Communities Household Panel (ECHP). I begin by considering the overall distribution of youth poverty across 11 European countries in comparison with older citizens, and with regard to the extent of poverty persistence across the panel. I then go on to examine the risk of entering and exiting poverty for young Europeans, especially with respect to the impact of leaving the parental home ("nest leaving"), youth unemployment and student status. I end by discussing the implications of these findings for European policies on youth and social inclusion. Firstly, however, we need to clarify the ways in which poverty is measured.

Cross-sectional poverty estimates

Three measures of poverty are commonly used:

Income poverty

This measure defines as poor those individuals living in households with equivilised incomes of less than 60% of the national median, as agreed at the 2001 Laeken Council.

Current lifestyle deprivation

This measure comprises an index of 13 household items, the absence of which can be taken to reflect an enforced lack of a socially desirable style of living (see Whelan et al., 2001). Since the distribution of these items (and hence also their relative desirability) is uneven across European societies, the items have been weighted according to the proportion of households within each country who have each item. The deprivation threshold identifies as poor the same proportion of households identified as poor using the 60% median income measure.

Core poverty

If the above measures related accurately to the same underlying concept of poverty, they should identify the same households and individuals as poor, but this is not always the case. Although the extent of the "overlap" between income and deprivation remains controversial, the notion retains considerable conceptual and intuitive validity. Here, the "core poor" comprises those individuals who are both income-poor and deprivation-poor.

Mean national rates of income poverty, deprivation and core poverty over the 1996-2001 period for young people aged 16-29 and for the adult population aged 30 and over are shown in Table 2 (below). Although higher rates of income poverty and deprivation are typical of the Mediterranean welfare regimes (Greece, Portugal and Spain, as well as Ireland), these data also show that rates of poverty amongst young adults in the "richer" northern states are often substantially higher than overall trends would suggest. Some of the highest rates of income poverty amongst young people (aged 16-29) are to be found in the Netherlands (19.3%) and Finland (20.5%), where they are at least twice as high as amongst adults aged over 30. Three clusters of countries can be identified:

- those where the income poverty rate for young adults is substantially higher than the rate for those aged over 30 (the Netherlands, Finland, Italy, France, Denmark);
- those where the income poverty rate for young adults is substantially lower than the rate for those aged over 30 (Ireland, Portugal);
- those countries where only marginal differences are observed (Greece, Spain, Belgium, Austria).

Table 2 – Income poverty, deprivation and core poverty rates in Europe by age, 1996-2001 (%)

	Income			Deprivation			Core		
	16-29	**30+**	**Diff.**	**16-29**	**30+**	**Diff.**	**16-29**	**30+**	**Diff.**
Ireland	14.9	21.8	-6.9	22.9	18.8	4.1	8.5	8.6	-0.1
Greece	16.8	19.6	-2.8	21.6	19.3	2.3	7.4	8.1	-0.7
Portugal	11.3	16.8	-5.5	18.6	18.2	0.4	5.2	7.1	-1.9
Spain	18.2	16.3	1.9	18.2	18.0	0.2	7.8	6.8	1.0
Italy	22.5	15.2	7.3	20.7	16.0	4.7	10.9	6.3	4.6
France	17.7	12.6	5.1	18.7	13.5	5.2	3.3	4.9	-1.6
Belgium	12.1	14.7	-2.6	14.3	12.5	1.8	5.0	4.5	0.5
Austria	9.5	11.2	-1.7	14.5	12.1	2.4	3.1	3.2	-0.1
Netherlands	19.3	7.1	12.2	15.5	10.5	5.0	8.5	2.5	6.0
Finland	20.5	10.3	10.2	17.7	9.4	8.3	8.0	2.3	5.7
Denmark	16.7	10.6	6.1	17.6	7.5	10.1	6.1	1.8	4.3
All	16.9	14.3	2.6	18.7	14.8	3.9	7.6	5.4	2.2

Source: ECHP Universal Data Base (UDB), 1996-2001.

Turning our attention to the investigation of deprivation reveals a more consistent pattern. In every country studied, deprivation is more widespread amongst young adults (aged 16-29) than amongst older citizens, though differences are very marginal in Spain and Portugal. This suggests that the "start up" costs associated with the transition to independent living (paying deposits on rental accommodation and mortgages, buying consumer durables, clothing for special occasions, etc.) may be offsetting the effects of comparatively high equivilised income in those countries where youth income poverty rates are lower than amongst older respondents. Young people thus require relatively higher incomes to achieve the same standard of living enjoyed by older citizens whose "fixed costs" in terms of capital outlay are typically lower. In general, the disparity between European countries in levels of deprivation is also lower than is typical for income poverty. We might therefore conclude that actual between-country variations in young people's standards of living are in fact not as large as would be suggested by the indirect income measures of poverty used in most official studies.

Finally, turning to "core poverty", we find that at any one point in time the proportion of young people both income-poor and deprivation-poor is highest in Italy (10.9%), the Netherlands (8.5%), Ireland (8.5%), Finland (8.0%) and Greece (7.4%). These results provide little consistent support for the proposition that rates of youth poverty reflect variations in the nature of welfare systems between the southern and northern European social welfare models. The most substantial disparity between rates of youth poverty and those of the population aged 30+ for "core poverty" is found in the Netherlands, Italy, Denmark and Finland.

Whilst high levels of youth poverty constitute an important policy problem in their own right, it may be that general poverty alleviation measures are likely to be effective in tackling youth poverty where rates of poverty amongst young people and amongst the adult population as a whole are similar. From a policy perspective, we might therefore view as most problematic those instances in which high levels of youth poverty are combined with substantial differences in poverty rates between

young people and adults of working age. In this regard, a fairly consistent pattern emerges with respect to the Netherlands, Finland, France and (to a lesser extent) Italy. Whether measured indirectly by income, or directly on the basis of material and social deprivation, or using a combination of these approaches, rates of youth poverty are not only high, but also much higher than one might expect given relatively low levels of poverty amongst the adult population as a whole. Despite the relatively comprehensive nature of welfare provision in these societies, it is thus clear that the goal of social inclusion remains an aspiration not fully realised in policy and practice. This is expressed most starkly in exclusionary practices and structures centred on gender, ethnicity and citizenship (see, for example Amineh Kakabaveh's chapter in this volume), but these findings also suggest that the intergenerational dimensions of social justice have yet to be fully addressed in relation to youth poverty.

Analysing poverty spells

Although these cross-sectional analyses are illuminating, the "snapshots" they provide still give a limited picture of the nature of youth poverty. There are three reasons for this. First, they disguise the extent of "churning" in the poor group, that is, they do not identify the fact that it may be different individuals who are poor each time the "snapshot" is taken. Second, cross-sectional analyses distort understanding of poverty spells, since those individuals observed as "poor" at a particular point in time will display significantly longer spells of poverty than those identified as "poor" within continuous panel studies. Third, and most importantly, cross-sectional analysis prevents us from understanding the long-term consequences of sustained exposure to poverty. Persistent poverty is not necessarily continuous, and can be conceptualised discontinuously as a recurrent experience of poverty over a long time period. Here I therefore define an individual as persistently poor where they experience income poverty, deprivation or core poverty (as defined above) for three or more periods over the five observations (Waves 4 to 8). Table 3 (below) shows the percentage of respondents experiencing recurrent poverty over the 1997-2001 period for the 11 countries considered here and for respondents aged 20-29, and 30+ years respectively.

With respect to income poverty, Table 3 (below) reveals a broadly similar pattern of results to the cross-sectional estimates. Recurrent income poverty is most widespread amongst young respondents (aged 20-29) in the Netherlands (26.3%), Italy (24.2%) and Finland (20.9%). However, comparison with the rest of the adult population reveals that the differences between younger and older respondents across countries is also substantial. The proportion of young Irish respondents experiencing recurrent income poverty (10.9%) is less than half that of respondents aged 30+ (24.1%). At the other end of the scale, more than one quarter (26.3%) of Dutch youth were recurrently income-poor – more than four times the proportion for older Dutch respondents (6.2%). As with the cross-sectional estimates, the disparity between recurrent poverty rates for young people and older respondents was highest in the Netherlands, Finland and Italy.

A similar picture emerges with respect to recurrent deprivation, though between-country differences are again smaller than for income. As with the cross-sectional estimates, this suggests that actual variations in standards of living across European societies may be rather less substantial than equivalent income-based measures suggest. Whilst rates of recurrent deprivation amongst young people tend to be highest in the Mediterranean countries, the disparity between poverty rates for young people and older adults is again highest in the Netherlands, Finland, Italy and, to a lesser extent, Denmark. Similar findings emerge when we consider the overlap between recurrent income poverty and deprivation. Here, we find again that rates of recurrent "core poverty" are much higher for young Dutch, Italian and Finnish respondents than might be expected on the basis of comparable estimates for adults aged 30+.

Table 3 – Recurrent income poverty, deprivation and core poverty by age, 1996-2001 (%)

	Income			Deprivation			Combined		
	20-29	**30+**	**Diff.**	**20-29**	**30+**	**Diff.**	**20-29**	**30+**	**Diff.**
Ireland	10.9	24.1	-13.2	22.6	21.4	1.2	6.5	9.9	-3.4
Greece	16.2	20.6	-4.4	22.5	19.2	3.3	6.3	7.8	-1.5
Portugal	11.6	17.7	-6.1	18.6	20.0	-1.4	8.3	7.5	0.8
Italy	24.2	14.7	9.5	22.6	15.1	7.5	12.5	6.4	6.1
Spain	18.1	15.8	2.3	16.4	17.4	-1.0	7.8	5.5	2.3
France	16.2	11.4	4.8	16.3	12.5	3.8	6.5	4.0	2.5
Belgium	8.9	13.1	-4.2	13.4	10.0	3.4	5.8	3.5	2.3
Austria	9.4	10.0	-0.6	12.5	11.8	0.7	2.0	2.5	-0.5
Netherlands	26.3	6.2	20.1	19.5	10.0	9.5	14.4	2.1	12.3
Finland	20.9	10.5	10.4	15.1	8.3	6.8	5.4	1.9	3.5
Denmark	9.4	10.3	-0.9	12.8	6.9	5.9	2.3	0.5	1.8
All	16.8	14.3	2.5	18.6	14.7	3.9	8.1	5.1	3

Source: ECHP UDB, 1996-2001.

With respect to young people, the relationships identified above certainly suggest that vulnerability to poverty across the lifecourse differs significantly from the model originally proposed by Rowntree. Across the sample as a whole, these data suggest that young Europeans are significantly more likely to experience income poverty than older citizens. This effect is amplified when we conceptualise poverty directly in terms of material and social deprivation, where the relationship between poverty and youth is more consistent across the 11 EU member states considered here.

Young Europeans are also more likely to experience recurrent poverty than older citizens, whether this is understood in terms of low income, deprivation or both. Arguably, the view that poverty amongst young people is transient, and that they will "grow out of it", is a normative perspective that has often informed policy responses to youth poverty. Underpinning such perspectives is an implicit distinction between a "deserving" and "undeserving" poor that accords greater moral weight to the vulnerability of some social groups, such as children or the elderly, than it does to others. Whilst in the long run poverty may indeed be episodic for many young people, this is not a situation unique to young people, nor does it obviate the need for a comprehensive strategic commitment to tackling low income and deprivation amongst Europe's young citizens.

Modelling youth vulnerability to poverty

It should be the task of future research to examine the long-term effects of sustained exposure to poverty for the quality of young people's transitions to adulthood. Here, I focus on explaining young people's vulnerability to low income and deprivation using discrete-time models of one-way transitions to examine the factors that predict entry into and exit from poverty. These analyses are based upon ECHP UDB person-period data on young people (aged 19 to 25 in 1996) for Waves 2 to 8 comprising 17,520 individuals and a total of 76,924 observations. The analyses estimate the odds of entering poverty for respondents who were not poor in the previous wave, and the odds of exiting poverty for those who were poor in the previous wave. Separate models are developed with respect to income poverty, deprivation and core poverty as defined above. In each case the models seek to determine the effects of young people's domestic and labour market transitions upon the odds of entering or exiting poverty, especially with respect to the impact of leaving the parental home, becoming unemployed and becoming a student.

Table 4 (below) shows the odds of entering and exiting poverty defined in terms of low income, deprivation and core poverty based on logistic regression. Leaving the parental home and being (or remaining) unemployed both substantially increase the risk of entering poverty for young Europeans aged 17-29. This is especially clear with regard to young people's income situation. Controlling for differences in age, gender, household type and national context, young respondents who had left the parental home in the past year were more than 11 times (11.59 to 1) more likely to become income-poor compared with those who continued living with their parents. In comparison, the effects upon young people's standard of living are much more modest, with nest leavers being more than twice as likely (2.33 to 1) to enter poverty compared with those who remained in the parental home. This disparity may reflect the relative sensitivity of income to short-term "shocks" that are often cushioned by withdrawals from savings in order to alleviate the direct effects of reduced income on individuals' standard of living.

Table 4 also shows that recurrent unemployment strongly increases the odds of entering poverty. Respondents who were unemployed in both waves were more than four times as likely (4.21 to 1) to become income-poor, and more than twice as likely (2.26 to 1) to become deprivation-poor, compared with those who never reported unemployment. At the same time, whilst leaving unemployment reduces the odds of becoming poor in comparison with those who were unemployed in both waves, this group are still at greater risk of income poverty and deprivation than those who were never unemployed. This pattern may reflect the long-term impact of unemployment upon individuals' well-being, that is to say, the after-effects of a severe "income shock".

The effects of being or becoming a student on the odds of entering poverty are less clear. Student status does significantly increase the odds of income poverty for the sample considered here, with those who became a student in the last year being 77% (1.77 to 1) more likely to become income-poor compared with those who were never students. However, leaving college or university has a more powerful effect, perhaps as a result of the delayed income shock of student debt and/or temporary labour market insecurity. More importantly, continuing students and those who left college or university in the last year appear to be at less risk of deprivation compared with their non-student counterparts.

Turning to country-level variations, these data approximate more closely to expectations based upon welfare regime theory than the descriptive results reviewed above initially suggested. For both income and core poverty, the odds of entering poverty are generally higher for respondents living in Mediterranean countries than they are for their northern European counterparts. It may be that the unexpectedly high rates of youth poverty observed in many northern European countries reflect differences in the timing of domestic transitions, with northern European young people leaving the parental home much earlier than their Mediterranean counterparts (Aassve et al., 2002), and perhaps also differences in household structure and labour market trajectories.

In comparison with poverty entry, the factors predicting poverty exit are less well specified due to small sample sizes of those leaving poverty. Nonetheless, the results are broadly consistent with expectations. Moving back to the parental home has a clear positive impact on the odds of exiting poverty. In comparison with respondents who always lived with their parents, those who returned to the parental home were twice as likely to escape income poverty (2.25 to 1) and deprivation (2.14 to 1), and eight times more likely (8.03 to 1) to avoid core poverty. At the same time, respondents who had remained living with their parents throughout were 45% more likely (1/0.69 to 1) to escape income poverty, and 18% more likely (1/0.85 to 1) to escape deprivation, compared with those who never lived with their parents during the period measured by the survey.

However, young people's domestic transitions are less important as predictors of leaving poverty than they are of entering poverty. Both insecurity in employment and student status are more important risk factors in obstructing routes out of poverty for young Europeans. Persistently unemployed respondents were three times (1/0.30 to 1) less likely to escape spells of income poverty, and two times (1/0.51 to 1) less likely to escape deprivation, compared with those who never reported unemployment. Similarly, respondents with any record of post-compulsory education were less likely to be able to escape income poverty than respondents who had not been students, although effects are less consistent for deprivation.

Table 4 – Odds of poverty entry and exit for young people (aged 17-29), logistic regression

	Poverty entry			**Poverty exit**		
	1. Inc.	**2. Dep.**	**3. Core**	**4. Inc.**	**5. Dep.**	**6. Core**
Domestic status:						
Always lived with parents	ref[1]	ref	ref	ref	ref	ref
Never lived with parents	2.56	1.53	3.49	0.69	0.85	[0.84]
Moved back to parental home	[1.59]	2.02	3.66	2.25	2.14	8.03
Moved away from parental home	11.59	2.33	6.06	[0.52]	[0.94]	[0.73]
Employment status:						
Never unemployed	ref	ref	ref	ref	ref	ref
Became unemployed	1.74	1.71	2.64	0.58	0.63	0.63
Left unemployment	1.96	1.38	2.47	0.52	0.80	0.80

1. "Ref" means the reference group with which the other categorised groups are being compared.

Always unemployed	4.21	2.26	5.15	0.30	0.51	0.41
Education status:						
Never a student	ref	ref	ref	ref	ref	ref
Became a student	1.58	1.18	1.33	0.67	[0.91]	0.64
Left study	1.74	0.79	1.23	0.50	1.20	[0.93]
Always student	1.44	0.66	1.25	0.44	0.88	0.59
Austria	ref	ref	ref	ref	ref	ref
Denmark	1.77	[1.18]	2.16	[0.96]	[1.05]	[0.84]
The Netherlands	2.02	[1.08]	3.07	[0.92]	[0.81]	0.60
Belgium	1.50	1.55	2.18	[0.96]	[1.07]	[0.68]
France	1.68	1.34	2.63	[0.94]	0.80	0.61
Ireland	1.94	1.51	3.21	[0.98]	0.72	0.59
Italy	2.97	1.81	5.37	0.68	[0.85]	0.56
Greece	2.65	2.13	3.87	[0.95]	[0.87]	[0.82]
Spain	2.73	1.54	3.32	[1.09]	1.01	0.66
Portugal	1.70	1.34	2.63	[0.82]	0.59	0.37
Finland	1.47	[1.18]	2.09	[1.01]	[0.87]	[0.71]
Constant	0.01	0.04	0.00	3.04	[1.31]	4.42
Nagelkerke R Sq.	.082	.043	.099	.095	.035	.064

Controlling for age, household type and sex (not shown). [ ] = not significant at the 95% confidence level.

To what extent do these findings vary across national contexts? Table 5 (below) shows significant country-level interactions for each of the variables of interest included in the income model of poverty entry (Model 1, above). This approach demonstrates the extent of variability in the social factors that predict entry into income poverty amongst Europe's young citizens. Of particular interest are the effects of welfare regime type, especially with regard to the distinction between northern "corporatist" and "social democratic" welfare regimes on the one hand and the "residualist" welfare model typical of Mediterranean Europe on the other.

Table 5 – The odds of becoming income-poor: country-level interactions

	County-level interaction	Odds
Household type:	DK * single household	3.40
	FI * single household	1.84
	IT * lone parent	0.35
Education status:	GR * never student	4.17
	IT * never student	3.91
	IR * never student	2.63

	FR * never student	2.17
	SP * never student	3.53
	PO * never student	2.77
Domestic transition:	GR * never lived with parents	0.66
	IT * moved in with parents	0.16
	NE * always lived with parents	0.39
	BE * always lived with parents	0.47
	FI * always lived with parents	0.19
Labour market transition:	DK * became unemployed	0.39
	GR * became unemployed	0.51
	SP * became unemployed	0.74
	BE * always unemployed	3.66
	FR * always unemployed	1.69
	IR * always unemployed	2.21
	IT * always unemployed	2.19
	SP * always unemployed	1.99
	PO * always unemployed	5.62

Selected coefficients. [ ] = not significant at 95% confidence level.

The most important country-level interactions relate to the differential impact of domestic and labour market transitions in shaping the risk of poverty. Here, the most substantial effects relate to interactions between student status and vulnerability to poverty entry. In southern European and/or predominantly Catholic countries (Greece, Italy, France, Spain, Portugal, Ireland), respondents who had never been a student were at substantially greater risk of becoming income-poor compared with those respondents with a record of post-compulsory education. In contrast, in northern European and/or predominantly Protestant countries student status increases the odds of entering income poverty.

The impact of unemployment on vulnerability to income poverty is less substantial and straightforward. Interpreting the effects of interactions in non-linear models is a complex task. However, the effects of recurrent unemployment appear to be considerably amplified in southern European countries and/or predominantly Catholic countries (France, Ireland, Italy, Spain, Portugal). As with student status, there thus appears to a reasonably clear divide between northern/Protestant countries and southern/Catholic countries. It may be that the additional "penalty" of recurrent unemployment in predicting poverty vulnerability in southern Europe may reflect underlying differences in the welfare mix between northern and southern European societies, and especially more limited availability of social transfer payments for unemployment in southern countries.

Turning finally to domestic transitions, the interactions again suggest an underlying distinction between northern and southern European societies. In comparison with nest leavers, young people who remained living with their parents received an additional "bonus" in avoiding poverty in several northern European countries (the Netherlands, Belgium, Finland). In view of the negative coefficient associated with leaving the parental home in the main effects model, the impact of nest leaving on the likelihood of becoming income-poor is especially acute in these northern European countries.

Discussion and conclusions

Across Europe, young people are especially vulnerable to income poverty as measured by the Laeken indicators. However, whilst comparative analyses have tended to focus exclusively on income measures of poverty, these data show that young Europeans as a whole are also more likely to experience both material and social deprivation and core poverty. Moreover, the experience of poverty is not confined to a small minority of "socially excluded" young people, but is very common for Europe's young people at various points in their transitions to adulthood. At the same time, these analyses show that young people are also more vulnerable to recurrent poverty than older adults, and it would be most surprising if such prolonged exposure did not seriously undermine young people's capacity for successful transitions to adulthood. Tackling youth poverty is thus important both as a policy objective in its own right, and as a lever in reducing the risk of more extreme forms of exclusion and marginalisation.

The models discussed above also demonstrate the importance of young people's domestic and labour market transitions in shaping their vulnerability to poverty. Leaving home, becoming unemployed and entering full-time post-compulsory education are all important predictors of vulnerability to poverty (see also Aassve et al., 2005). At the same time, these analyses suggest that there are important between-country variations in the relative weight of such factors in predicting entry into and exit from poverty. In particular, substantial differences are evident with respect to the effects of nest leaving, unemployment and student status between the "corporatist" and "social democratic" welfare regimes of northern Europe and Scandinavia, and the "residualist" model typical of Mediterranean European countries. Clearly, these differences reflect cross-national variations in the transition profiles of European youth but, as Daniel Blanch shows in his chapter on Galician youth in this volume, such differences in the timing of domestic and labour market transitions means that the effects of domestic position on youth inclusion are different in nature as well as degree across European societies.

What then are the overall policy implications of these analyses for the future direction of youth policy in Europe? To the extent that one can speak of an integrated European framework for youth policy, the development of youth inclusion policies have largely focused on combating social exclusion, preventing social "deviance", and promoting the social integration of young people primarily through active labour market policies. In contrast, efforts to combat poverty amongst Europe's young citizens through the promotion of income-maximisation strategies, for example through improved social welfare provision and upgraded minimum wage legislation, have in general been conspicuous by their absence. Clearly, caution is also needed in assessing the policy implications arising from the link between student status and poverty in some countries. Where becoming a student brings a high risk of poverty, the factors which cause this should be investigated and addressed and the findings should certainly not be interpreted to suggest a downplaying of

widening participation policies – not least because the long-term financial and material benefits of higher education cannot be estimated within this context.

However, the policy emphasis on combating social exclusion, discrimination and social "deviance" largely reflects a perception of youth as a policy problem rather than a resource (Biggart et al., 2004). At the same time, the focus upon "exclusion" rather than poverty has all too often been interpreted narrowly in terms of labour market non-participation, with the necessary corollary that the "integration" of youth is to be achieved through labour market insertion. In addition to the theoretical and conceptual shortcomings of this "social integrationist discourse" (Levitas, 2005), discussed by Helen Colley in her chapter in this book, this strategy is unlikely to be effective – not least because, whilst youth unemployment is a strong predictor of poverty, many of Europe's "poor" young people are in fact neither unemployed nor seeking work. Poverty is thus more widespread amongst European youth than is generally acknowledged. Importantly, it affects large numbers of young people who are in education, employment or training, and who are therefore usually defined as "socially included".

Notwithstanding these general observations, the above analyses demonstrate just how little we currently know about the extent and dynamics of youth poverty in Europe – and especially about their long-term effects upon the quality of young people's transitions to adulthood. These findings have also focused primarily upon inter-generational inequalities within individual nation states rather than on spatial inequalities in levels of youth poverty across Europe as a whole. Certainly it is clear that, at a European level, rates of youth disadvantage are highest in southern and eastern Europe. However, what is equally striking, as illustrated here, is the disparity in access to social rights across the lifecourse in countries which are usually viewed as having low levels of inequality. Moreover, the degree of variability across Europe in the factors that predict entry to and exit from poverty also needs be acknowledged in the design and implementation of polices to eradicate youth poverty. National and transnational anti-poverty initiatives therefore need to be tailored to supporting young people transitions in a diverse range of settings across Europe, for example with respect to the timing of domestic and labour market transitions, rather than assuming a traditional, linear – and outmoded – model of young people's routes to adult independence.

References

Aassve, A., Francesco, C., Billari, B., Mazzuco, S. and Ongaro, F. (2002), "Leaving comparative analysis of ECHP data", *Journal of European Social Policy*, 12(4), pp. 259-275.

Aassve, A., Iacovou, M. and Mencarini, L. (2005), "Youth poverty in Europe: what do we know?" ISER Working Paper 2005-2. Colchester: University of Essex, Institute for Social and Economic Research.

Biggart, A., Bendit, R., Cairns, D., Hein, K. and Mörch, S. (2004), "Families and transitions in Europe". EUR20796. Luxembourg: European Commission.

Catan, L. (2004), *Becoming adult: changing youth transitions in the 21st century*. Brighton: Trust for the Study of Adolescence.

CEC (Commission of the European Communities) (2001), "A new impetus for European youth", COM(2001)681 final. Brussels: CEC.

Dennis, I. and Guio, A.-C. (2004), "Poverty and social exclusion in the EU", *Statistics in Focus Series*, 16/2004. Luxembourg: Eurostat.

Levitas, R. (2005), *The inclusive society? Social exclusion and New Labour*, 2nd edn. London: Palgrave Macmillan.

Millar, J. (2002), "Transitions from youth to adulthood", in Barnes, M., Heady, C., Middleton, S., Millar, J., Papadopoulos, F., and Tsakloglou, P. (eds.), *Poverty and social exclusion in Europe*. Cheltenham: Edward Elgar.

Mizen, P. (2003), *Changing state of youth*. London: Palgrave.

Rowntree, B.S. (1901/2000), *Poverty, a study of town life*. Bristol: The Policy Press.

Whelan, C., Layte, R., Maître, B. and Nolan, B. (2001), "Income, deprivation and economic strain: an analysis of the European Community Household Panel", *European Sociological Review*, 17(4), pp. 357-372.

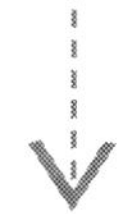

5. Depending on their parents: risks of social exclusion among youth in north-western Spain

Daniel Blanch

Introduction

This chapter will examine the risks of social exclusion for youth in the autonomous region of Galicia, located in the north-west of Spain.[1] Galician youth constitute a good example of potential exclusion due to several social characteristics of the region, particularly: low mobility, late emancipation, traditional family structures and negative social capital. European, national and regional policies have been implemented in the last decade in order to mitigate factors leading to social exclusion, but they easily miss the broader picture and overall complexity of incorporating youth fully into society. Policies are often focused on specific salient aspects of public problems and may not address the underlying social factors leading to youth exclusion.

Studies based on large-scale quantitative data are often unable to examine local challenges fully, due to their level of aggregation. Our research complements such studies by presenting a series of fine-grained insights that have been teased out of qualitative research concerning the dilemmas that youth face with regard to social inclusion and exclusion. These insights into the motivations of young people and the pressures they experience provide a vital perspective on the challenges facing them in today's world. Understanding this perspective is essential if effective policy and practice are to be developed.

Through the use of discussion groups in our research, we have endeavoured to enter the deeper realm of young people's opinions and mindsets regarding social inclusion in a context that is postmodern in attitudes but traditional in structure. These discussion groups were carried out with 108 students over the last nine years, divided into 27 groups that met weekly throughout the school year for a period of one hour. Discussion groups provide an in-depth look at individuals' lives and motivations. According to Blumer:

1. I would like to thank the organisers and participants of the Youth Research Partnership Seminar on Social Inclusion and Young People for their helpful feedback. Special thanks are also due to my research colleagues at CIDEFA Research Centre, particularly Craig Charnley and Elisa Rustenbach, for their work in compiling data, commenting on hypotheses and contributing their expertise to this paper. Any errors in this paper are entirely the author's.

"A small number of individuals, brought together as a discussion or resource group, is more valuable many times over than any representative sample. Such a group, discussing collectively their sphere of life and probing into it as they meet one another's disagreements, will do more to lift the veils covering the sphere of life than any other device that I know of" (cited by Flick, 1998, p. 116).

The findings of our study show that Mediterranean youth face problems which are quite different from the challenges confronting youth in northern Europe, and this chapter begins by outlining these. In addition, due to its particular characteristics, the region of Galicia demonstrates a certain distinctiveness vis-à-vis other regions in Spain, which will also be described. In consequence, broad national and European policies need to be reinforced by additional regional initiatives that address unique regional-level problems. After presenting our findings on the risks of social exclusion for Galician youth, I shall therefore briefly examine various policies at the several governmental levels in Galicia, consider their limitations and discuss ways in which these might be overcome.

Our findings complement other research reported in this volume. Siyka Kovacheva's research on youth in eastern Europe (see Chapter 3) offers some clear similarities to the habits and attitudes of Mediterranean youth, especially the ways in which they conduct their relationship with their parents. A variety of interesting findings also arise from the broad statistical data presented in Eldin Fahmy's chapter (4). He states, regarding domestic transitions, that "interactions are again suggestive of an underlying distinction between northern and southern European societies with respect to the factors shaping young people's vulnerability to poverty in Europe". This fits well with our research, which indicates that the behaviour patterns of youth in Mediterranean countries tend to be family dependent. Southern European youth seek to avoid poverty by maintaining financial dependence on parents and late emancipation from the family home. But this comes at a price, which they will tell us about in this chapter.

Social exclusion risks for youth: labour market challenges

Recent studies have begun to distinguish several types of exclusion (Kieselbach, 2004). While much of the research focuses on economic exclusion due to unemployment and difficulties in entering the labour market, we find this to be only one element of the larger issue. Exclusion may also be social, institutional, cultural or even spatial/physical (Littlewood and Herkommer, 1999, p. 15). The following factors tend to place youth at risk of exclusion in Galicia:

- difficulties entering the labour market;
- low mobility, insufficient foreign language skills;
- late emancipation from parental home;
- inter-generational transmission of traditional localist culture;
- low levels of state subsidies or aid to youth;
- negative social capital and low conventional political participation.

For youth in Spain, entry into the labour market is a particularly difficult step in the process of social inclusion. It is likely that youth are significantly influenced to stay at home by the high unemployment rate, which has reached 24% among female youth in Galicia (Xunta de Galicia, 2004, p. 101). The marked improvement in youth unemployment figures since 1994 still leaves Spain in a mid-range position vis-à-vis other European countries, as shown in Table 1.

Table 1 – Seasonally adjusted unemployment rates for youth under 25 in percentage of workforce, ranked by country in descending order of most recent data

Country	1994	2005
Greece	28	27
Italy	29	2
Belgium	23	22
France	29	22
Finland	34	20
Spain	40	19
Luxembourg	7	18
Portugal	15	16
Germany	16	1
Great Britain	16	14
Austria	6	10
Ireland	23	8
Denmark	10	8
Netherlands	11	8

Source: Eurostat 2006.

Yet in Spain, regions with lower rates of unemployment still demonstrate high percentages of youth living at home, much higher than in the north of Europe (Leal-Maldonado, 2002, pp. 256-7). This suggests that the unemployment rate is not the whole picture.

A notable fact in relation to job placement in Spain is that youth may have difficulties entering the labour market even if they are highly qualified. Spain is an exception to the Western norm, in that a college degree in this country does not ensure higher earnings, better employment options or a job in their field of training. In contrast with other countries, a lack of adequate academic qualifications is not a key predictor of social exclusion for youth in Spain (Kieselbach 2004, p. 41).

Since job options are very limited close to home, many young people decide to look for work outside of Spain. The best opportunities to find jobs tend to be in countries where Spanish is not spoken, which means that language skills and personal adaptability also come into play. A lack of adequate language skills thus becomes another barrier to integration into society, as it limits emancipation options. Table 2 reveals the difficulties that Spanish youth face when crossing the language barrier, especially compared to the Nordic countries and Luxembourg (see also Chapter 15 by Christiane Weis). Even though students' language skills have been improving in Spain, it is still a problem for almost half the country's youth.

Table 2 – Percentage of youth saying language difficulties would be their main barrier for studying abroad, by country

Country	1997	2001
Spain	51	47
Ireland	41	47
Great Britain	48	41
France	35	40
Portugal	48	39
Italy	41	38
Germany	27	28
Greece	27	24
Belgium	32	23
Austria	21	23
Netherlands	21	22
Denmark	16	16
Finland	17	16
Luxembourg	13	12
Sweden	20	12

Source: Eurobarometers 47.2 and 55.1.

Although economic self-sufficiency is important for youth, it does not fully explain the process of emancipation, as young people in Spain delay departure from home for an additional two years on average after they become financially independent (Leal-Maldonado, 2002, p. 254). Research has also found that time is a factor in exclusion: the longer youth remain outside the labour market, the more likely it is that they will move towards a situation of exclusion (Kieselbach, 2004, p. 41). Unemployment and lack of economic self-sufficiency may well function as deterrents to the social inclusion of Mediterranean youth, but there are clearly other factors as well, which we shall now examine.

Youth emancipation in Spain

One of the distinguishing characteristics of Spanish youth is their late departure from home compared to other youth in the West. Table 3 illustrates this Mediterranean tendency, represented here by four Southern countries that evidence the slowest emancipation rates in Europe. This may in part be due to the fact that governmental subsidies for youth housing have only recently been offered.

Table 3 – Age at which 50% of youth are living away from home by country.

Country	Women	Men
Italy	27.1	29.7
Spain	26.6	28.4

Greece	22.9	28.2
Portugal	25.2	28.0
Austria	23.4	27.2
Ireland	25.2	26.3
Belgium	23.8	25.8
Germany	21.6	24.8
France	22.2	24.1
Great Britain	21.2	23.5
Netherlands	21.2	23.3
Finland	20.0	21.9
Denmark	20.3	21.4

Source: European Communities Household Panel, cited in Iacovou, 2001.

The percentage of Galician youth that have left home happens to be lower than that of any other Spanish region: 28.6% (Leal-Maldonado 2002, p. 256). Over 70% of young Galicians live at home until age 30 (Xunta de Galicia, 2002), and the average age of emancipation, rather than decreasing, has increased over the last decade (Moreno-Minguez, 2002, Table 1).

Once again forming a Mediterranean cluster, youth in Spain, Greece and Italy tend to rely on their families for income more than in other European countries. The opposite is evident in Great Britain and Denmark, where the percentage of youth dependent on their families for income is less than a third of what it is in these three Mediterranean countries (Table 4).

Table 4 – Percentage of youth aged 15-24 living on parental resources by country

Country	**1997**	**2001**
Italy	68	74
Greece	51	71
Spain	62	67
Luxembourg	58	66
France	48	61
Belgium	48	58
Portugal	51	54
Germany	38	46
Netherlands	33	42
Austria	41	42
Finland	41	40
Sweden	34	39

Ireland	38	32
Great Britain	17	21
Denmark	19	19

Source: Eurobarometers 47.2 and 55.1.

So how does the dependency of Mediterranean youth on parental resources affect their relationship with their parents? Although families provide the needed security for youth, keeping them from financial hardship, this can easily involve significant limitations on young people's choices. We shall now examine to what degree youth dependency affects family relationships, and what sort of constraints are placed on young people.

Close-knit Galician families limit young people's options

Research carried out by CIDEFA Research Centre sheds light on the feelings students express concerning family relationships, social inclusion, and the process of leaving home and seeking work (see Appendix B in Blanch et al., 2003). CIDEFA's research has focused on comparing and contrasting the results of broad quantitative studies, such as the Eurobarometers, with our own data from in-depth discussions held in groups and carried out over a number of years with a broad range of students at the University of Santiago, in the capital of Galicia. In this chapter we will draw on the quantitative data and, particularly, our qualitative investigation, both of which lead us to conclude that family conflict is not generally a central element of youth concerns.

Most Spanish parents now maintain a model of open tolerance towards their children, providing youth with a margin of freedom. As a norm, young people feel that the family places a higher priority on maintaining its own unity than on determining how youth should live their lives (see Gaviria-Sabbah, 2002, p. 4; Moreno-Minguez, 2002). This translates into a relatively comfortable situation for young people at home. One student interviewed by CIDEFA expressed herself in this way: "Living with parents is a selfish option that means being cared for by your folks and having a good standard of living".

Spaniards live at home longer than other Europeans, delay the reproduction process, and then generally leave home in order to get married. Although Spanish youth tend to live out a very different love life from what their parents envisioned, this does not lead to a very different social structure – young Spaniards still overwhelmingly choose marriage over cohabitation and raise their children in close contact with their own parental home.[2] In response to why they would choose to get married instead of living together, 72% of youth say it is due to pressure from their families (Moreno-Minguez, 2002). Spanish families are intent on maintaining their structure from one generation to the next.

The parenting style that most Galician youth experienced was one of negotiation, of ignoring differences in various areas as long as the family could remain a unit. In other words, in few cases did confrontations lead families to break up. Serious conflict was generally avoided for the greater good of keeping the family together. For this reason the distance between parents and youth on a variety of matters does

2. However, in contrast with prior generations, they now choose to form the smallest families in Europe. So Spain has gone from having the largest number of people per household, to one of the lowest fertility rates.

not typically lead to lasting divisions or separation of the family unit. Over 80% of Galician youth state that their relationship with their parents is good or very good (Xunta de Galicia, 2004).

This sort of negotiated agreement seems to work well for bridging the gap between the values of the elder and younger generations, allowing many issues to fall into a grey zone that is not fundamental for the family, while a few key loyalties remain strong. Some of the highest values are a commitment to care for elders, to tight family ties and not to "publicly mar the family's good name". So to the extent that Galician families have eluded some of the most divisive inter-generational issues, families remain relatively strong. As one student emphasised in a CIDEFA interview, "Family transcends all, they are the most important relationships".

So we find that there are certain benefits of Mediterranean culture for young people:

- families provide needed financial and social support;
- families tend to avoid conflict that would break the family structure;
- pressure to "grow up" remains low until about age 30;
- societal tension is diffused as youth express novel ideas but remain within the traditional social system.

This family dependency does not mean that there are no clashes, but it does imply that there must be a certain number of common attitudes and values in order to assure that family life will continue to remain stable. Research suggests that Spanish youth typically have most differences with their parents on issues of personal relationships (youth seek less commitment and more flexibility), entertainment (youth prefer staying out late), religious values (youth are less devout), and the role of women in society (youth overwhelmingly support gender equality in the working world). They do not tend to conflict significantly on issues regarding priorities in life (family over work), or most social practices like marriage (Moreno-Minguez, 2002).

Traditional family values do not limit freedom of thought for today's youth in Galicia, but they do limit their margin for action. Even though they hold drastically different values from their parents, 8 out of 10 participants in the discussion groups considered the younger generation as conformist rather than rebellious. This would seem to be evident in the fact that few youth have actually opted for lifestyles that are far removed from traditional options – there are very few unmarried mothers, couples in long-term cohabitation, or individuals living alternative lifestyles. Although it has increased over the years, the number of unmarried mothers is still very low in Galicia: only 14% of mothers were unmarried in the year 2000, up from 9% in 1994, but still well under the national average of 18%, or the European average, which is twice as high (Eurostat, 2006b). Yet changes have occurred as the departure from home is delayed, which in turn delays childbearing. The average age for a Galician woman to have her first child is now 31, up from 29.4 in 1996 (Instituto Galego de Estatistica, 2005). The statistics also show a very low number of marriages and of children per fertile woman, as the region is second to last in Spain on both measures.

Galician youth therefore tend to opt for freedom of attitudes and opinions, but stay within the realm of the family's protection and aid. This may be seen as a protective mechanism that ensures economic support and access to the family's resources, but it does not lead youth towards independence. In the words of one student, "In

Spain, young people have no power, no independence. We study, but have no power to change the world – our protective parents give us no margin to do that".

Even when young people seek to move beyond the protection of their parents and enter the labour market, they encounter a variety of constraints, so that a lack of mobility can become a limiting factor (see Xunta de Galicia, 2004). Often the idea of finding a local job that provides closeness to family is so strong that some youth opt for turning down opportunities that require moving away from the local area. A localist culture that emphasises family ties and regional traditions has a positive side as it provides safety in the small local society of home and friends, but can lead towards exclusion from the larger society or from a reasonable job and future. Localist culture tends to become a trap when youth seek to enter the labour market or emancipate from the parental home, as it limits options. Living, working or studying outside Galicia is not currently perceived as a positive long-term experience that enriches lives (Xunta de Galicia, 2004, p. 99).

This leads to a situation where youth express strong support for a modern de-structured lifestyle, but find that they are constrained when it comes to living out that lifestyle. Even when they are able to move away from home, a localist narrative often comes into play, suggesting that leaving home should not involve breaking with family, friends and familiar surroundings. Galician youth express the view that culture pulls them towards home, at a price, as they surrender a portion of their autonomy. Our research suggests that, in these circumstances, youth dependency is a factor leading towards social exclusion.

Youth as citizens: regional culture and social capital

Another factor affecting youth in Galicia, both regarding mobility and inclusion, is the distinctive regional culture. A problem of cultural exclusion can arise in areas which have a prominent alternative culture that seeks to build on its differences with the dominant culture. In Galicia, a region with its own language distinct from Castilian Spanish, studies have shown that there is a certain degree of cultural cleavage that highlights regional uniqueness vis-à-vis the dominant Spanish culture. (For extensive research on Galicia's national character and cultural differences, see Maiz, 1997.) As one student expressed, in a view that is typical of a significant portion of youth in our study, "Spain's past centralism makes it harder for me to identify with Spain than with Europe – I have no fear of Europe". This distancing from the rest of Spain can form a barrier to easy personal interfacing with cultures of other regions, which in turn can lead to a localist life strategy focused on setting up life in a way that is coherent with family traditions, and ignoring or seeking to elude global trends that work against a life built principally around a local context.

In addition, research on social capital has highlighted that negative social capital can be a factor hindering the economic and social development of regions and countries (Pharr and Putnam, 2000). Negative social capital includes a variety of associated factors including a lack of interpersonal trust, of collective agency, of institutions that are collectively respected and of links between people, such as associations and clubs, which provide a constructive network for society. These factors come into play when analysing social exclusion, since they tend to show a weakness in the fabric of society that often affects youth deeply.

The level of social capital in Galicia is generally low with regard to participation in associations and other activities that fall outside the immediate circle of friends and family (Blanch, 2005). Tight family and social networks remain the norm, and outside these circles there is a rather high level of distrust, which works against allowing co-operative relations on a horizontal level. Yet youth in Galicia have demonstrated over the last few years that, although a negative culture of political participation persists concerning voting and traditional forms of participation, young people are politically active. Non-conventional forms of participation have been demonstrated recently in, for example, volunteering in ecological disasters, street marches to protest governmental policies in education and foreign policy, and ad hoc activism. These forms of non-conventional participation are generally not fully recognised in the public sphere as legitimate and important functions of citizens, yet they tend to be the most frequent alternatives for youth to express their ideas about the realm of politics. Even though social capital indicators such as levels of association, interpersonal trust and political confidence have not increased in Spain, unconventional participation levels suggest that youth do engage in collective activity, but have a sense of exclusion from conventional politics. One student put it this way: "We can only get things to happen when we struggle [against the system], because those who have power ignore us and make laws without thinking about what is right or wrong for our [youth] interests".

The European Commission (EC) White Paper "A new impetus for European youth" suggests that young people are keen on democracy, but mistrust institutions and old mechanisms:

> "It is up to the public authorities to bridge the gap between young people's eagerness to express their opinions and the methods and structures which society offers. Failure to do so might fuel the 'citizenship' deficit, or even encourage protest" (EC, 2001, p. 10).

Politicians are now recognising this gap and seeking to address it. Belgian Prime Minister Verhofstadt (2006) has proposed a Manifesto for a New Europe in order to delineate a European project capable of attracting younger generations. In a follow-up to the EC White Paper on youth, the Commission proposes "greater participation by young people in the life of the community in which they live", involving lines of action such as identifying "more carefully the obstacles which prevent specific groups from participating ..." (EC, 2003, pp. 5-6). In this chapter I have endeavoured to clarify some of the obstacles to youth inclusion, and possible solutions, focusing on mainstream youth rather than specific at-risk groups. If defined narrowly, social exclusion misses the problems that affect millions of average young people who are unable to fully participate in society. Merely fostering employment is insufficient, as exclusion can also result from social structures and practices.

Taking into consideration the "no" votes to the European Constitution in several national referenda, the social unrest that took place in France in 2005 and the ongoing migration and labour-market issues arising from European Union enlargement, it is clear that social issues are deeply intertwined with European policies. So at this point let us turn to the policies being carried out with regard to social inclusion issues faced by youth. It is evident that the various levels of government will address issues somewhat differently, based on their resources and perspectives. Top level policies have been successful in providing the momentum for addressing social exclusion, but in Spain the regions are so diverse in their needs regarding youth that subsidiarity becomes the key, as policies can be designed to fit specific regional needs. In the past, Galician policies have traditionally focused more on the elderly than on youth. This is now changing, as new policies come into force intended to address the chronic localism and lack of mobility.

Social inclusion policies

Several initiatives from the Council of Europe and the EC have in recent years attempted to address the issue of social inclusion. In particular, the EC has led member states to create national action plans for social inclusion. European policy has been to influence members to make social inclusion a key part of their agendas, exerting pressure to get states to adjust their national objectives and policies to fit with the European initiatives. These plans have had mixed results in the various European countries. Generally they appear to have fostered third sector involvement in social inclusion plans, but have not actually revolutionised this area significantly (Brandsen et al., 2005). Policies addressing social exclusion tend to focus on easily identifiable issues and groups, while leaving the larger theoretical debate to academics and third sector agents.

Selected social inclusion policies affecting youth

European:

- EC Guided National Action Plans on Social Inclusion (2000)
- White Paper: "A new impetus for European youth" (2001)
- European Youth Pact (2005)

National:

- Spain's III National Action Plan for Social Inclusion 2005-06
- Youth Plan for 2005-08

Regional:

- Social Inclusion Plan of Galicia for 2001-06
- Galicia's Strategic Youth Plan for 2004-07

Spain's III National Action Plan for Social Inclusion was approved by the Spanish Government in September, covering the 2005-06 period. It follows the EU guidelines for increased access to jobs and other resources for those in situations of risk of exclusion, involving prevention of exclusion, actions to protect the most vulnerable groups and people, and attempts to mobilise and to facilitate participation in this process by all pertinent social agents. Its strategic lines of action span broad areas of social need. One of the key elements in this whole process is the involvement of third sector agents. They constitute an integral part of making the avoidance of exclusion reach as far as possible into society, in order to become truly multidimensional (Montagut, 2005). In Spain, over 500 third sector organisations were approached in the consultation process developing the national action plan for social inclusion (Ministerio de Trabajo y Asuntos Sociales, 2005). However, their involvement in the process occurred only after the draft documents on social inclusion had been prepared.

Traditionally social inclusion policies have not ranked high on the Spanish political agenda, as retirement and aging tended to be viewed as more significant (Brandsen et al., 2005, p. 18). In addition, the complexity of integrating and co-ordinating the various agencies and governments involved, from local to regional to national, became evident as they have attempted to address social exclusion risks. In Spain the regional governments have significant competencies in the social arena, so their presence and involvement is essential. The numerous social pro-

grammes implemented by the Spanish regions run alongside the national initiatives of the Spanish central administration, channelling resources towards these objectives. Minimum income schemes have been implemented at a regional level in Spain, as well as housing, education and health initiatives for individuals with exclusion risks (see Almenara, 2004, p. 12). Yet table 5 shows how, after Italy, Spain has the lowest percentage of funding dedicated to social inclusion among these European countries.

Table 5 – Percentage of total national social protection budget dedicated to social inclusion

Country	1991	2002
Netherlands	2.8	5.2
Portugal	0.4	4.6
Denmark	4.1	3.6
Greece	1.1	2.3
Luxembourg	1.0	2.3
Ireland	1.7	2.3
Sweden	0.0	2.2
Finland	2.2	2.1
Belgium	2.0	1.9
Germany	1.8	1.7
France	0.9	1.4
Austria	1.2	1.4
Great Britain	0.8	0.9
Spain	0.4	0.8
Italy	0.1	0.2

Source: Eurostat, SEEPROS, cited in Consejo Economico y Social, 2005.

The region of Galicia developed its own Social Inclusion Plan for 2001-06. Monitoring of the social inclusion process in Spain has now provided some evidence of the extent of impact that these policies have had (see Almenara, 2004). Galicia's plan has been criticised for placing excessive emphasis on elderly and disabled persons when unemployment was "one of the main variables explaining poverty and social exclusion as well as a marked feminisation of the problem" (Almenara, 2004, p. 23).

Only recently has there been a move to address youth needs through policies specifically designed for young people. The Spanish Government set up a Youth Plan for 2005-08, with the main objective being to encourage the emancipation of youth. This plan will be funded with 2.3 billion, to be allocated to youth employment, education and housing (Instituto de la Juventud, 2005, p. 1). It also offers new institutional possibilities for youth to participate in designing Spain's youth policies.

Galicia's regional Strategic Plan for Youth (Plan Estratexico de Xuventude) was designed to cover the years 2004-07. With the recent change in the regional government,[3] modifications will be introduced into this plan, which proposes a variety of measures that are intended to favour emancipation and increase youth mobility and participation. This plan envisions that Galician youth would become mobile as a rule, rather than as the exception. This is to be done by emphasising linguistic skills that facilitate mobility in order to provide greater connection with the rest of the European Union.

Youth policies are a key tool designed to address the challenges that arise from a lack of mobility and slow emancipation. The weak development of the Spanish welfare state in this policy area has meant that attempts to address social exclusion risks are only in their initial phases. Now that we have examined some of the risks facing youth in Galicia and the policies intended to address them, we shall conclude our study with a brief overview of our findings.

Conclusions

In southern Europe, youth have only recently appeared on the institutional agenda as a priority, and much remains to be done in order to work towards full inclusion. Galician youth suffer from a sense of exclusion from society's productive framework due to a late and difficult emancipation, poor labour market options, a negative socialisation concerning politics and citizen participation, and a strong transmission of inter-generational values that encourage localism. In response to this the Galician regional government has begun to implement policies to facilitate mobilisation and emancipation, which have yet to reach large numbers of youth. The Spanish Government has made a more concerted effort in this direction in accordance with EU guidelines. However, policies tend to address matters in a piecemeal fashion, and do not capture the overall sense of exclusion that a Spanish student can feel at age 30, living at home, unable to find work locally and with little freedom to move far from home.

At home, youth tend to be eclipsed by their elders, so that young people's presence is one of dependence, and their influence is mostly limited to their circle of peers. Outside the home, youth tend to adopt unconventional forms of political participation, which can lead to a sense of exclusion if they remain outside the realm of recognised legitimate expressions of political ideas. This is compounded by Galicia's historically distinct position in relation to the Spanish state. As citizens, Galician youth need to feel that they have a recognised legitimate voice, a presence and some sort of influence.

Galicia's shift from a pre-modern economic and societal structure to become part of a global economy involves a conflict between modernisation and a cultural paradigm in the region that encourages geographical immobility, strong family ties, economic constraints on emancipation, with norms that emphasise localism and tradition. All of this combines to slow down the transition process of Galician youth from the family into society, making the family's social contract of self-protection and survival weigh more heavily than young people's quest for independence and emancipation. Thus, in spite of a strong tendency towards globalisation, individualisation and specialisation, Galicia struggles with past tendencies towards localism, traditionalism and immobility. Galician youth seem to choose compro-

3. In June of 2005 the conservative Popular Party of Galicia was replaced in the regional government by a coalition of the Socialist Party of Galicia and the Galician Nationalist Bloc.

mise over conflict, allowing traditions to retain a powerful influence in their lives, delaying their inclusion in society. Policies designed to facilitate their emancipation could empower youth to move beyond family resources, allowing them to establish a life of their own as full participants in society.

References

Almenara (2004), "Second monitoring report of the 'Group of non-governmental experts in the fight against poverty and social exclusion' on the National Action Plan for Social Inclusion 2003-2005 of Spain" (online). Madrid: Almenara Estudios Economicos y Sociales, S.L. (accessed 16 September 2005). Available at: www.almenaraestudios.com.

Blanch, D. (2005), "Between traditional and postmodern: youth political participation in Galicia", in Forbrig, J. (ed.), *What about youth political participation?* Strasbourg: Council of Europe.

Blanch, D., Rustenbach, E. and Charnley, C. (2003), "Youth in Galicia". Paper presented at the European Sociological Association Conference, 23-26 September, Murcia, Spain.

Brandsen, T., Pavolini, E., Ranci, C., Sittermann, B. and Zimmer A. (2005), "The National Action Plan on Social Inclusion: an opportunity for the third sector?". Third sector European Policy Working Paper 14 (online). London: London School of Economics and Political Science (accessed 17 July 2005). Available at: www.lse.ac.uk/collections/TSEP/.

Consejo Económico y Social (2005), "Informe sobre el borrador del III Plan Nacional de Acción para la Inclusión Social del Reino de España, 2005-2006". Colección Informes, N.4/2005 (online). Madrid: CES (accessed 14 July 2005). Available at: www.ces.es.

European Commission (April-June 1997), "Eurobarometer 47.2: Young Europeans". Brussels: Commission of the European Union.

European Commission (2001), "A new impetus for European youth". White Paper COM(2001)681 final. Brussels: Commission of the European Union.

European Commission (April-May 2001), "Eurobarometer 55.1OVR: Young European Citizens". Brussels: Commission of the European Union.

European Commission (2003), "Follow-up to the White Paper on a new impetus for European youth", COM(2003)184 final. Brussels: Commission of the European Union.

Eurostat (2006a) (12/2006 – 1 February 2006), "Euro-indicators news release" (online). Luxembourg: Eurostat Press Office (accessed 25 October 2005 and 18 May 2006). Available at:
http://epp.eurostat.cec.eu.int .

Eurostat (2006b) (59/2006 – 12 May 2006), "The family in the EU25 seen through figures" (online). Luxembourg: Eurostat Press Office (accessed 18 May 2006). Available at: http://epp.eurostat.cec.eu.int.

Flick, U. (1998), *An introduction to qualitative research*. London: Sage Publications, LTD.

Gaviria-Sabbah, S. (2002), "Retener a la juventud o invitarla a abandonar la casa familiar. Análisis de España y Francia", *Estudios de Juventud*, 58, pp. 1-6.

Iacovou, M. (2001), "Leaving home in the European Union". Working Papers of the Institute for Social and Economic Research, No. 2001-18. Colchester: University of Essex.

Instituto de la Juventud (Injuve) (2005), "El plan de Juventud 2005-2008 apuesta por el empleo, la vivienda y la formación de los jóvenes". Nota de prensa (online). Madrid: Injuve (accessed 18 June 2006). Available at: www.mtas.es/injuve/contenidos.downloadatt.action.id=151994487.

Instituto Galego de Estatistica (IGE) (2005), "Galicia en cifras" (online). Santiago: IGE (accessed 18 June 2006). Available at: www.ige.eu/ga/estructura/documentos/folletos/MNP_2004F.pdf.

Kieselbach, T. (2004), "Desempleo juvenil de larga duración y riesgo de exclusión social en Europa: Informe cualitativo del proyecto de investigación YUSEDER". *Estudios de Juventud*, 65, pp. 31-49.

Leal-Maldonado, J. (2002), "Retraso de la emancipación juvenil y dificultad de acceso de los jóvenes a la vivienda", in Iglesias de Ussel, J. (ed.), *La sociedad: teoría e investigación teórica*. Madrid: CIS.

Littlewood, P. and Herkommer S. (1999), "Identifying social exclusion", in Littlewood, P. (ed.), *Social exclusion in Europe*. Aldershot: Ashgate.

Maiz, R. (1997), *A idea de nación*. Santiago de Compostela: Xerais.

Montagut, T. (2005), "The third sector and the policy process in Spain". Third sector European Policy Working Paper 2 (online). London: London School of Economics and Political Science (accessed 10 July 2005). Available at: www.lse.ac.uk/collections/TSEP/.

Moreno-Minguez, A. (2002), "El mito de la ruptura intergeneracional en los jóvenes españoles", *Estudios de Juventud*, 58, pp. 1-16.

Ministerio de Trabajo y Asuntos Sociales (MTAS) (2005), *El Periódico*, 8 September. Madrid: MTAS.

Pharr, S. and Putnam, R. (2000), *Disaffected democracies: what's troubling the trilateral countries?* Princeton: Princeton University Press.

Romar (2005) Espana, unico pais de la OCDE donde una carrera no garantiza un trabajo. *La Voz de Galicia,* 14 September, p. 84.

Verhofstadt, G. (2006), *The United States of Europe*. London: Federal Trust for Education and Research.

Xunta de Galicia (2002), *Enquisa Xuventude Galega*. Santiago: Xunta.

Xunta de Galicia (2004), "Plan Estrategico de Xuventude: da información a participación, 2004-2007" (online). Santiago: Xunta (accessed 11 July 2005). Available at: www.rix.org/datos/publicaciones/planestratexico04 07.

6. European policies on social inclusion and youth: continuity, change and challenge

Helen Colley

Introduction

Like a number of those who contributed papers to the Youth Research Partnership seminar and chapters to this book, many youth researchers and practitioners have devoted their efforts to supporting the fight against poverty and social exclusion within the framework set by European and national policies. They work to advance the *realpolitik* of which Howard Williamson speaks in Chapter 2. But as Williamson also points out, deeper theoretical understandings – however taken for granted or tacit – serve to shape both policy and practice in fundamental ways. The way we think about social inclusion shapes what we do about it. There is, then, a parallel need to consider research which engages in critical analysis of policies on social inclusion for young people, making explicit and questioning the assumptions that underpin them. If social exclusion can be seen as a "box" in which young people become trapped, we need to ensure that social inclusion policies do not become another type of "box" in which our ideas and practice can become trapped. We need to "think outside the box" on policy as well, and to do so, we need to understand how that "box" too has been constructed.

Some previous work in the Youth Research Partnership (Lentin, 2004; Colley, 2005) shows that this requires a historical perspective. By this, I do not just mean giving a chronological account of these policies over time, but resisting ahistorical accounts that would strip policies of their social, economic, political and cultural context, and of the complexities and contradictions in their development. This is a two-way process. Many stakeholders and voices input into European policy, and, of course, the principle of subsidiarity emphasises agreement across all the member states. But there are concerns that not all stakeholders or voices are heard or attended to in making policy, and that once policy has been made at European level, it can drive practice at the national and local level, particularly through funding mechanisms and auditable targets (Brine, 2003).

This chapter discusses some of the issues that are often taken for granted or obscured when we locate ourselves and our practice within the social inclusion policy "box". It reviews some of the research that has tried to unpack that "box" and make its construction more visible, through critical analyses that highlight questions of social justice. I hope that these critiques will help those working with

less advantaged young people, by providing a sense of both the limitations and opportunities that European policy currently provides. Inevitably, my remit here can only summarise briefly a few important areas of research, but I hope it can point readers in the direction of more specific lessons related to their own particular area of work and concerns. It should be our job to "think outside the box" in terms of our own practice, as well as in terms of young people's experience of being boxed into a position of social exclusion. Let us begin, then, by looking back in some detail at the policies which first placed social inclusion centre stage on the European scene.

Early policy: the inter-relationship of social and economic strategies

Ruth Levitas (1996) offered an early overview of early policy on social inclusion, which I draw on substantially here. Two White Papers, one on economic and one on social policy published respectively in 1993 and 1994, can be seen as landmarks in establishing social exclusion as a key issue for European governments. *European social policy – A way forward for the Union* (EC, 1994) noted a growing social crisis which had to be addressed:

> "The marginalisation of major social groups is a challenge to the social cohesion of the Union ... At present, with more than 52 million people in the Union living below the poverty line, social exclusion is an endemic phenomenon ... It threatens the social cohesion of each Member State and of the Union as a whole" (EC, 1994, pp. 36-37).

At the same time, it treated these concerns as inextricably connected with the threat of economic crisis:

> "This is not just a question of social justice; the Union simply cannot afford to lose the contribution of marginalised groups to society as a whole ... the Union needs to ensure that the most vulnerable ... are not excluded from the benefits of – and from making an active contribution to – the economic strength of a more integrated Europe" (EC, 1994, p. 37).

Explanations for the cause of this double threat were located in contingent factors, specific to a period which had seen a series of co-ordinated global recessions, from the oil crisis of 1973 to the latest downturn starting in 1991; and in which new technology had come to play a crucial role.

> "It is clear that contemporary economic and social conditions tend to exclude some groups from the cycle of opportunities ... social exclusion stem[s] from the structural changes affecting our economies and societies" (EC, 1994 pp. 36-37).

Accordingly, the twin responses proposed were "competitiveness" and "social progress", presented in harmony as "two sides of the same coin" (EC, 1994, p. 4):

> "Continuing social progress can be built only on economic prosperity, and therefore on the competitiveness of the European economy ... While wealth creation is essential for social progress, the social environment is also an essential factor in determining economic growth. Progress cannot be founded simply on the basis of the competitiveness of economies, but also on the efficiency of European society as a whole" (EC, 1994, pp. 4-5).

The overwhelming emphasis of policy solutions was clear. The first guiding principle established was: "Social and economic integration: employment is the key" (EC, 1994, p. 4). Welfare assistance was to be replaced as a priority by employment generation, and the first full chapter of the White Paper was entitled "Jobs: the top priority".

> "For the Union to reconcile high social standards with the capacity to compete in world markets, it is therefore necessary to give the highest priority to creating new jobs, enabling everyone to integrate into the economy and society" (EC, 1994, p. 4).

This White Paper on social policy noted risks in pursuing economic competitiveness as the route to social inclusion, since increases in productivity and efficiency might result in job losses rather than job creation. Nevertheless, the key underpinning of the strategy was an approach of human capital development targeted at the supply side of the labour market:

> "All Member States have expressed their determination to improve the quality of their education and training systems to better meet the challenge of long-term competitiveness, and to provide the supply of a highly skilled and adaptable workforce. A qualified and well-motivated workforce is a cornerstone of a competitive economy. This is vital as individuals will in future have to change careers or jobs more frequently during their lifetimes" (EC, 1994, p. 15).

It is here that the White Paper located young people. Although young people were not mentioned as being among the most vulnerable groups in society, the document stated that "unqualified school-leavers inevitably become the hard-core of the long-term unemployed" (EC, 1994, p. 15). Priorities therefore focused on the extension and improvement of vocational training and apprenticeships, along with other measures such as tackling illiteracy, vocational guidance provision, higher education and business partnerships, and an emphasis on the need for young people to acquire foreign language, entrepreneurial and information technology skills.

The strategies proposed for social policy therefore drew heavily on the economic White Paper "Growth, competitiveness, employment" (EC, 1993). Here too, the social and the economic aspects of both the problem and its solutions were presented as inseparable. The central goal to ensure Europe's future prosperity was:

> "... finding a new synthesis of the aims pursued by society (work as a factor of social integration, equality of opportunity) and the requirements of the economy (competitiveness and job creation)" (EC, 1993, p. 3).

Such a goal was, however, threatened by the effects of globalisation, especially increased competition from the US and Japan. Unemployment was presented as the most serious block to combating this threat, along with the drain that it represented – through welfare assistance – on public resources which could otherwise be "channelled into productive investment" (EC, 1993, p. 40). The emergence of "the knowledge economy" and information technologies was seen as creating challenges for transformation that European businesses have to seize, in order to stimulate growth and expand employment. Here, even more explicitly than in the White Paper on social policy, it was young people's lack of skills which was viewed as a prime cause of social exclusion:

> "*... too many young people leave school without essential basic training ... the failure of education ... is a particularly important and increasingly widespread factor of marginalisation and economic and social exclusion.* In the Community, 25 to 30% of young people, who are the victims of failure, leave

the education system without the preparation they need to become properly integrated into working life" (EC, 1993, p. 118, original emphasis).

This was to be addressed as a dual social and economic problem, through the elevation of skill levels:

"The basic skills which are essential for integration into society and working life include a mastery of basic knowledge (linguistic, scientific and other knowledge), and skills of a technological and social nature, that is to say the ability to develop and act in a complex and highly technological environment, characterised, in particular, by the importance of information technologies ... People's careers will develop on the basis of the progressive extension of skills" (EC, 1993, p. 120).

The Youthstart Initiative (discussed further below) was central to this policy, promising a guarantee of further education, training, work experience or voluntary activity to all young people under 18. More than ten years later, both socio-economic conditions and policies have moved on in Europe. In what respects has policy altered in this time, and in what respects has it continued in the same vein?

Policy on social inclusion and youth today: continuity and change

If the White Papers of 1993 and 1994 had a strong sense of urgency in relation to economic competitiveness and social cohesion, the most recent European policy documents on these issues are marked more by a sense of emergency. In 2000, with the adoption of a new strategy at the European Council in Lisbon, the EC looked optimistically to a "European renaissance" in which Europe "can be a beacon of economic, social and environmental progress to the rest of the world" (EC, 2005a, p. 4). In the face of a "quantum shift" in the economic landscape, the Lisbon Strategy aimed to make the European Union.

"the most dynamic and competitive knowledge-based economy in the world, capable of sustainable economic growth with more and better jobs and greater social cohesion" (European Parliament, 2000, p. 11).

However, explicit concerns were voiced by Nicole Fontaine, President of the European Union in 2000, in her speech on the original launch of the Lisbon Strategy. She argued that Europeans:

"... are scandalised by untrammelled capitalism, whose relocations, social dumping, ruthless exploitation of the disparities between the social and fiscal legislation of the Member States and remorseless pursuit of profit at the expense of working men and women have a direct and traumatic impact on their lives, both as communities and as individuals" (Fontaine, 2000, p. 5).

She went on to provide a very different explanation of some causes of social exclusion:

"Unregulated mergers, based merely on dominant capitalist concerns, have a devastating effect on the Union's social cohesion. That face of the European Union is unacceptable to men and women who wake up one morning to discover that the company they work for has changed hands and that they are at the mercy of their employer's economic strategy options. The effect on the lives of those people, their families and their entire region is traumatic and, let's face it, inhuman" (Fontaine, 2005, p. 7).

This very blunt rejection of the capacity of economic market functioning to create the conditions for social inclusion, and the naming of capitalism as fundamental to the problem of social exclusion, poses a major challenge to those who focus on the development of human capital as the key to both economic and social policy.

However, by 2005, the strategy was relaunched in the face of deep concerns about its progress at the midway stage:

> "Today, we see that progress has at best been mixed ... there has simply not been enough delivery at European and national level. This is not just a question of difficult economic conditions ... it also results from a policy agenda which has become overloaded, failing co-ordination and sometimes conflicting priorities ... Time is running out and there can be no room for complacency" (EC, 2005a, pp. 4-5).

The response has been to reassert the priority, established in the earlier White Papers discussed above, of employment strategies as a means to address both economic and social problems:

> "... renewed growth is vital to prosperity, can bring back full employment and is the foundation of social justice and opportunity for all ... We need a dynamic economy to fuel our wider social and environmental ambitions. This is why the renewed Lisbon Strategy focuses on growth and jobs ..." (EC, 2005a, p. 5).

> "Growth and jobs are the next great European project" (EC, 2005a, p. 13).

Apart from the tone of alarm, then, there is considerable continuity between this communication and the White Papers of 1993-94, in the assumed unity between social and economic spheres of life, and in strategies which prioritise economic responses as the solution to social problems. Accordingly, proposals still focus strongly on "investing more in human capital through better education and skills" (EC, 2005a, p. 10), and this remains the key concern with regard to young people, particularly given the persistence of high drop-out rates from education and training, through a new European Youth Initiative.

There are, however, also changes as well as continuities in recent policies, and three are particularly significant here in relation to social inclusion for young people. First, the Lisbon Strategy itself places far greater emphasis than the previous White Papers on the role of the "knowledge economy". Its importance is no longer seen primarily as the technological facilitation and competitive advantage of businesses, but as fundamental to social inclusion through not just "more" but also "better" jobs (EC, 2005a, p. 26 ff.). This draws on a widespread and dominant discourse about changes to the world of work since the decline of the manufacturing sector. In this new scenario, the knowledge-based service sector promises higher skilled and higher paid jobs that are also attractive and socially inclusive because they are creative and empowering. It is couched in exciting and optimistic terms, referring to "the European adventure", and contrasting it favourably with old forms of production:

> "In advanced economies such as the EU, knowledge, meaning R&D [research and development], innovation and education, is a key driver of productivity growth. Knowledge is a critical factor with which Europe can ensure competitiveness in a global world where others compete with cheap labour or primary resources" (EC, 2005a, p. 21).

Within this scenario, young people will benefit through the opening up of "new career prospects" (EC, 2005a, p. 27). We can also note here the change to more favourable economic conditions at the start of the 21st century than prevailed in the recession of the 1990s: "The Union is experiencing its best macro-economic outlook for a generation" (European Parliament, 2000, p. 11).

Second, following the Kock report in October 2004, there was a concerted attempt to place the difficulties young people faced through unemployment more centrally to the Lisbon Strategy, and to create greater coherence across a range of policy fields in order to address this matter. In early 2005, the initiative was taken to develop a European Youth Pact (EC, 2005b), promoting specific measures to improve employment, social cohesion, education, training and mobility, as well as the reconciliation of family and working life. Youth policy was operationalised within the European Employment Strategy, the Social Inclusion Strategy, and the Education and Training 2010 Work Programme.

The Youth Pact is certainly the most high profile youth policy development in Europe to date, and the first time that youth policy has focused on employment for young people in addition to its traditional emphasis on active citizenship. While those practitioners involved in youth work and informal education may find this focus a challenge to their traditional remit, it also opens up opportunities for them to bring their expertise in the sectors of education and training to an unprecedented degree, and Chapters 7 and 8 by Beatrix Neimeyer and Andreas Walther in this book testify to the potential of this synergy. However, as the editors of this book point out in Chapter 1, there are significant questions posed by the content of the Youth Pact, in particular whether the same balance that the document proposes between economic strategies and strategies for active citizenship will actually be maintained in practice.

Third, a White Paper on the specific subject of young people, "A new impetus for European youth", was published by the EC in 2001, after wide consultation across the youth sector. This not only represents a much stronger and more comprehensive policy focus on youth than was evident in the 1990s. It also represents a rather less utilitarian view of young people than is expressed either in those early White Papers or in the recent Lisbon Strategy documents. This is signalled by four key messages, which emphasise the need to recognise and provide material support for: the active citizenship role that young people wish to play; their non-formal learning; their autonomy; and their demands for social inclusion and human rights for all.

While the White Paper on youth acknowledges employment as crucial to social inclusion, it highlights that, despite improved economic conditions and two decades of policy focused on social inclusion via employment, "young people are willing to work, but finding a good job is getting harder" (EC, 2001a, p. 38):

> "the transition between education, training and the labour market ... has objectively deteriorated in the past 20 years ... Youth unemployment rates remain high compared with general employment rates ... Precarious forms of employment have become more widespread. Wages have decreased compared to those of adult workers ... Even a good educational qualification does not automatically guarantee them a job, as competition for employment has become fiercer" (EC, 2001a, pp. 38-39).

A further significant change is that this White Paper discusses young people's political dissatisfaction with both national and European governance, and economic globalisation. In at least partial contrast to both the Lisbon vision and the statement of "European values" contained in earlier social inclusion policies, which emphasised the market economy alongside other factors, young people give primacy to ideals of peace and democracy:

> "It is obvious to all that the clear affirmation of an area of rights and freedoms is much more necessary today than that of an economic Europe" (EC, 2001a, p. 53).

The youth White Paper indicates the tensions between broader policy and the views of youth, especially in relation to the supposed harmony of economic and social objectives. In a highly prescient passage, it notes that young people's mistrust of traditional democratic structures and governmental institutions might "even encourage protest" (EC, 2001a, p. 10):

> "Young people in Europe form part of societies which are open to outside cultural and economic influences. The world is their frame of reference ... At the same time, they dispute some of the consequences of globalisation on grounds of social justice, openness and 'sustainable' development ... *This relationship between young people and globalisation, which is mixed to say the least, is a sign of malaise and must not be ignored*" (EC, 2001a, pp. 10-11, emphasis added).

In the light of these tensions, we can ask an important question that formed a powerful theme in a previous Youth Research Partnership seminar: when a particular issue (such as social inclusion) becomes the focus of policy attention, what becomes visible and what becomes invisible?

Social exclusion: a problematic way of thinking about society?

Ruth Levitas (1996) provided one of the earliest critical analyses of the social and economic White Papers of 1993 and 1994. She argued against the way in which these documents elided economic efficiency and social cohesion, particularly their tendency to define social exclusion as being outside the labour market, with the parallel definition of social inclusion as being in paid employment. While making aspects of the problem visible, this dissolution of civil society into market relations rendered others invisible:

> "It is a discourse unable to address the question of unpaid work in society (work done principally by women), or of low-paid work, and completely erases from view the inequality between those owning the bulk of productive property and the working population, as well as obscuring the inequalities among workers. It presents 'society' as experiencing a rising standard of living by defining those who have not done so, who have become poorer, as 'excluded from' society, as 'outside' it" (Levitas, 1996, p. 7).

On the one hand, Levitas highlighted the danger of ignoring the poverty and social problems facing employees in low-quality, low-paid work: we cannot assume that all "inclusion" in employment is beneficial, as Fahmy's chapter in this book also suggests. This concern for the working poor has been borne out by subsequent evidence. Five years later, the annual report on employment trends in Europe (EC, 2001b) showed that a quarter of the workforce were in "dead-end" or "low pay/productivity" jobs, with young people disproportionately represented in this category. Only around 13% of young people in "dead-end" jobs were transitioning into better jobs a year later, while almost 30% were dropping into unemployment or inactivity. "Bad" jobs represent a real trap (see also Capillari, 2002). A more recent Eurostat

report (Bardone and Guio, 2005), using data from the 15 EU member states in 2003, shows 11 million workers living in poverty, with a further 9 million household members affected by it. Once again, young workers are at higher risk than adults. Although Nicole Fontaine (2005) pointed to the need for a redistribution of wealth in order to combat such "inhuman" aspects of capitalism, the main redistribution proposed by the economic and social policy White Papers is from spending on welfare assistance to subsidising the low wages offered by employers.

On the other hand, Levitas (1996) also warned against a way of thinking about "socially excluded" people as an underclass outside of the "mainstream", or treating social exclusion as "their" problem rather than a problem at the heart of our whole society (see also Jarl-Aberg, 2005). Though often excluded from paid work, women are integrated into society (unequally) through their unpaid work as carers. Though often excluded from welfare benefit rights, many migrant workers are integrated into society (unequally) through precarious, low-paid work. Though areas of employment like the financial and "dot.com" sectors may represent the most advanced expressions of the new service economy, they also integrate (unequally) large numbers of poor and marginalised cleaning, catering, delivery and maintenance staff, often from Europe's former colonies – we have to consider all of the workers in a sector, not just the most visible and successful (Sassen, 1996; Nolan, 2003). In a previous book in this series, John Wrench (2004) has shown how anti-discrimination measures to increase under-represented minority ethnic groups in employment may be diluted by newer "diversity management" approaches that sound inclusive but avoid confronting racism. The work of Shahrzad Mojab (2006) and Jackie Brine (1998, 1999) reveals how disadvantaged women, both native-born and immigrant to Europe, are in practice more often treated as "trainees" rather than "learners", and may even find themselves deskilled rather than better educated, because of the impact of European policies and their funding mechanisms on vocational education and training programmes. Without taking these issues into account, calls for social solidarity are reduced merely to individualistic moral exhortations, rather than ensuring that solidarity is actively fostered by the structures we create for our society (Levitas, 1996).

Byrne (1999) has argued that this social segregation is increasingly becoming a problematic reality, as the end of the economic expansion following the Second World War has resulted in new socio-economic conditions. In the language of chaos theory and complexity, society has shifted from a "torus" (doughnut) form in which most people were able to benefit from incremental upward mobility. It has now bifurcated into a "butterfly": contiguity of social positions has disappeared, and conditions of social inclusion and exclusion are quite separate; minor changes can propel people into poverty; and it can be very difficult to return back across the narrow boundary. Such an analysis resonates strongly with the accounts of "yo-yo" transitions by Kovacheva and Pohl and by Walther in this book.

This analysis, however, resists presuppositions that such conditions lie somehow in the abstract functioning of socio-economic structures beyond the realms of agency. As Gorman also argues in her chapter, such an ahistorical view of social exclusion as "systemic" ignores the use of state power by the capitalist class, and the practices at every level by which people enact its relations of ruling. Both the development of part of the working class and the underdevelopment of others, to form a reserve army of labour, are complementary and active strategies for capitalism, which reproduce the same hierarchical division among workers in Europe as they do for the Third World (Byrne, 1999). What, though, of the Lisbon vision, which promises that growth will bring social inclusion through not just more, but better jobs? What evidence does the last decade offer that this promise can be kept?

Social inclusion: can the promise of more and better jobs be kept?

The policy linkage between economic growth and social cohesion is heavily reliant on the optimistic forecast, central to the Lisbon Strategy, that a "paradigm shift" has taken place in the world of work; that new, post-Fordist forms of work organisation and information-based services now dominate the economy; and that the "knowledge society" will foster a virtuous high-employment, high-skills, high-pay, and high-trust economy (Brown and Lauder, 2003; Capillari, 2002). Debates on this paradigm shift have polarised this extreme against an opposite, cataclysmic prophecy that predicts social antagonism and collapsing employment in the grip of a vicious, low-skill economy. Both positions, however, have been criticised for being ahistorical, lacking empirical evidence and ignoring global tendencies – the "ungrounded predictions of the visionaries" (Nolan, 2003, p. 479, see also Thompson, 2003). More nuanced and partial accounts of shifts in the nature of work may be far more accurate.

What, then, of the "better jobs" promised by the knowledge economy? First, the growth in "knowledge work" has to be disaggregated in order to get a true picture of the situation. An expanding body of evidence from some European countries, the US and Australia (Fleming et al., 2004; Felstead et al., 2002; Nolan 2003; Thompson et al., 2001) shows that most occupational growth in knowledge-based services is dominated by jobs which entail low-grade, routinised handling of information, such as keyboard operation and data inputting, often with high levels of workplace surveillance and control. These are a far cry from the autonomous, creative and empowering jobs in knowledge production and management, which are implied by the "knowledge economy" rhetoric, but enjoyed only by a small minority of professional and managerial-level employees. Even in the fast-growing "dot.com" sector, the largest increases in employment are to be found among shelf-stackers, warehouse keepers, drivers and telephone operators: namely, those who facilitate the delivery of goods for e-commerce (Nolan, 2003). Moreover, the other fastest-growing occupations in the UK, for example, are in low-paid personal services such as hairdressing, care of children and the elderly, and domestic house-keeping. This expansion is fuelled by the polarisation of unequal incomes: many poor people now rely for work on servicing the personal needs of those who are better-off.

If the promise of better jobs may be exaggerated, can we at least hope for more jobs? Thompson (2003) argues that policies on economic growth as the route to social cohesion hark back to the reciprocity of the social contract that existed as a result of the post-war settlement and Keynesian economic strategies. This has today been replaced by a new and more tenuous type of settlement, related to so-called "knowledge work", and based on the development of human capital through lifelong learning. However, tensions in this settlement are produced by the actual conditions of the labour market. The operation of capitalist markets, and especially the dominance of finance capital, continues to result in overproduction and downsizing, rather than growth in jobs, or continuity and stability of employment for workers. At the same time, work has qualitatively intensified, especially through the demand for greater employee commitment in the form of emotional and aesthetic labour – but such commitment is difficult to maintain in conditions where labour is becoming ever more exploited and ever more contingent. These pressures are becoming evident even in Germany, which arguably contrasts most in its high-skill/high-pay

strategies with, for example, the UK. Thompson suggests that employers may want and intend to keep their side of the growth-cohesion bargain, but are increasingly unable to do so.

Such evidence and analyses point to a contemporary context in which globalisation, shareholder interests, and systemic rationalisation disrupt the very connectedness of the economic and social on which European policy for social inclusion is founded. They resonate more with the political cautions expressed in the White Paper on youth than with the other policy documents we have considered here. But education and lifelong learning for employability are the cement which should bind the social and economic in these policies. Do they offer to re-knit the disconnection?

Can employability link economic and social goals?

Employability has become a key concept in a situation where employment itself cannot be guaranteed. It was central to the Youthstart Initiative funded by the EC from 1995-99 to improve young people's school-to-work transitions and their social inclusion through labour market integration. A distinctive aspect of Youthstart lay in the "comprehensive pathways" and "stepping stones" approach it took to overcoming complex social and economic disadvantage. The policy documents outlining the initiative focused on empowerment for young people, client-centred support for their individual goals and a holistic ethos:

> "The empowerment stage concerns activities that give young people the tools and confidence to take control of their own pathway ... It is about empowering young people to plan their own future and to understand and capitalise on their own potential" (EC, 1998, p. 12).

However, the key funding targets set for Youthstart projects defined these pathways in terms of their employment-related direction and destinations, without taking account of the low-quality training and low-paid jobs that were often the only options available to many disadvantaged young people (Colley, 2003a). This rather undermines claims for their empowering effect.

Official documents from the Youthstart Initiative spelled out its "holistic" approach:

> "Each of the stages of the pathway is associated with bringing about a *significant shift in the values and motivation of the young people*, their skills and abilities and in their interaction with the wider environment. The overall objective is to move the young person from a position of alienation and distance from social and economic reality, to a position of social integration and productive activity" (EC, 1998, p. 6, emphasis added).

"Empowering activities" such as mentoring were supposed to "reinforce the acceptance of values and attitudinal change amongst the young people" (EC, 1998, p. 12, emphasis added). As the largest Youthstart mentoring project in the UK put it, "mentors" primary task of influencing behaviours, and by implication attitudes, is a fundamental one' (Ford, 1999, p. 18, emphasis added). Such an approach contains questionable normative assumptions, however (Colley, 2003a). Which values and attitudes are to be inculcated? In whose interests? What of the economic and social realities that do confront these young people? Or the poor communities in which they are, for better or worse, integrated?

Some have argued that such a view of employability has "more to do with shaping subjectivity, deference and demeanour than with skill development and citizenship" (Gleeson, 1996, p. 97). Indeed, it can be seen as a very narrow instrumental view of young people's transitions and learning, in stark contrast with the emphasis on active citizenship in the White Paper on youth (EC, 2001):

> "... so commonly expressed now in the reductionist terms of the requirements of international economic competitiveness, [current policies on youth transitions] are almost exclusively concerned with the production of future workers with particular skills or dispositions ... [T]he work ethic and human capital theory generate between them a very utilitarian version of what it is to be a young person in contemporary society" (Maguire et al., 2001, p. 199).

There is, then, a tension between the Youthstart Initiative's claim to promoting holistic support for young people, and its economically instrumental vision of education and training. Holism treats the person as an organic and complex whole, connected in dynamic ways with their environment. By contrast, the pursuit of "employability" seems to atomise young people's dispositions, and dictate their responsiveness to already-prescribed categories of ideal-typical employee attributes determined elsewhere (Colley, 2003b). As we have already noted above, an increasing element of employability is a willingness to deploy one's very emotional and aesthetic self at work. The danger is that hearts and minds become the raw material of professional "support" and "guidance" interventions, which aim to reform young people as saleable commodities in the competitive labour market.

Conclusion

If the critiques reviewed in this chapter hold true, employability can represent only a weak link between the labour market and social inclusion. Defining employability in terms of individuals' characteristics obscures its dependence on conditions in the labour market, and their role in determining the chances of getting a job (Brown, Hesketh and Williams, 2002). As Niemeyer explains in her chapter in this book, at best this risks simply changing the order of the queue at the factory gate, without reducing it substantially. At worst, it risks placing the blame for "social exclusion" at young people's own feet. The White Paper on youth seems to offer the potential to open up broader discussions and different perspectives on social inclusion, most importantly from the point of view of young people themselves (du Bois-Reymond, 2004). But the lower status of the youth sector in the policy-making hierarchy, compared to both employment and education, makes it less likely that this potential will be fully exploited.

One thing that all the researchers reviewed here have in common is that they highlight practices which contribute to social exclusion, including those which are sedimented even in policies, structures, institutions and practices which are supposed to promote social inclusion. By better understanding the assumptions that underpin European policy, and being able to think about them critically, we will be better equipped to engage in the *realpolitik* that is so necessary: to influence policies and shape our own practice in ways that really do break down the barriers facing disadvantaged young people.

References

Bardone, L. and Guio, A.-C. (2005), "In-work poverty", *Statistics in Focus*, 5/2005. Brussels: Eurostat.

Brine, J. (1998), "The European Union's discourse of equality and its education and training policy within the post-compulsory sector", *Journal of Education Policy*, 13(1), pp. 137-152.

Brine, J. (1999), *Under-educating women: globalizing inequality*. Buckingham: Open University Press.

Brine, J. (2003), "The Europeanization of vocational training: policy, politics and practice of the European Social Fund", in European Conference on Educational Research, University of Hamburg, 17-20 September (accessed 12 September 2006). Available at:
www.leeds.ac.uk/educol/documents/00003516.htm.

Brown, P., Hesketh, A. and Williams, S. (2002), "Employability in a knowledge-driven economy" (Working Paper 26). Cardiff: Cardiff University School of Social Sciences.

Brown, P. and Lauder, H. (2003), "Globalisation and the knowledge economy: some observations on recent trends in employment, education and the labour market" (Working Paper 43). Cardiff: Cardiff University School of Social Sciences.

Byrne, D. (1999), *Social exclusion*. Buckingham: Open University Press.

Capillari, L. (2002), "Do the 'working poor' stay poor? An analysis of low pay transitions in Italy", *Oxford Bulletin of Economics and Statistics*, 64(2), pp. 87-110.

Colley, H. (2003a), *Mentoring for social inclusion: a critical approach to nurturing mentor relationships*. London: RoutledgeFalmer.

Colley, H. (2003b), "Engagement mentoring for socially excluded youth: problematising an 'holistic' approach to creating employability through the transformation of habitus", *British Journal of Guidance and Counselling*, 31(1), pp. 77-100.

Colley, H. (2005), "Formal and informal models of mentoring for young people: issues for democratic and emancipatory practice", in Chisholm, L. and Hoskins, B. (eds.), *Trading up: potential and performance in non-formal learning*. Strasbourg: Council of Europe.

du Bois-Reymond, M. (2004), "Youth – Learning – Europe: ménage à trois?", *Young*, 12(3), pp. 187-204.

European Commission (EC) (1993), *Growth, competitiveness and employment: the challenges and ways forward into the 21st century*. Luxembourg: Office for Official Publications of the European Communities.

EC (1994), *European social policy: a way forward for the Union*. Luxembourg: Office for Official Publications of the European Communities.

EC (1998), *Unlocking young people's potential*. Luxembourg: Office for Official Publications of the European Communities.

EC (2001a), *A new impetus for European youth*. Brussels: Commission of the European Communities.

EC (2001b), *Employment in Europe 2001: recent trends and prospects*. Luxembourg: Office for Official Publications of the European Communities.

EC (2005a), *Working together for growth and jobs: a new start for the Lisbon Strategy*. Brussels: Commission of the European Communities.

EC (2005b) "Communication from the Commission to the Council on European policies concerning youth: addressing the concerns of young people in Europe – Implementing the European Youth Pact and promoting active citizenship". Brussels: Commission of the European Communities (accessed 14 June 2006). Available at: http://ec.europa.eu/youth/whitepaper/post-launch/com_206_en.pdf.

European Parliament (2000), "European Council, Lisbon: conclusions of the Presidency" (accessed 20 February 2006). Available at: www.europarl.eu.int/bulletins/pdf/1s2000en.pdf.

Felstead, A., Gallie, D. and Green, F. (2002), *Work skills in Britain 1986-2001*. Nottingham: DfES Publications.

Fleming, P., Harley, B. and Sewell, G. (2004), "A little knowledge is a dangerous thing: getting below the surface of the growth of 'knowledge work' in Australia", *Work, Employment and Society*, 18(4), pp. 725-747.

Fontaine, N. (2000), "President's speech to the European Council meeting on employment, economic reform and social cohesion: towards an innovation and knowledge-based Europe" (accessed 20 February 2006). Available at: www.europarl.eu.int/bulletins/pdf/1s2000en.pdf.

Ford, G. (1999), "Youthstart Mentoring Action Project: project evaluation and report". Stourbridge: Institute of Careers Guidance.

Gleeson, D. (1996), "Post-compulsory education in a post-industrial and post-modern age", in Avis, J., Bloomer, M., Esland, G., Gleeson, D. and Hodkinson, P., *Knowledge and nationhood: education, politics and work*. London: Cassell.

Jarl-Aberg, C. (2005) "Ni Putes Ni Soumises" (Neither Whores Nor Submissive), in European Youth Research Partnership Seminar on Social Inclusion and Young People, Budapest, 31 October-2 November.

Lentin, A. (2004), "The problem of culture and human rights in the response to racism", in Titley, G. (ed.), *Resituating culture*. Strasbourg: Council of Europe.

Levitas, R. (1996), "The concept of social exclusion and the new Durkheimian hegemony", *Critical Social Policy*, 16(1), pp. 5-20.

Maguire, M., Ball, S.J. and Macrae, S. (2001), "Post-adolescence, dependence and the refusal of adulthood", *Discourse*, 22(2), pp. 197-211.

Mojab, S. (2006), "War and diaspora as lifelong learning contexts for immigrant women", in Leathwood, C. and Francis, B. (eds.), *Gender and lifelong learning: critical feminist engagements*. London: Routledge.

Nolan, P. (2003), "Reconnecting with history: the ESRC future of work programme", *Work, Employment and Society*, 17(3), pp. 473-480.

Sassen, S. (1996), "New employment regimes in cities: the impact on immigrant workers", *New Community*, 22(4), pp. 579-594.

Thompson, P. (2003), "Disconnected capitalism: or why employers can't keep their side of the bargain", *Work, Employment and Society*, 17(2), pp. 359-378.

Thompson, P., Warhurst, C. and Callaghan, G. (2001), "Ignorant theory and knowledgeable workers: interrogating the connections between knowledge, skills and services", *Journal of Management Studies*, 38(7), pp. 923-942.

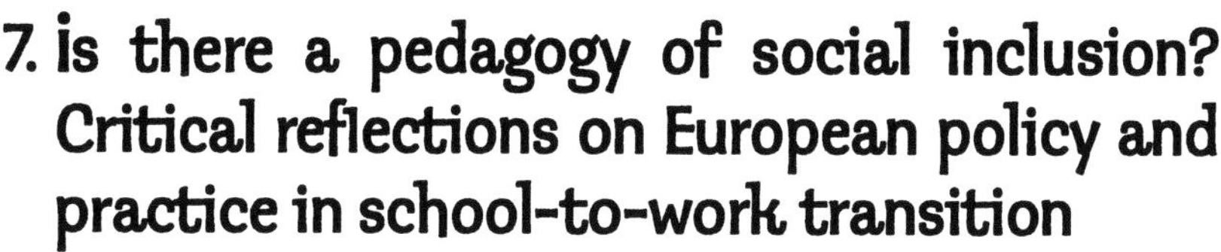

7. is there a pedagogy of social inclusion? Critical reflections on European policy and practice in school-to-work transition

Beatrix Niemeyer

introduction

This chapter will discuss how the idea of social inclusion represents challenges for educational policy and practice in Europe, drawing on findings from a European research project on reconnecting disadvantaged young people with vocational education and training (VET). It focuses on the "risk zone" of transition from school to work. In many European countries, this transition takes places via an intermediate stage of VET, but the most disadvantaged may experience problems of exclusion from VET itself. The chapter therefore examines school-to-VET transitions specifically, and the "system of schemes" which has been established in almost every European country to bridge the growing gap between general education and the labour market.

At the macro- as well as at the micro-level, the problem of school-to-work transition is often viewed from an economic perspective, highlighting employers' demands for vocational skills and employability, and active labour market policies for achieving these. A second common perspective focuses on the social effects of exclusion, highlighting pedagogical support and educational strategies in general. In contrast with these two prevailing approaches, I will explain the concept of situated learning in learning communities centred on practice as a model to re-think and re-conceptualise policies and practice, by aiming at both social and vocational integration. In this model, learning itself is considered as a social process: learners and those who facilitate learning are engaged in common activities, and learning itself is viewed in terms of social participation – belonging and becoming – rather than simply acquiring knowledge and skills. The idea of situated learning therefore helps to overcome the limitations of thinking about informal and formal learning as separate and distinct, and encourages us to see them as closely inter-related dimensions of the same process.

In addition to this multidimensional perspective on learning, the European context also means that the transcultural dimension of school-to-work transition and VET arrangements needs to be included in a context-sensitive way, since policies and practices have to be adapted to specific national and cultural settings. Moreover, I will end by suggesting that this concept of a community of practice is also helpful as an analytical framework for critically examining current European policies for social inclusion, and for identifying key areas for improvement.

The problem of social inclusion in learning

"The question is outstanding on how to encourage young people's sense of belonging to the European project and how to get young people to believe that being a citizen of

Europe offers the security which is desperately sought by young people in the increasingly individualistic and globalised world."

This is how the problem of social inclusion was outlined in the call for Youth Research Partnership Seminar on Social Inclusion and Young People on which this book is based. From this point of view, the problem seems to be how to mediate the "European idea" to young people. But the reciprocal relationship between macro-level European policy and micro-level individual lifecourses seem to drift into opposite directions for many young people. What does lifelong learning mean for somebody whose motivation to learn has come to an early end in the institutions of formal education? While learning is believed to open the door to the knowledge society, which type of knowledge and which ways of learning will be valued there? Who holds the keys to this door, and thereby rules on inclusion as well as on exclusion? These are crucial questions, not only for European social policy, but also for national and regional level policies, where social inclusion should be enacted in institutions and programmes and experienced at the micro-level of educational practice.

The focus of my reflections will be on school-to-VET transition as a decisive process for social inclusion, from society's as well as from the individual's perspective. In particular, I will examine the "system of schemes" which have been implemented in most member states to bridge the gap between general education and entry into the labour market. As Helen Colley points out in her chapter in this book, existing policies and programmes build on two presuppositions: firstly, that job placement is the one and only indicator for quality and success; and, secondly, that individual success in learning creates the one and only entrance ticket to social and vocational participation. However, there is a structural as well as an individual dimension to the problem of social inclusion. Consequently, we have to ask not only if young people are adequately prepared for VET systems, but also if VET systems are adequately prepared for young people – especially for those who are disadvantaged in relation to the mainstream. We should keep in mind, however, that educational systems have a selective function, and themselves produce social exclusion. Given a drastic lack of training places and jobs in a restructured labour market throughout Europe, and the high level of youth unemployment (see Figure 1) the establishment of schemes and special support programmes may change the order in the queue at the company gates, but it will not broaden those gates to let more young people in (Galuske, 1998).

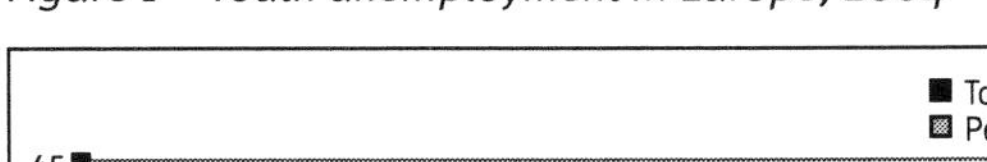
Figure 1 – Youth unemployment in Europe, 2004

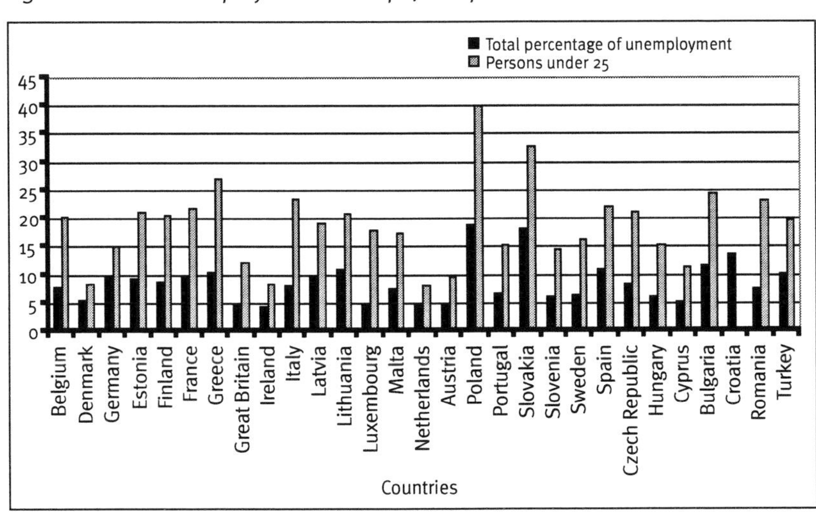

Source: Eurostat 2005.

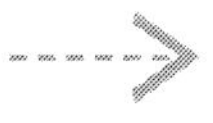

If the labour market and institutions of formal education both produce and maintain excluding effects, how could the idea of social inclusion as a political target make any difference? The expression "social inclusion" is an original European invention, introduced by politicians in the European Commission because "the Member States expressed reservations about the word 'poverty' when applied to their respective countries. 'Social exclusion' would then be a more adequate and less accusatory expression to designate the existing problems and definitions" (Berghman, 1995, p. 5). In the policy arena, social inclusion tends to be downsized into a technical problem: identifying significant indicators, measuring and reporting on them. It is treated in a way that renders personal problems invisible. This also tends to be the approach in the academic field. A lot of effort is put into the description of significant indicators, main target groups, etc., yet little is known about how social inclusion could positively be achieved. There are not many researchers who dirty their hands with participating in field research to learn about the subjective dimension of exclusion: the personal challenges young people face every day in dealing with the multifaceted effects of a risky life.

With the focus on risky transitions from school to work, inclusion is often reduced to the issue of job placement. In vocational education and training, this results in an emphasis on technical skills development and qualification in response to the requirements of the economy. VET is supposed to support young people with qualification deficits to become adequately prepared for the labour market. However, in contrast with this narrow and functional understanding of qualification, VET may also aim at more holistic personality development, which corresponds to the notion of citizenship. Such an approach presupposes a type of VET which is more adequately prepared for young people, and for their expectations and needs within their complex life worlds. In line with this, Andreas Walther (Chapter 8 in this volume) prefers the concept of citizenship, which incorporates the subjective dimension of the reciprocal relationship between the individual and society, to that of inclusion. "Citizenship" points to the competence and ability, as well as the right, to participate and engage in social processes and systems. By contrast, the concept of inclusion does not make visible or challenge the existence of an excluding social system, and thus reproduces the boundaries of that society. In summary, then, social inclusion has been developed as a political goal rather than an analytical concept, and the notion certainly needs further unpicking. For the purposes of this chapter, though, let us see how an economic view of social inclusion impacts upon VET provision.

School-to-VET transition as a risk zone: pedagogical answers to economic questions

Becoming an actively participating citizen includes more than just negotiating a successful school-to-work-transition. Indeed, Kronauer (2002) has identified six different risks of exclusion:

- exclusion from the labour market;
- economic exclusion, which does not necessarily mean the same;
- social exclusion;
- cultural exclusion;
- institutional exclusion;
- spatial exclusion.

It is without doubt, however, that labour is a key element for social inclusion. It should allow for economic independence; in addition, the position in the labour market is closely linked to the social status of a person and also shapes personal identity. For the majority of young people, therefore, becoming an adult means finding an appropriate place in the labour market.

Parallel to changes in educational policy, the context and rules of work, patterns of employment and the utilisation of human resources have also changed. The intensity of work is growing rapidly, the risks of market fluctuations are increasingly delegated to individual employees and teams, and organisations are becoming the prime reference for individuals' identification (Field, 2001; Silverman, 1999; Heikkinen and Niemeyer, 2005). This is the context in which the "problem groups" of mainstream education and employment are defined and diagnosed, and measures for solving the problem in a most "cost-effective" way are developed.

In the revised European Charter on the Participation of Young People in Local and Regional Life, adopted by the Congress of Local and Regional Authorities of Europe in May 2003, we read that: "The active participation of young people in decisions and actions at local and regional level is essential if we are to build more democratic, inclusive and prosperous societies" (Council of Europe, 2003, p. 2). Concerning sectoral policies, the Charter argues that youth employment should be promoted and unemployment combated, because:

"When young people are unemployed or living in poverty they are less likely to have the desire, resources and social support to be active citizens in local and regional life. Young people who are unemployed are likely to be among the most excluded in society and therefore local and regional authorities should develop policies and promote initiatives to reduce youth unemployment" (Council of Europe, 2003, p. 4).

The EU Council explicitly recommends the elaboration of accompanying programmes for the members of socially disadvantaged groups leading to employment and to avoid an interruption of career through enhancement of employability, administration of human resources, organisation of work processes and lifelong learning. The approach of social inclusion policy should be multifaceted and focusing on target groups such as children in poverty (Council of Europe, 2003, p. 11).

These statements quite clearly describe a policy of programmes and schemes, with the effect of establishing special pathways – offering "special" access for "special" people. There is a basic pedagogical dilemma resulting from this. School-to-work-transition can be identified as being of critical importance for social inclusion and participation; but although there are strong structural reasons for the emergence of this "risk zone", the approaches to meeting this challenge are mainly training initiatives aimed at improving the individual. Responding to this mismatch is difficult.

The majority of the member states have launched specific programmes to support young persons at the risk of being excluded from the labour market. However, these programmes differ great in terms of duration, funding and pedagogical approaches. We can identify four main aspects of these differences:

- how programmes are generally situated in the respective national landscape of education and labour;
- how programmes are legitimised via prevailing paradigms of disadvantage;
- dominant expectations that society has of young people;
- how youth unemployment is perceived.

In relation to these aspects, the following types of programme can be distinguished:

- programmes which aim to open up alternative individual experiences and broaden the mainstream pathway of schooling, building on the idea of individual personal development, with high options for occupational choice to be achieved by general education;
- measures aiming to compensate structural deficits and shortcomings of the apprenticeship market. Usually, access to these programmes is linked to the identification of individual deficits, thus stigmatising the participants;
- "workfare" programmes oriented to improving employability with varying combinations of general and technical education, building on a model of early economic independence and a comparably short period of youth;
- programmes which aim to address the shortage of workplaces as well as a lack of training, with an extension of schooling and emphasis on work placement.

At the conceptual level, programmes and schemes mostly seek to build on a combination of general education with workplace experience and/or training and social support, although the relation of education and training varies in quantity and quality. In practice, however, this "alternance principle" can be difficult to maintain, as we can see from a previous period in which school-to-work transitions first became risky.

Alternance seemed to be an appropriate solution when the first post-war wave of youth unemployment challenged established educational systems in the late 1970s. At that time, it involved alternating periods of training, education and work experience that were deemed necessary to bridge young people into mainstream VET and labour market positions from which they had been displaced by social and economic conditions. Such programmes were established in the German-speaking countries, France and the Benelux countries, to overcome the fact that mainstream educational routes were too narrow, unattractive, or difficult to access for young people. But in the following period, continued displacement and disappointed expectations created motivational problems that simple application of the "alternance" principle could not tackle. From the case of Germany, we can learn that alternance, as a basic principle of VET, may guarantee a high quality of training. However, since it depends on the economy offering sufficient places for work experience and training, it is difficult to implement when unemployment is high. As such, it cannot help to prevent large-scale youth unemployment (Dietrich, 2003; Hammer, 2003).

At the same time, another branch of theory and practice focused on the underlying causes of disengagement, building on social theory, and using the methods of "social pedagogy" and youth work (Evans and Niemeyer, 2004). For example, in Germany in the early 1990s, social workers became regular members of the staff running re-integration programmes. They offered general support with social problems as well as guidance and counselling of vocational orientation processes (Eckert, 1999; Biermann and Rützel, 1999). While these approaches were able to demonstrate theoretical coherence and practical successes in engaging young people (at least in the short term), vocational achievement and recognition in the labour market were lacking.

Reconsidering this history of school-to-work schemes, the "V" and the "E" of VET – the vocational and the educational – appear like competing elements. The vocational approach focuses on matching individual competences to the needs of the labour market; building on the assessment of qualifications, acquired in modular forms of training; and enhancing employability. The educational approach, on the other hand, is more holistically aimed at personal development, by offering social support and including multiple contexts of learning and activities.

After a subsequent period of serious practical attempts to integrate social and vocational support and training, today the gap seems to be becoming wider again. This gap can be identified at the micro-level of educational practice as well as at the macro-level of policy and planning. Training geared to enhancing employability seems to be counterposed to education aimed at creating an emancipated citizen. One of the most basic contradictions is that ever more training programmes seek to enhance young persons' employability, while there is simply too little employment available for all of them. So such programmes, apart from their filtering effect and their fine-tuning of the selective mechanisms of the general educational system, have the important task of preserving the ideology of the labour society – one which sees the important task as training young people in the virtues of the labour market, such as punctuality, courtesy or accurateness.

Situated learning: changing the perspective

The concept of situated learning in learning communities centred on practice has been developed in the context of an EU Socrates project, Re-enter: improving transition for low achieving school-leavers to vocational education and training, which I undertook with partners from Finland, UK, Belgium, Portugal and Greece from 1999 to 2001 (Evans and Niemeyer, 2004). This project analysed best practice examples for re-engaging young people with learning and training. Its findings highlight the social nature of learning processes, thus building on the original model of situated learning (Lave and Wenger, 1991), but also showing how it should be adapted it to the specific needs and conditions of the target group: young people who experienced serious troubles with learning in formal contexts.

Socio-anthropological perspectives came into the frame for understanding learning in the 1990s, with Lave and Wenger's (1991) influential study of workplace interactions and the ways in which workers' skills were constructed, recognised and ascribed value in workplace settings. This social process of learning can be considered as a gradual process of growing participation in communities of practice. Originally, a "community of practice" was seen as a group of experts collaborating to accomplish a common aim. According to this concept, learning is a simultaneous process of belonging (to a community of practice), of becoming (developing an identity as member of this community), of experiencing (the meaning of the common work task) and doing (as practical action contributing to the common work task) (Wenger, 1999, p. 5). While this social theory of learning was developed in the context of workplace learning, building on ethnographic research, the Re-enter project showed that it also provides valuable insights for programmes aiming to counter social and vocational disengagement.

Theories of learning have been developed predominantly in the context of established learning settings. Yet in many cases, these are exactly the learning contexts in which young people have previously experienced failure. This means that they are unlikely to be the best places for positive engagement, or for forging a new sense of themselves or their abilities. The concept of situated learning questions schooling as the unique location of learning processes, and stresses the importance of other learning environments. It values informal ways of learning, and emphasises the potential of settings in which learning may be unintentional. It is based on the importance of work experience and practical action for enhancing processes of learning and understanding (which is, of course, a common theme in existing theories of vocational education and training), but crucially it shifts the focus from the individual to the social components of learning. This allows for an extended view of competences and competence development: situated learning is not about the specialised training of particular skills, but about experience and competence in participation. It includes the process of coming to share in the cultural attributes of participation: values and beliefs, common stories and collective problem-solving strategies of the learning community centred on practice.

While theories of situated learning appeared promising in offering the potential for a more holistic formulation of VET, one that could go beyond the former twin-track approaches of vocational and social pedagogy, we have worked towards an expanded set of ideas that differ from Lave and Wenger's (1991) framework in some significant respects. Based on the analysis of good-practice examples in the six participating countries we have developed a set of criteria for learning communities centred on practice, which combines the social aspects of learning, the crucial element of participation and the time and space for reflection. Our approach highlights the following features, while recognising the socially situated nature of the learning:

- the individual biography of each young person is highly significant for their engagement in the learning environments and "communities" in question;
- the programmes' explicit goals are to foster learning, in order that people can move through the programme and move on beyond it. The communities are therefore communities of learners, and the primary goals are learning and moving on;
- the concepts of "novice" and "expert" do not have the same salience as in Lave and Wenger's (1991) notion of communities of practice, which focuses mainly on the integration of novices into an existing group of experts. In the context of VET for young people, newcomers bring capabilities with them, they participate, move through, and eventually move on with strengthened capabilities which they share along the way. Expert status here comes with the responsibility for creating and maintaining the environment for full participation.

Engagement in intended learning is often the single biggest challenge, since without engagement there is no motivation and no learning. Our expanded concept thus sees learning as situated in three ways:

- in practical activity;
- in the culture and context of the workplace/learning environment;
- in the socio-biographical features of the learner's life.

Our concept of learning communities centred on practice thus builds on the importance of situated learning, with the core idea that learning is an interactive social process rather than the result of classroom instruction. The four dimensions of learning as doing, experiencing, belonging and becoming seem crucial to reconnect young people at the risk of becoming disengaged. Throughout our project, it was a common international experience that work-related forms of learning which go beyond mere technical qualification, and which promote these dimensions of learning, help considerably to increase the motivation of young people for education and training. Participating in a work process encourages young people to take on responsibility and to develop commitment. Practical work in a team helps to

make learning success visible, and to experience one's own contribution to it as personal success. Working in an authentic, rather than simulated, context highlights the importance of one's own work. Authentic training places, which have a close link to the local labour market and offer customer contact, help to provide evidence of the significance and importance of the individual's work, provided these places have been chosen properly according to the interests, abilities and needs of the young person.

Effective engagement and learning therefore requires a balance between the challenges of authentic work contexts and the time and space necessary for reflection on that experience. It also requires an approach that integrates the development of technical, practical, basic and personal skills. I turn next, then, to look at the ways in which learning communities centred on practice can offer such a balanced approach.

The learning community centred on practice

The concept of learning communities centred on practice builds on the outstanding importance of the community itself for processes of situated learning. To reconnect disengaged young people, it is crucial that they share the meaning of a common activity. Furthermore, they need the opportunity to experience their participation in a very practical sense. The learning community centred on practice plays such an important role, because it helps to rebuild an identity in the working context. It also serves to support problems in learning, and as a means of social background, ensuring appropriate behaviour. In addition to this, the idea of a learning community views young people as potential experts, thus focusing on learners' abilities rather than their deficits. It highlights the common efforts of both co-learners and adults, who interactively frame and shape this process as it develops.

The learning community centred on practice is not only a working team, but a group of members with different individual bodies of competence. The development of the individuals, as well as of the group, arises from the heterogeneous structure of the learning community centred on practice and the specific conflict-solving strategies within the group. Learning is understood primarily as participation. The novice is taking part in the activity of a learning community centred on practice. His or her status as a learner is accepted by other members, and more experienced members are ready to allow novices access to themselves and their community in order to make learning possible.

Communities of practice exist not only among young learners and their trainers, but they can be identified on the institutional and at the structural level as well. Here, they are shaped by interactions among the community of educational staff in particular institutional contexts. For example, the staff working on a programme – teachers, trainers and social workers – can be seen to engage in a common process of sharing competence, experience and expertise amongst themselves. Their opportunities for participation in decision making impact upon their motivation to work. The institution's affordances for – or constraints upon – flexible and open learning practices are significant influences on learning. Where an institution promotes and supports a common aim of cross-professional collaboration, individuals' perspectives are enriched, as is the educational approach of the team. It can itself operate as a learning community centred on practice. Its members profit from each other's practice and know-how, and through shared reflective processes, they are able to accumulate a common body of experience and knowledge and create a

common history. New programmes are built on the experience of earlier ones, and this history itself becomes a database of know-how and good practice. A culture of self-evaluation and reflection seems essential to this process.

Situated learning, in this sense, is not limited to the organisation of learning situations and the delivery of vocational qualifications, but also relates to the structures of the institution in which it takes place, and the readiness to learn of its employees and co-workers. In the case of schoolteachers, for example, it is evident that the professional actions, norms and values that individuals adopt are related to the institutional setting in which they work. Distinct professional models of practice also operate at the structural level, and can be seen in the division between the academic disciplines of vocational and social pedagogy. In addition, those who represent institutions, and who are concerned with the planning, funding, and researching of re-integration programmes, also form a community of practice. Well-situated learning should aim to link all these levels of community together and be ready to develop, re-new and re-adapt continuously the social body of competence among its members.

A further challenge is how to transform this accumulated experience into a more general pedagogy of social inclusion. Communities of practice, and (we might add) collaborative networks between them, depend on relations between persons (Lave and Wenger, 1991) and between individuals' experiences and programme histories. But unless they are stabilised by adequate structures and maintained by adequate resources, they are likely to remain weak and sporadic, to depend on the efforts of individuals and to lack a sustainable perspective. The quality and history of communities of practice in VET can therefore be taken as an indicator of the degree to which national policies for re-engaging young people are inclusive. While inclusiveness has been widely accepted as a shared vision at the policy level and among most practitioners, still the realities of collaborative structures and arrangements all too often show that this vision is not carried into practice. To do so would, of course, imply rethinking the problems of school-to-VET transition, not only in the field, but also in terms of funding and legislation. Only a joint effort will help to progress towards the aim of assuring the right to participate in the social community at all levels.

Challenges in thinking about situated learning

There are also other challenges in developing this social theory of situated learning, and putting it into pedagogical practice. On the one hand, the approach assumes that the community is ready and willing to open itself up to newcomers or learners; on the other hand, it also assumes a willingness to share the meaning of the common activity and the community's underlying values. This concept of a learning community centred on practice therefore has three presuppositions:

- that the aim is commonly shared, and that all members of the group will identify with it – which is more likely to be achieved for a work task or a material product than for a school test, for example;
- that the common expertise is able to achieve this aim – which is more easily arranged outside of a classroom;
- that structures promoting hierarchy and competition do not work against this common aim.

In these terms, the theory appears to be highly idealistic and optimistic. While it highlights the social dimension in the process of learning, it does not sufficiently reflect a number of related issues:

- questions of power and hierarchies;
- questions of selection and exclusion;
- structures of educational systems;
- and questions of individual abilities and limits to learning.

Certainly these aspects need further research. Furthermore, the concept of situated learning has been subject to critique, because it is not clear how it allows participants to move on and beyond a community, or whether they are limited to remaining within and reproducing its social boundaries (Heikkinen, 2004). Thus the concept of situated learning itself is socially situated. If applied uncritically, it can help to serve strategies for new qualification policies dominated exclusively by workplace and employer demands, and neglecting any responsibility on the part of the established agents of education. It is self-evident that the problem of social inclusion will be sharpened rather than solved by such arguments and strategies. Our expanded concepts of situated learning have to include the critical dimension of social participation. Participation thus includes the right to criticise, the ability to learn how to criticise constructively, and thereby the opportunity to influence and shape the values and strategies of a learning community centred on practice. If this critique can be addressed in these ways, our project findings suggest that learning communities centred on practice have great potential for creating social inclusion, and can usefully serve as a model to foster reflective processes about VET at all levels: policy making, institutional arrangements and practice.

What about European added value?

The approved strategy to achieve social inclusion are common agreements and national action plans building on human resource development, IT competences and lifelong learning, which altogether are expected to lead to economic growth in a prospering Europe with free markets and social justice. These instruments of national action plans present a new dimension of political strategy as the EU level impacts on national policies. Projects and initiatives are competing with – or may be even replacing – established structures in the area of youth work as well as in VET (Heikkinen and Niemeyer, 2005). The unification of scales, measures and money seems to be the model for further standardisation in the field of education. In this process, established national welfare systems, which have in the past been capable of addressing social inclusion, lose some of their significance and are increasingly determined by a common set of indicators imposed from above. Norms and values rooted in national culture are marginalised in favour of the common goal of creating the European project. But can this strategy be successful? The idea of an "enlightened", reflective Europe inhabited by emancipated citizens is competing with a concept of short-term campaigns, projects, reports and initiatives.

I argue here that this also entails a transcultural dimension of learning. Since national integration practices are rooted in their typical cultural contexts, this needs adequate identification and consideration, and their specific value should be acknowledged. Recommendations for improving VET programmes should therefore take thorough account of cultural differences, and of national particularities in educational and welfare policies, and of practitioners' established approaches and

needs. Such consideration might be effected in the context of joint activities like exchange visits, research projects or research seminars. It is in itself an ongoing practical process that allows learning from each other's experiences, while avoiding simplistic borrowing of policies and initiatives.

However, there remains "the problem with the apples and the pears": as noted above, all these types of school-to-VET support programmes differ greatly in terms of duration, funding and pedagogical targets from country to country. They are influenced by each country's respective historical, economic and political structures, and by the specific cultural concepts of youth and education that have emerged from these. The political and educational responsibility for re-integration programmes, and for the pedagogical approach they promote, are shaped by two main factors: the prevailing welfare policy on the one hand, and the established mainstream routes of education (that is, in the case of disadvantaged youth, primarily the system of VET) on the other. Welfare systems and VET structures determine the ways in which alternative trajectories from school to work are provided for young people at risk of social exclusion (cf. Walther in this volume). They influence the ways in which disadvantage is defined, as well as the pedagogical approach of support programmes (cf. Pohl and Walther, n.d., and Evans and Niemeyer, 2004). There are four different models of welfare and VET systems to be distinguished in Europe, which carry specific – and differing – risks of exclusion (Stauber and Walther, 2001). Figure 2 presents a model of the relation between the types of re-integration programmes, the types of welfare systems and the types of VET systems in the countries participating in the Re-enter project.

Figure 2 – Four models of transition regimes in Europe

Type of model	Welfare paradigms	Organisation of VET ⬍ Resulting risks	Intention of programmes
Scandinavian model	• social security and education as a civil right	• school based VET ⬍ • transition into the labour market • chill out at school	• enhancement of individual development • broadening of the mainstream
Liberal model	• free individual in a flexible market economy • high risk of social exclusion	• market dependent ⬍ • risky transitions • Level of qualification	• promoting employability • bridging function
Corporatist model	• Systems and access to social security depend on position in the labour market	• dual system ⬍ • conditions of access • drop out rate • lack of training places	• compensation of structural deficits • establishment of a parallel system
Mediterranean model	• partial systems of social security • high importance of informal structures	• school based and/or market dependent ⬍ • not very formalised • weak structures • little esteem	• acknowledgement and valuing of VET • introduction of formal structure • enhancing job placement

This may serve as an analytical framework for further transnational considerations, but it should be kept in mind that it presents an abstract typology, and that in practice, mixtures of all types are more likely to occur. We should also note that re-integration programmes aiming to support transitions from school to VET are situated in a field of educational policy and practice, which is itself subject to constant change and development. Given these widely differing contexts, each model is challenged by the concept of situated learning in a specific way. Consequently, different conclusions need to be drawn, and different focuses will be set in policy as well as in practice. Some examples may illustrate key areas for improvement at different levels (for a fuller discussion, see Niemeyer, 2004 and 2006).

At the macro-level of policy and planning, in countries with a strong school-based VET system, an approach based on situated learning challenges the established institutional barriers. Re-integration activities need to provide more authentic working experience and reduce the impact of classroom learning, which provides certification for some young people, but is not necessarily a positive learning environment for others. By contrast, in countries with a strong non-formal VET system and little institutionalised VET, learning seems to be more closely situated in communities centred on practice. However, assessment of competence and acknowledgement of informal learning need to be further developed.

At the meso-level enacted by institutions and programmes, in countries with a strong school component of VET (the Nordic countries as well as Germany, with its strong formal structures and in-built hurdles), the community-of-practice aspect needs to be strengthened. Collaboration between schools and out-of-school institutions should be encouraged in order to open up broader options of choice, and to provide more supportive approaches, both between institutions and for individual learners.

At the micro-level of educational practice, in countries with a strong tradition of informal learning, this offers good opportunities for young people who have difficulties in more formal settings. It is often in small enterprises that these young people can start to become more and more engaged. A relatively strong culture of self-employment, especially in the countryside, will also provide much family support. This form of parenting provides surroundings which are safe, but also normative and disciplining, possibly with too little tolerance for non-traditional behaviour (see, for example, Daniel Blanch's and Amineh Kakabaveh's chapters in this book, on Galician and Kurdish youth-family relations). So in the southern European countries (and, we might add, in migrant communities), where the family plays a strong role in social support for young people, improving social inclusion could also mean allowing for more economic and social independence among youth.

is VET adequately prepared for young people?

To return to the initial question in the title of this chapter: is there a pedagogy of social inclusion? I think there is still a big gap between theory and practice in providing answers to this question. While there is a broad collection of good practice examples from all over Europe, their effect on mainstream educational policy and practice is not as evident. At the conceptual as well as at the practical level, different approaches to vocational training and social pedagogy seem to be acting in different spheres. VET research does not tend to consider issues of social inclusion, nor does VET practice usually address excluded youth. On the other hand, social work and youth work activities tend to neglect the importance of employment for social integration. Thus the distinction between formal and informal learning is maintained.

I argue strongly here that we need to think about bringing both approaches together. I therefore suggest the concept of situated learning in communities centred on practice as an instrument to integrate both tracks, to develop a common perspective and to adjust their respective activities. To engage in meaningful socially situated activities is essential for young people at risk of becoming disaffected. Rediscovering the educational potential of meaningful work helps greatly to motivate this engagement, though this presupposes an acknowledgement that work has a value in itself for the attainment of citizenship. The actual shortage of training places in a restructured labour market with scarce opportunities, however, makes it necessary to develop a wider notion of work, including voluntary work. For example, in a society where inclusion builds exclusively on employment, there is virtually no opportunity for the legitimate participation of newcomers – not even at the periphery. While different national and cultural contexts also value differing strategies of participation and inclusion, various possibilities of engaging in meaningful practical activity can be provided, as Walther shows in his chapter.

Although this specific concept of situated learning has first been elaborated with a focus on the micro-level of integrative work practices (Evans and Niemeyer 2004), the idea of learning communities centred on practice may also be transferred to the context of planning and decision making. Here it could serve as an instrument to foster self-reflection among both learners and those who facilitate learning, and to develop indicators for socially inclusive policy strategies and programmes. The central challenge, then, in relation to learning communities centred on practice, is to develop a pedagogy for social inclusion that links broad experiences of practice to a pedagogical theory that integrates both social and vocational learning. There is already importance evidence that more socially inclusive approaches to VET can be advanced through such efforts – even in the current labour market context – if resources and encouragement can be provided at the European level for developing practice and for further research.

References

Berghman, J. (1995), "Social exclusion in Europe: policy context and analytical framework", in Room, G. (ed.), *Beyond the threshold: the measurement and analysis of social exclusion*. Bristol: Policy Press.

Biermann, H. and Rützel, J. (1999), "Didaktik der beruflichen Bildung Benachteiligter", in Biermann, H., Bonz, B. and Rützel, J. (eds.), *Beiträge zur Didaktik der Berufsbildung Benachteiligter*. Stuttgart: Holland and Josenhans.

CEDEFOP (1998), *Training for a changing society. A report on current vocational education and training research in Europe*. Thessaloniki: CEDEFOP.

Council of Europe (1996), European Social Charter (revised) (online). Strasbourg, Council of Europe (accessed 29 March 2006). Available at:
http://conventions.coe.int/treaty/en/treaties/html/163.htm.

Council of Europe (2003), Revised European Charter on the Participation of Young People in Local and Regional Life (online). Strasbourg, Council of Europe (accessed 29 March 2006). Available at:
www.coe.int/t/e/cultural_cooperation/youth/TXT_charter_participation.pdf.

Dietrich, H. (2003), "Scheme participation and employment outcome of young unemployed people: empirical findings from nine European countries", in Hammer, T. (ed.), *Youth unemployment and social exclusion in Europe*. Bristol: The Policy Press.

Eckert, M. (1999), "Prozesse sozialer Integration oder Ausgrenzung – Die Funktion von beruflicher Sozialisation und Arbeit in der Entwicklung Jugendlicher", in INBAS, *Betriebliche Realität in der Ausbildungsvorbereitung – Chancen und Grenzen*. Frankfurt am Main: INBAS.

Eurostat (2005), *Eurostat Yearbook 2005*. Brussels, European Commission (accessed 6 October 2006). Available at: http://epp.eurostat.ec.europa.eu/portal/page?_pageid=1334,49092079,1334_49092794&_dad=portal&_schema=PORTAL.

Evans, K. and Niemeyer, B. (2004), "Re-enter and reconnect – but whose problem is it?", in Evans, K. and Niemeyer, B. (eds), *Reconnection: countering social exclusion through situated learning*. Dordrecht: Kluwer.

Field, J. (2001), *Lifelong learning and the new educational order*. Wiltshire: Trentham Books.

Galuske, M. (1998), "Abkehr von der 'Heiligen Kuh'! Jugendberufshilfe nach dem Ende der Vollbeschäftigungsillusion", *Jugend Beruf Gesellschaft*, 49(1), pp. 6-14.

Hammer, T. (ed.) (2003), *Youth unemployment and social exclusion in Europe. A comparative study*. Bristol: The Policy Press.

Heidegger, G. (1997), "The social shaping of work and technology as a guideline for vocational education and training", *Journal of European Industrial Training*, 21(6), pp. 238–247.

Heidegger, G., Adolph, G. and Laske, G. (1997), *Gestaltungsorientierte Innovation in der Berufsschule* (Shaping oriented reform in vocational schools). Bremen: Donat.

Heikkinen, A. (2004), "Re-enter initiatives in the context of integrative vocational education and training", in Evans, K. and Niemeyer, B. (eds.), *Reconnection: countering social exclusion through situated learning*. Dordrecht: Kluwer.

Heikkinen, A. and Niemeyer, B. (2005), "Schlüsselqualifikationen für verschlossene Türen?" (Key qualifications for locked doors?), in Niemeyer, B. (ed.), *Neue Lernkulturen in Europa*? Wiesbaden: VS Verlag für Sozialwissenschaften.

Kronauer, M. (2002), *Exklusion. Die Gefährdung des Sozialen im hoch entwickelten Kapitalismus*. Frankfurt am Main: Campus.

Lave, J. and Wenger, E. (1991), *Situated learning. Legitimate peripheral participation*. Cambridge: Cambridge University Press.

Niemeyer, B. (2004), "CRIS-Collaboration, reflexivity, inclusiveness and situated pedagogy. Transcultural recommendations for the improvement of the quality of re-integration programmes" (online). Flensburg: Berufsbildungsinstitut Arbeit und Technik, University of Flensburg (accessed 29 March 2006). Available at: www.biat.uniflensburg.de/biat.www/index_projekte.htm.

Niemeyer, B. (2006), "Zwischen Schule und Beruf – Dilemmata einer europäisch vergleichenden Übergangsforschung". Europäische Zeitschrift für Berufsbildung.

Pohl, A. and Walther, A. (no date), "Bildungsprozesse in der Jugendarbeit im Europäischen Kontext. Expertise im Rahmen der 'Konzeption Bildungsbericht: vor und außerschulische Bildung' am Deutschen Jugendinstitut, München". Munich: Deutsches Jugendinstitut (accessed 29 March 2006). Available at: www.dji.de.

Silverman, M. (1999), *Facing postmodernity*. London: Routledge.

Stauber, B. and Walther, A. (2001), "Misleading trajectories: transition dilemmas of young adults in Europe", *Journal of Youth Studies*, 4(1), pp. 101-118.

Wenger, E. (1999), *Communities of practice. Learning, meaning and identity.* Cambridge: Cambridge University Press.

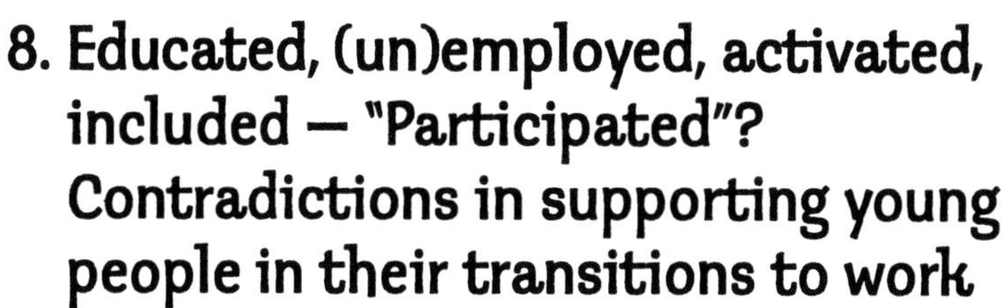

8. Educated, (un)employed, activated, included – "Participated"? Contradictions in supporting young people in their transitions to work

Andreas Walther

It is a widely shared assumption that young people's transitions to work are today characterised by new opportunities and new risks while social inequalities prevail. Although youth unemployment, dropping-out from education or training, fixed-term contracts or informal work, and "status zero" situations – being neither included in education, training and work nor registered unemployed – do not concern all young men and women, it can be argued that coping with uncertainty and insecurity has become a general demand. Youth transitions are becoming increasingly individualised and destandardised due to a profound process of flexibilisation which – reinforced by trends of globalisation – has decoupled formerly standardised links between education and employment. Rather than following collective patterns, young people increasingly have to take individual decisions, such as staying on in education, reducing aspirations if jobs are difficult to find, moving out from the parental home, etc. Individuals' motivation thereby becomes a crucial factor in social integration and social reproduction, and with this, questions arise as to what extent young people are passive or active in shaping their biographical transitions.

This chapter aims to explore possibilities and dilemmas in supporting young people in the active management of their transitions, from a comparative perspective. It is based on the findings of the EU-funded study "Youth Policy and Participation" (YOYO) on the "potentials of participation and informal learning for young people's transitions to the labour market". The study involved nine countries – Denmark, Germany, Ireland, Italy, Netherlands, Portugal, Romania, Spain and the UK – and consisted of biographical interviews with young people and case studies examining the potential of projects addressing youth transitions in a participatory way.[1] The chapter continues by reflecting the relationship between young people's motivation,

1. The YOYO project has been carried out in the framework of the EGRIS network (European Group for Integrated Social Research) and funded by the European Commission's Fifth Framework Programme for Research under the Key-Action "Improving the Socio-Economic Knowledge Base" between 2001 and 2004. The project has been co-ordinated by IRIS (Institute for Regional Innovation and Social Research), Tübingen. Research partners were based in Munich and Dresden (Germany), Leiden (Netherlands), Copenhagen (Denmark), Coleraine (Ulster, UK), Bologna (Italy), Valencia (Spain), Lisbon (Portugal), Bucharest (Romania), and Cork (Ireland). An executive summary, working papers and other materials can be downloaded from the project website: www.iris-egris.de/yoyo.

social inclusion and citizenship. Then some exemplar case studies are presented. The conclusion of the chapter discusses under what conditions participation can be a way to solve the dilemmas resulting from the social inclusion of young people.

Who is "active" in social inclusion and citizenship?

The way in which individuals pursue their lives within the frame of socially recognised rights and responsibilities in modern societies is institutionalised by the status of citizenship. In the early post-war years, Thomas Marshall reconstructed the making of the modern citizen as a historical process, during which first civil rights, then political rights, and finally social rights were established (Marshall, 1950). In this framework, citizenship was connected to a (gendered) life course regime of "education – employment/family work – retirement", and depended on the assumption of full employment and the growth rates of Fordist large-scale production and consumption. In this context, young people's citizenship rights could legitimately be postponed, as future fulfilment seemed guaranteed. The renewed attention paid to questions of citizenship at the beginning of the 21st century results from the fact that this connection is clearly no longer reliable. In fact, the shift from linear towards "yo-yo" transitions, which are reversible and fragmented, confronts young men and women with the contradictory demand of reconciling autonomy and dependency across different life spheres (Walther et al., 2002). Access to full citizenship is also narrowed, especially for so-called disadvantaged young people.

Since the late 1990s, the policies which have been implemented to secure the transitions of disadvantaged youth from school to work have been characterised by a discourse which has shifted from the perspective of "social integration" towards "social inclusion". What is the difference between these two apparently similar terms? Social integration describes both a process and state of society which, ideally, results in a balance between individual aspirations and collective demands. This has been described as a dialectic relationship between the social structures in which individuals find themselves and their own agency through which they may also reproduce these structures. Social inclusion starts from the perspective of insiders in a society who define the "outsiders" as those who need to be included. This means that inclusion in fact builds on mechanisms of exclusion (cf. Weber, 1920), just as education builds on the distinction of (adult) teachers and (young) learners. Both social inclusion and education thereby start from a power relationship, and this entails the risk that social integration is reduced to systemic integration according to functional imperatives in which individuals have the passive role of "being educated", "being employed", "being included".

However, inclusion does not occur mechanically by "putting" young people into education or work, but depends on their individual decisions to engage actively in constructing their biographies. This is where motivation comes into play, and relates to a currently significant policy approach, that of "activation". Active labour market policies, with their focus on bringing people into the labour market rather than paying benefits, depend on the active collaboration of individuals. Activation starts from the assumption that unemployed people are passive – either in terms of "learned helplessness" and a "culture of dependency", or in terms of a rational choice model of preferring benefits to work – and therefore need incentives to become active (cf. Kronauer, 1998). Entitlements for support increasingly are coupled with conditions, obligations and responsibilities. In its most rigid form, activation imposes negative incentives such as reducing benefit levels and sanctioning passive job search by benefit cuts, commonly known as "workfare" (Lødemel and Trickey, 2001; van Berkel and Hornemann Møller, 2002).

Activation policies obviously rely on a somewhat simplistic motivation theory which links politically undesirable choices by individuals – such as passive job search behaviour and "undeserving" poverty – to negative consequences. In contrast, psychology explains motivation as the result of the interaction between interest and experiences of self-efficacy (Bandura, 1997; Deci and Ryan, 1997; Walther et al., 2004). Motivation can be intrinsic if a goal is self-chosen, or extrinsic if it is imposed by someone else. The latter suggests that motivation is less sustainable because it is only effective as long it is needed to avoid the negative incentive. While motivation is often viewed in policy contexts as an individual characteristic, it results from experiences which are structured by unequal access to resources and opportunities. In fact, the persistence of the "status zero" phenomenon (Williamson, 1997) results from the fact that the more rigidly activation policies are applied, the more young people have only the possibility of disengaging and dropping out in order to remain actors in their own lives.

A more agency-related concept of citizenship is that of "participation", since this is considered to re-balance systemic demands and subjective needs in terms of being active, taking on responsibility, identifying with shared goals, and having power. Participation is a buzzword in current policy discourses. However, if we look at how the concept of participation is referred to in these discourses, we find a broad range of meanings in different policy sectors which can be distinguished as "soft" and "hard" (see Figure 1; Walther et al., 2006).

Figure 1 – Hard and soft policies addressing youth in transition

	"Soft"		**"Hard"**
Rationale	Individual development Subjective dimensions Local level		Allocation/normalisation Systemic dimensions National level
Sector	**Youth policy** **Youth work** **Youth information**	**Education + training** **Welfare policy**	**Labour market policy**
Aims	Self-realisation Political education Civic socialisation Community development	Selection / human resources Civic education Prevention of/compensation for social problems	Labour allocation Segmentation Employability

In the following, reference is made to the European policy level: we may start from the "soft" end with the area of youth policy documented by the European Commission's White Paper on youth (EC, 2001a) or the Council of Europe (Williamson, 2002). Here, young people are addressed as individuals within a perspective of empowerment. The reliance on non-formal education stands for a belief in the potential, abilities and interest of young people to learn, and represents the main method of participation. Youth policy is "soft" because it is voluntary, in most cases related to the areas of leisure and culture, and operates with limited funds on the local level. If we shift towards education and training, we find that schools or apprenticeship schemes generally do not foresee any active influence on the part of young people, or do so only with regard to marginal issues. However, in the context of the discourse of lifelong learning, individuals have been re-discovered as subjects who engage in learning only if it is relevant for them and if they can reconcile it with their wider lives (EC, 2001b; see also Chapter 7 by Beatrix Niemeyer in this volume). In the context of welfare policies multidimensional strategies like the ones promoted in the EU's Social Inclusion Process suggest the need to address individuals via a holistic perspective. However, in this context participation means to be part of a system which is defined by the relation between individual contributions and benefits and which is evaluated merely against quantitative indicators such as rates of poverty, activity and unemployment (EC, 2003). Finally, in labour market policies like the European Employment Strategy, the objectives of employability and adaptability imply an understanding of participation as being part of the workforce, which is regulated by a market system of supply and demand.

Different meanings of participation can therefore be distinguished. First, there is a distinction between active and passive participation; that is to say, between individuals having a direct influence on matters which concern them, and simply taking part in formal programmes. Second, participation can either be an objective or an integral principle of policies. Do young people have to be prepared for participation at some later stage, or are policies based on the assumption that participation has to be learned "by doing" and by experiencing the possibility of exercising influence? In general, in the "soft" sector active participation is an integral principle of expressing one's subjectivity; whilst in the "hard" policy sector participation is passive, and is largely reduced to attendance on training programmes or being part of the workforce. The latter is not necessarily voluntary, and it can be postponed after adaptive preparation and reduced to low status positions. Youth transitions are largely regulated by "hard" policies. While the European Youth Pact (EC, 2005) may be interpreted as claiming to reconcile "soft" and "hard" policies, to do so in practice would imply a more radical change in the sense of a fundamental re-balancing of power differentials between policy sectors related in the direction of empowering young people's subjective needs and interests.

The relation between "hard" and "soft" policies varies across contexts of different "transition regimes". Inspired by the Esping-Andersen model of welfare regimes (Esping-Andersen, 1990; Gallie and Paugam, 2000), transition regimes cluster according to national constellations with regard to socio-economic structures; state institutions; cultural values and patterns; and their dependency on specific paths of modernisation. The relation between social security, school, vocational training, labour market, gender-related trajectories, interpretations of "disadvantage" (structural versus individualised) and dominant concepts of "youth" creates different "climates of normality" for young people's transitions to work and adulthood, and with regard to young people's citizenship status. While individualisation and de-standardisation of transitions is taking place all across Europe, this takes different forms in different countries and regions, where global concepts such as activation may be interpreted and put into practice differently (Walther, 2006; see also Beatrix Niemeyer's Chapter 7).

Participation in de-standardised transitions: "hard" and "soft"

The YOYO project was concerned with the biographical perspectives of young men and women in relation to the new demands of getting started and keeping on moving in investing in their careers. As a first step, explorative interviews were conducted with young people who had experienced processes of "cooling out", that is reducing their aspirations due to mechanisms of selection (Goffman, 1962), and whose motivation was therefore expected to be seriously damaged. As a contrast group, young people in situations such as self-employment were interviewed, since they were likely to have combined formal and informal resources within individualised "choice biographies" (du Bois-Reymond, 1998; see also Colley et al., 2003), and therefore might serve as "models" for transition policies. Thematically, these interviews centred around career aspirations and experiences with institutional actors in formal transition systems, but also explored these processes within informal contexts such as networks, youth cultures or the family. The focus of the analysis was to reconstruct what we termed young people's "motivational careers". The so-called biographical "trendsetters", for instance, distinguished between (frustrating but strategically necessary) formal education and subjectively meaningful learning processes, and they relied strongly on informal networks (cf. Raffo and Reeves, 2000). In contrast, the more disengaged young men and women generally distanced themselves from learning, without distinguishing between formal education and training and alternative forms of learning. Prevailing negative experiences with institutions were reflected in internalised individual ascriptions of failure and generalised into a self-concept of being a "loser" or "victim". These also led to a withdrawal from counselling, education or training measures. This process occurred especially amongst young men. Young women more often seemed to succeed in "saving" their motivation for more promising opportunities, although this was not necessarily sufficient to overcome barriers of gendered labour market entrance.

Against this background, the objective of the YOYO project was to investigate to what extent the choice biographies of "trendsetters" might serve as models for supporting "disadvantaged" youth in their transitions to work. Biographical self-determination was the key perspective, with motivation as a subjective dimension and participation as a structural one. Therefore, as a second step, case studies of projects were carried out which appeared to address young people's transitions using a more participatory approach. Despite this purposively selected sampling, only a few of the analysed projects in fact corresponded to this ideal combination of "hard" and "soft" policy principles. The sample proved to be highly heterogeneous, with strong contrasts between youth work and employment schemes. Therefore comparison in a strict sense was not possible, and the model of "transition regimes" that we used was applied simply as a framework of reference to relate differences and similarities to wider contexts.

In the following section of this chapter, five different project types are discussed with regard to their understanding of participation, the scope of participation they promote, and their effectiveness in re-motivating young people. The examples stand in the context of different regime types, which are briefly introduced.

Sub-protective transition regimes: the case of Italy

Italy is typical of the "sub-protective" transition regime, which is characterised by a considerable lack of reliable vocational training, youth policies and welfare structures for young people. The relation between education level and labour market destinations is blurred: the permeable school system provides three out of four school-leavers with a school qualification giving access to higher education, but more than one third of young people under 25 are unemployed – across different levels of education. Transitions primarily mean long waiting phases, dependency on the family of origin and/or involvement in the informal economy. Young women's career opportunities are particularly limited, while family dependency more often means control and restriction of autonomy. Consequently, young people lack a well-defined social status:

> "We are alone! If you have some friends, fine ... otherwise ..." (female, 19 years).

This structural deficit is especially obvious in the south, in cities like Palermo, where 60% of young people are unemployed. Since the 1990s, however, the third sector has been growing significantly and many community and youth organisations have emerged. One is ArciRagazzi, an association aiming at providing young people with a horizon of autonomy through community-based activities of cultural practice. The work is based in groups characterised by high social and cultural heterogeneity, in which "peer learning" has led to high levels of cohesion. Although the project does not dispose of systematic links with the labour market or other transition actors, the project workers and managers see it as relevant for young people's transitions to work:

> "We would not be so well accepted by the young people, if they saw us as a measure of professional orientation ... Experimenting is the most important thing in the transition to work, to have time and opportunities to see what you want ... The experience of developing and realising their own ideas can help the young people to invest their creativity also beyond the limits of the association" (project worker, ArciRagazzi).

For some of the young men and women interviewed, simply starting off as a service user has turned into voluntary engagement and into the early stages of a freelance career, as they manage a self-administrated children and youth centre in a deprived neighbourhood (Lenzi et al., 2004):

> "You can be yourself ... I mean, nobody should tell you, 'do this, do that'. You should decide yourself, just try things out. During this one year in the project we have made mistakes – but, OK, this was growing up, a way of self-training ... They trusted me and gave me the opportunity to design my future ... Dreaming of the stable job is a waste of time ... You have to create your own job, invent new professions, realise your desires" (female, 20 years).

Employment-centred transition regimes: the case of Germany

The "employment-centred" transition regime is represented by Germany. Here, the standard lifecourse prevails as the main point of reference, reflected in objectives such as "training for all". However, the combination of a selective school system and a rigidly standardised system of vocational training leaves increasing numbers of young people excluded from regular training. They are labelled as "disadvantaged" – interpreted primarily in terms of learning and socialisation deficits – and channelled into pre-vocational schemes, which have the task of making young people "fit" for being placed in training or work after the intervention. Social work and youth work professionals admit that much "motivational work" is necessary, due to a high level of stigmatisation and uncertain outcomes. In this context, young people's transition experiences reveal a tension between biographical orientations towards the standard lifecourse and neglected desires for autonomy:

> "You get pressure: you must, you must – training, training, training ... there's no way of experimenting with other ways" (female, 21 years).

They experience the employment service as highly alienating – "They are not in the mood for helping you, they treat you like a cow" – while they see it as a matter of luck whether the programmes in which they are placed improve their chances of entering regular training or not.

Mobile Youth Work, in Stuttgart, is an outreach service supporting young people in deprived neighbourhoods with counselling and leisure-time opportunities. While this often includes also assisting "their" young people to find an apprenticeship or a job, mobile youth work within the local transition system also serves as a "door opener" to reach young people who have withdrawn from employment services and careers guidance. This represents an ambiguous approach between low threshold support and increasing control. However, as youth workers are not recognised actors in the formal transition system, their only resource is a trustful relationship, and their only possibility is offering support. This also includes a stance of not withdrawing support if young people take counterproductive decisions, such as dropping out from a practice placement because they do not feel respected by the employer (Pohl and Stauber, 2004).

> "Young people need a place to act out this clash: why do you need an upper secondary certificate to work in a bakery? They need a real person to talk to about this injustice, and maybe later on they see that, OK, this is unjust, but this is how it is. I have to look for another opportunity ... Otherwise he or she takes this as a personal offence by society" (project manager).

In this safe context, which many young people refer to as "family", they even accept pressure by project workers to apply for apprenticeship places as an expression of care and recognition:

> "Sometimes she [project worker] really was a pain in the ass, hassling me about writing applications ... But she took her time ... If nobody really cares, you get the impression that nobody gives a shit whether you get something or not" (female, 18 years).

A good example is the success story of a young man who – with the help of the youth workers – starts an apprenticeship to improve his chances in a pending trial at court:

> "After six months I really was fed up. I thought to myself, I will continue until the trial, then I will leave. Then the trial came, it went well. Seven months of the first year [of the apprenticeship] passed. I said to myself, 'At the end of the year there's a bonus payment, I might as well wait until then'" (male, 23 years).

The youth workers accept this pragmatic orientation to training, and step-by-step, by setting himself meaningful and reachable aims, he successfully completes the apprenticeship:

> "The longer I was there, the more my interest grew – to get a good qualification, to be really involved."

Universalistic transition regimes: the case of Denmark

Denmark belongs to the "universalistic" transition regime cluster, in which participation is not reduced to youth policy, but is a basic principle of general and vocational education. The education system aims first of all at motivation for personal development and only secondly at direct labour market relevance. To a certain

extent, this can also be said for activation measures allowing choice between alternative options and offering positive (material) incentives. For example, in cases of long-term unemployment, those who undertake self-initiated projects (for example, on environmental protection) still qualify for receipt of social benefits. As young adults from the age of 18 enjoy full citizenship status, they are entitled to an educational allowance for the duration of initial vocational training or higher education, regardless of the income situation of their parents. For those at risk of early school leaving, apart from pre-vocational initiatives (the so-called "production schools"), measures exist aimed at motivating young people in ways that can create a subjectively meaningful learning biography. One example – which despite its success has since been ended by the liberal-conservative government – is Open Youth Education. Although concentrating on early school-leavers, this national programme was open to all young people:

> "It is not up to us to decide why a young person does not want to take on a traditional youth education. We cannot force him or her to do so, at least not in the kind of society we wish to have. But we can try to create incentives and believe that because they are getting started at something, he or she will discover they are actually able to do something" (ministerial official, Open Youth Education).

In Open Youth Education, students arranged individual education plans with only a few compulsory elements, while non-formal and peer learning and even trips abroad were foreseen as the principal activities. In developing and realising their education plans, young people were supported by personal advisers whose role was defined by:

> "... never imposing limitations or restrictions but of course by directing the attention to possible problems of different options" (adviser, Open Youth Education).

Young people have internalised this optimistic approach towards an education-based life plan. The statement "it is my education, I take the decisions" (female, 18 years) stands for both the willingness to take responsibility and for the fact that experimentation and individual choice of lifestyles – even if "deviating from the straight way adopted by all" – are supported, as long as they are pursued within the system (Bechmann Jensen and Holmboe, 2004).

Post-socialist transition regimes: the case of Romania

The post-socialist countries can only be allocated to existing regime types by reductive simplification. While sharing the heritage of a socialist or communist regime in which lifecourses were stable but the extent of choice was restricted, processes of re-standardisation and de-standardisation since 1989 have taken different forms and directions. In Romania, aspects of de-standardisation prevail and imply precariousness for large segments of the population. While the education system is organised comprehensively, neither general nor vocational education keep pace with changing labour market demands. In view of drastically decreasing social benefits, the coping strategies of young adults are structured by precarious informal work, plans for emigration, or the accumulation of education and training that they may one day capitalise on in the labour market. SOLARIS in Pitesti is at first glance a normal training provider, offering a range of vocational qualifications, computer and language courses. However, as a non-governmental organisation (NGO), what they offer is more flexible in terms of meeting the demands of both young people and employers. Courses are not organised in a participatory way – they are not even free, except in cases of extreme social disadvantage – but because they are not linked to the state, the project enjoys a high level of credibility among young people which relates to different dimensions:

> "It was a friendly relationship, not like the relation between teachers and pupils in school" (male, 25 years).

> "NGOs offer young people what public education institutions do not provide: non-formal courses with qualifications that are actually demanded on the labour market" (project worker, SOLARIS).

In the end, the mere existence of such a project is perceived by young adults as a space of possibilities which can influence their own lives in the context of change and uncertainty. This also includes voluntary or even professional work within the project (Marcovici et al., 2004):

> "Before, I never was involved in social activities ... I only was interested in myself and my friends ... Through this course I understood that each of us can do something. If we avoid this responsibility, we'll never have any excuse in case of failure" (male, 27 years).

Liberal transition regimes: the case of the UK

The "liberal" transition regime in Europe is mainly represented by the UK, seen as the pacemaker for neo-liberal activation policies and a re-balancing of "rights and responsibilities". Young Britons are entitled to welfare benefits independently from their family from the age of 18, while allowances and wages in training and employment options tend to be only slightly higher than the level at which benefits are set. Corresponding to the primacy of market and individual provision in this regime, youth is viewed as a transitional status which should be replaced by economic independence as soon as possible. This is reflected by the programme "New Deal for Young People", which offers job-seekers an orientation phase, after which they are obliged to opt for employment (in some cases subsidised), training, voluntary work or environmental work. Unless they accept such a placement, their benefits are reduced or suspended. This programme has also been extended to single parents, although this also includes childcare support, and to the disabled.

Lifting the Limits was a pilot project for lone mothers in a rural area of Northern Ireland. Most of the young mothers had been on benefits for a long time before they entered the project. Like self-fulfilling prophecies, their self-concepts reflected the discourse of a "dependent underclass" and the effects of repressive activation policies. This can be seen in the response of one young woman when introduced to the project:

> "It was a big 'no way'. Being on benefits for three years I had begun to lose sight of my personal goals. I was afraid to come off benefits; afraid to go back to work; afraid to set goals, but most of all afraid to fail" (female, 23 years).

The project succeeds in buffering external pressures. The young women are employed, receive a wage and are trained for eighteen months as community leaders. The project manager describes the meaning "participation" has for her/him:

> "... a kind of self-determination ... having freedom of choices ... having the self-confidence to stand up and say, 'This is the choice I want to make and these are the right choices'... For us it means that these young people are adults and

have a right to determine the programmes they engage in ... If ... young people don't feel that their views are valued and respected ... they are not going to engage" (Director, Lifting the Limits).

Participants in the project receive a qualification corresponding to Level 3 out of five levels in the modularised British system of national vocational qualifications (NVQS). This provides them with the entry requirement for access to higher education in youth and community work. While central elements of the course consist of practical outreach projects, in which participants work with other young mothers in the community, the project is also characterised by peer learning and mutual support (Hayes and Biggart, 2004):

"It felt amazing ... being able to do that I suppose showed me that I could do everything I wanted to do, despite having a child" (female, 23 years).

"A few of us went through difficult things during the project, you know, outside of work, and everyone was always involved in supporting each other" (female, 23 years).

Dilemmas for participation: balancing autonomy and responsibility

There was clear evidence that the projects described above have succeeded in re-motivating young people for active engagement in their transitions to work and in developing a reflexive learning biography. However, only Lifting the Limits was able to secure biographical perspectives in a sustainable way by providing both "hard" and "soft" resources. We have to say "was", because this project shares with all the others a precarious funding situation: after the end of the pilot programme, it was not incorporated into mainstream policies and funding was stopped. Open Youth Education was ended due to a lack of political will to maintain it; transition-related funding for Mobile Youth Work was stopped after one year and re-directed towards social work in schools; while young adults at ArciRagazzi continue to be dependent on their families in order to secure their precarious biographies. This may be interpreted as a clear trend of convergence across Europe towards a model of activation that restricts individual autonomy. Nevertheless, case study analysis allows us to identify those elements of a participatory approach that enable young people to become subjects of their own lives (cf. Rabe and Schmid, 2000). This implies conceptualising individuals as principally interested in being active, even if their coping strategies lack the resources and recognition which are necessary to become productive. Consequently, positive rather than negative incentives should be applied in order to provide the necessary resources, opportunities and competencies for successful outcomes.

First of all, this is reflected by possibilities of choice, as is the case in the universalistic transition regime, where a range of recognised options is materially secured. Choice that allows for decisions with which the young person can subjectively identify, and thereby for intrinsic motivation, includes keeping processes of guidance and counselling open, rather than imposing adaptation to what seems "realistic" right from the beginning. This is illustrated by the example of Mobile Youth Work. From a more general perspective, this can imply the modularisation of qualifications to mediate better between systemic and subjective interests and to give young people the possibility of engaging – and trying options out – step-by-step. Lifting the Limits and ArciRagazzi provide evidence that so-called "disadvantaged" young people do not necessarily have to compensate for deficits before taking responsibility for something "real". In interpreting transition problems which result

from competition for scarce positions in a tight labour market, the concept of "disadvantage" has not only proved to be an obstacle for competence development, it also hides existing competencies (Walther et al., 2002). Non-formal education, or the recognition of competencies acquired outside of any pedagogical setting, can therefore be a form of participation – unless informal spheres of life become formalised themselves, and thereby exposed to the pressure of capitalisation (Colley et al., 2003; Chisholm et al., 2005). A prerequisite for participation is the provision of social spaces which are open for young people to shape, and of access to flexible support, tailored to each individual's needs.

Participation evolves in relationship to other individuals and to social contexts, and thus depends on trust and confidence between project workers and young people. The example of Mobile Youth Work reveals a differentiation between a socio-political and a pedagogical interpretation of activation: while the political approach demands individual activity as a prerequisite for support, the pedagogical approach offers support for exploring and challenging individual strengths. This does not exclude conflict: inasmuch as individualisation implies diverging interests, participation necessarily has to provide spaces for conflict instead of hiding them through asymmetric structures (Stevens et al., 1999).

It may be concluded that participation can only contribute to solving the dilemmas related to young people's social integration and citizenship if it is not reduced to a "soft" pedagogical understanding, but extends to the "hard" structural and socio-political level. Enabling responsibility requires securing negotiation power through rights and resources, and validating the participatory expertise of the "soft" policy sectors, especially youth work, in the context of transitions to work. However, the current trend, represented by the dismantling of workers' participation in the economy and the undermining of individual autonomy by activation policies, seems to point in the opposite direction. If a passive version of participation is used to replace social rights, thereby obscuring structures of power and inequality, it risks becoming a "new tyranny" (Cooke and Kothari, 2001). Under conditions of individualisation, the status of citizenship – that is the trinity of civil, political and social rights – needs to be proved by "lived citizenship": the subjective possibilities for individuals to lead their lives in a socially recognised way (Hall and Williamson, 1999). This means that social policies may fail in providing citizenship and social integration if they do not involve the target groups in interpreting their needs – as well as their rights and responsibilities (Fraser, 1989). Welfare and active forms of participation therefore need to be inter-related, to avoid both the imposition of bureaucratic norms and the individualisation of risk and exclusion.

References

Bandura, A. (1997), *Self-efficacy: the exercise of control.* New York: W.H. Freeman & Co.

Bechmann Jensen, T. and Holmboe, A. (2004), "Youth policy and participation. Case study report Denmark", YOYO working paper (online). Copenhagen: University of Copenhagen (accessed 25 June 2006). Available at: www.iris-egris.de/yoyo.

Böhnisch, L. and Schröer, W. (2002), *Die soziale Bürgergesellschaft.* Weinheim' Munich: Juventa.

Chisholm, L., Hoskins, B. and Glahn, C. (eds.) (2005), *Trading up – Potential and performance in non-formal learning.* Strasbourg: Council of Europe.

Colley, H., Hodkinson, P. and Malcolm, J. (2003), *Informality and formality in learning*. London: Learning and Skills Research Centre.

Cooke, B. and Kothari, U. (eds.) (2001), *Participation – The new tyranny?* London/New York: Zed Books.

Deci, E.L. and Ryan, R.M. (1985), *Intrinsic motivation and self-determination in human behavior*. New York: Plenum Press.

du Bois-Reymond, M. (1998), "'I don't want to commit myself yet.' Young people's life-concepts", *Journal of Youth Studies*, 1(1), pp. 63-79.

Esping-Andersen, G. (1990), *Worlds of welfare capitalism*. Cambridge: Polity Press.

European Commission (EC) (2001), "A new impetus for European youth". White Paper of the European Commission. Luxemburg: Office of Publications of the European Communities.

Field, J. (2000), *Lifelong learning and the new educational order*. Stoke-on-Trent/Sterling: Trentham Books.

Fraser, N. (1989), *Unruly practices: power, discourse and gender in contemporary social theory*. Minneapolis: University of Minnesota Press.

Gallie, D. and Paugam, S. (eds.) (2000), *Welfare regimes and the experience of unemployment in Europe*. Oxford: Oxford University Press.

Hall, T. and Williamson, H. (1999), *Citizenship and community*. Leicester: Leicester Youth Work Press.

Hayes, A. and Biggart, A. (2004), "Youth policy and participation: case study report UK", YOYO working paper (online). Coleraine: University of Ulster (accessed 25 June 2006). Available at:
www.iris-egris.de/yoyo.

Lenzi, G., Cuconato, M. and Laasch, C. (2004), "Youth policy and participation: case study report Italy", YOYO working paper (online). Bologna: University of Bologna (accessed 25 June 2006). Available at:
www.iris-egris.de/yoyo.

Lødemel, I. and Trickey, H. (eds.) (2001), *An offer you can't refuse. Workfare in an international perspective*. Bristol: Policy Press.

Marcovici, O., Constantin, A., Stupcanu, A., Dalu, A. and Iacob, L.B. (2004), "Youth policy and participation: case study report Italy", YOYO working paper (online). Bucarest: Agency of Youth Initiative Support (accessed 25 June 2006). Available at:
www.iris-egris.de/yoyo.

Marshall, T. (1950), *Class, citizenship and social development*. Chicago: Chicago University Press.

Pohl, A. and Stauber, B. (2004), "Youth policy and participation: case study report West Germany", YOYO working paper (online). Tübingen: Institute for Regional Innovation and Social Research (accessed 25 June 2006). Available at:
www.iris-egris.de/yoyo.

Rabe, B. and Schmid, G. (2000), "Strategie der Befähigung: Zur Weiterentwicklung der Arbeitsmarkt und Rentenpolitik", *WSI-Mitteilungen*, 2000(5), pp. 305-313.

Raffo, C. and Reeves, M. (2000), "Youth transitions and social exclusion – Developments in social capital theory", *Journal of Youth Studies*, 3(2), pp. 127-146.

Rychen, D.S. and Salganik, L.H. (2003), *Key competencies for a successful life in a well-functioning society*. Cambridge: Hogrefe and Huber.

Stevens, A., Bur, A. and Young, L. (1999), *Partial, unequal and conflictual: problems in using participation for social inclusion in Europe*. Canterbury: University of Kent.

van Berkel, R. and Hornemann Møller, I. (eds.) (2002), *Active social policies in the EU. Inclusion through participation?* Bristol: Policy Press.

Walther, A. (2000), *Spielräume im Übergang in die Arbeit. Junge Erwachsene im Wandel der Arbeitsgesellschaft in Deutschland, Italien und Großbritannien*. Weinheim, Munich: Juventa.

Walther, A., Stauber, B., Biggart, A., du Bois-Reymond, M., Furlong, A., López Blasco, A., Mørch, S. and Pais, J.M. (eds.) (2002), *Misleading trajectories: integration policies for young adults in Europe?* Opladen: Leske + Budrich.

Walther, A. , Stauber, B., Pohl, A., Biggart, A., Hayes, A., Burgess, P., du Bois-Reymond, M., Jensen, T.B., Lenzi, G. and Plug. W. (2004), "Youth policy and participation. The potential of participation and informal learning in young people's transitions to the labour market". Final report. Tübingen: Institute for Regional Innovation and Social Research.

Weber, M. (1920), *Wirtschaft und Gesellschaft*. Tübingen: JCB Mohr.

9. Monitoring policy development in the field of education for active citizenship

Bryony Hoskins

Creating social cohesion in Europe has been and continues to be a challenge for policy makers across Europe. Given this, we need to be able to monitor and evaluate policies that tackle this issue in order to improve them, and one method for doing so has been the use of indicators and benchmarks. These tools consist of setting policy objectives and then measuring progress towards them through agreed targets. They thus provide a snapshot of the state of play in a country, and/or a comparison over time and between different countries.

This chapter will focus on one specific aspect of social inclusion – active citizenship – and consider how indicators can be used to evaluate policies directed towards increasing the number of active citizens in European countries. In particular, it will discuss a research project called Active citizenship for democracy, hosted in the Centre for Research on Lifelong Learning (CRELL), and created in co-operation with the Council of Europe Directorate of Education. CRELL has recently been set up by the European Commission Directorate Education and Culture and the European Commission Directorate General Joint Research Centre, to support the monitoring of the Lisbon Strategy in the field of education. Within this remit, the research project on active citizenship aims to propose indicators on education and training for active citizenship, and on active citizenship in practice. (Education and training for active citizenship is taken to include all types of learning: formal, non-formal and informal.) The project is wider than a youth research project, as it will consider all age groups in the context of a lifelong learning strategy. It is supported by a research network comprising key experts from across Europe with expertise in the different types of learning opportunities for active citizenship the knowledge, skills and competencies required for the practice of active citizenship and active citizenship itself.

Using indicators to evaluate policy on active citizenship is an underdeveloped field of research, and is only now beginning to take shape as political awareness around the need for active citizens is growing. In the last year, research has started to be published from projects funded by the European Commission on this topic. The Commission financed studies on "Indicators for monitoring active citizenship and citizenship education" by the consultancy Regioplan (Weerd et al., 2005) and EUYOUPART – Political Participation of Young People in Europe: Development of Indicators for Comparative Research in the European Union by the consultancy

SORA (Ogris and Westphal, 2005). Using indicators in the youth field was also explored by a Council of Europe expert group (Council of Europe, 2003).

Other research on education and training for active citizenship is more developed. In terms of formal education and active citizenship, a number of pan-European research projects have been carried out by the Council of Europe, the International Association for the Evaluation of Educational Achievement (IEA) (broader than Europe) and Eurydice (the information network on education in Europe). The Council of Europe have published widely on the topic of education for democratic citizenship, including identifying competencies (Veldhius, 1997; Audigier, 2000); exploring quality assurance (Birzea et al., 2005); and developing a coherent framework for education for democratic citizenship (Birzea, 2000). The IEA international study on civic education completed across 24 countries in 1999 generated a number of publications demonstrating international trends in civic knowledge and the teaching of civics in schools (Torney-Purta et al., 1999; Torney-Purta et al., 2001). This study will be repeated in 2008/9 and will form an important part of fulfilling the data needs on indicators for education for active citizenship. In 2005, Eurydice completed a study on citizenship in the school curriculum, national education policy and teacher training (Eurydice, 2005).

In the non-formal learning sector, and in co-operation between the European Commission and the Council of Europe, youth research from across Europe has been compiled on volunteering (Williamson and Hoskins, 2006) and the types of volunteering that offer learning opportunities for citizenship (Mutz and Schwimmbeck, 2006). In the area of youth political participation across Europe, further research was compiled (Forbrig, 2005) that highlighted new forms of political participation, such as fluid networks of people gathering in short-term projects. Such projects aimed, for example, to create political change (Griffin, 2005) or to support the community in an environmental crisis (Blanch, 2005). They tend to require no membership and make less use of organisational logos than traditional political formations (Pleyers, 2005). This evidence is complimented by research completed for the European Commission in the field of adult learning (Holford and van der Veen, 2003) that sees these new forms of participation as learning environments, where experiences of informal learning in one context can be transferred to another.

This chapter will explore how and why indicators are useful for evaluating education policy in the particular context of "active citizenship for democracy". It will address a number of questions: what policies are directed towards this field, why governments are interested in it and what is meant by active citizenship. Finally, it will discuss what indicators would be appropriate for this field. In view of the early stage of the project, the chapter will present the current framework which has been developed for the creation and selection of indicators.

Use of indicators in policy making

In order to make decisions about which policy to introduce, and to evaluate the policy outcomes of a particular topic on a European-wide scale, we have to be able to map out the state of play in Europe and compare the situation from one country to another. One method for doing this is the use of indicators. In some areas there may be a great deal in common across Europe, but in others we find greater disparity, for example, the percentage of early school-leavers in some southern European countries is comparatively lower than in north, east and west Europe.

Indicators can provide an evidenced-based link to ensure congruence between social circumstances and social policy. Having made the comparisons, it is then possible for countries to learn from each other. In countries where the indicators demonstrate successful scores – high quality activities or results – it is possible to look for good practices and explore the strategies used to achieve these results. In countries where the scores are less successful, it is important to support policy development towards redressing the issues. The sharing of good practices can be useful to support countries' policy development. However, it is always necessary to understand the social, historical and cultural context in which a policy strategy is used, in order to judge whether its application in a different national context is appropriate. Using the same indicators over time gives a signal as to whether there is an improvement as a result of policy initiatives – although non-governmental activities also play an important role. In general, governments prefer to be considered as performing well with high quality activities and results, so using indicators provides peer pressure between countries to get the policies right.

One argument for governments to use indicators is that monitoring services which underpin them make the information gathered more accessible to individual citizens, civil society and the media. Results are presented as specific numbers, which can be displayed in user-friendly tables or graphs, so that it is relatively easy to make comparisons between countries. Audiences can then interpret the story that the indicators tell, and make their own evaluation from the results. Appropriate use and communication of indicators can therefore render governments more accountable, since they help to make policy monitoring transparent, and empower citizens (Lievesley, 2005). Citizens are thereby able to debate policy developments, providing a tool to promote good governance and democracy (Council of Europe, 2003). It is also interesting to note that some NGOs use indicators to compare and evaluate governments' policy developments for advocacy in civil society, for example:

- The World Wildlife Fund (WWF) has two indicators, the Living Planet Index and the Ecological Footprint (WWF, 2006);
- Transparency International, a non-governmental organisation (NGO) devoted to combating corruption, has indicators on the perception of corruption (Transparency International, 2005);
- Social Watch, an international watchdog citizens' network on poverty eradication and gender equality, has indicators on development (Social Watch, n.d.).

A powerful argument can be made based upon the results given to the public, and attention can be drawn to policy needs in these fields.

At the same time, we must note that caution is needed to ensure that indicators are not badly created, misread or misunderstood as the last word on a topic. Indicators need to be created with care and transparency of purpose. They are only the starting point of discussion on policy evaluation. As the term itself suggests, they can only provide an indication of what is going on at one particular moment, and cannot substitute for further in-depth and comparative research that helps to explore the complexities of active citizenship across Europe. It is a mistake to assume that indicators give the full picture of a situation, as this may lead policymakers to concentrate on hitting particular targets rather than improving the situation overall. This danger here, noted often at the seminar on which this book is based, is that of "hitting the target and missing the point". Giving adequate information about the limitations of the data is one way to ensure that this does not occur.

In the European context, indicators have been created to establish whether progress has been made on the Lisbon 2010 goals towards Europe becoming the "the most competitive and dynamic knowledge-based economy in the world, capable of sustainable economic growth with more and better jobs and greater social cohesion" (European Council, 2000). The open method of co-ordination was the policy tool used to create European common objectives on education. These objectives refer to the quality and effectiveness of European education in the context of globalisation and of wider societal goals of participation and inclusion. To evaluate the common objectives on education, 29 indicators and five benchmarks have been agreed. An example of these is the indicator on the completion of upper-secondary education, and the benchmark of 85%. A report has been created each year to demonstrate progress made on the indicators and benchmarks (see European Commission, 2006). However, none of the indicators that have been agreed with the European Union member states so far have referred to active citizenship, and so the CRELL project has been set up to support the creation of indicators in this field.

Active citizenship is embedded into Education Objective Number 2, "facilitating the access of all to education and training systems", but there are currently no agreed indicators specific to active citizenship established for this objective. It has therefore been difficult to establish whether progress has been accomplished in this area among the member states, and active citizenship takes only a minor place within the progress report. In order to develop education and training opportunities for learning active citizenship, indicators for this need to be agreed, so that policy implementation can be monitored.

What are the policies relevant to active citizenship?

The choice of indicators should reflect the aims and objectives for the implementation of policy in the field in order to provide adequate evaluation. Thus it is necessary to explore what policy makers are trying to achieve by implementing policies relating to active citizenship. In this section of the chapter, I will explore why national governments are interested in increasing active citizenship.

One of the predominant concerns of politicians recently is political apathy towards traditional forms of democracy (voting and mainstream party membership), and an increasing lack of trust in political parties and politicians. In many cases, apathy is rapidly changing into resentment, as we have seen in young people's demonstrations in France in 2005 and 2006, with protests in the suburbs, the universities, and among young people opposing proposed changes to employment law affecting them. Traditional engagement in civil society is in general low across Europe, for example, voting (except in Italy in 2006, with an increase in the levels of participation), membership and participation rates in political parties and NGOs. The reduction of membership of NGOs is of particular concern in relation to the continuation of civil society and accountability of governments.

Some social scientists link the decline in traditional forms of participating to increasing individualisation and globalisation, in which governments are seen to have less control over decision-making processes (Pleyer, 2005). Instead global corporations are seen to have the power. The lack of involvement of citizens is considered to pose a long-term risk to democracy and to the continuing legitimacy of governing institutions at a European, national and local level. However, new forms of participation are on the rise, such as one-off issue politics – where persons participate and help others in the community in a crisis, attend a demonstration or organise a single protest, rather than becoming a member of an NGO (see Chapter 5 by Daniel Blanch, also Blanch, 2005). Another new form of participation on the rise is ethical consumption – a person purchasing a certain product because it is made and traded in a way that is not damaging to the environment, or that is not unfair to producers in underdeveloped countries, for example. There is an interest amongst policy makers in understanding these new forms of participation, including those which are not in the formal political domain, and the extent of new forms of civil renewal.

In contrast to concerns related to apathy, there are serious anxieties related to extremist and non-democratic political engagement such as the recent terrorist activities that caused large-scale loss of human life (in the US in September 2001, in Madrid in March 2004, and in London in July 2005). A need to increase the levels of education, specifically on democracy, intercultural learning and human rights, has been considered an important long-term tool to reduce terrorist activities (Council of Europe, 2006). In many ways, this issue is closely related to policy discussions on racism and migration. The rise in Islamophobia in Europe and violent actions and intolerance demonstrated towards Muslim migrants as a result of terrorism is of concern, and has been closely monitored by the European Monitoring Centre on Racism and Xenophobia (Allen and Nielsen, 2002) along with racist acts towards other minority communities. Concerns of integration equally refer to the respect of minorities for the majority population, and the wording in the definition below from the active citizenship for democracy project uses the term "mutual respect" to refer to this. The rise in intolerance and racism enhances pre-existing difficulties in migration and citizenship – interest is increasing on debates about who should be allowed to be a citizen of their country. These combine with various forms of citizenship training and culturally developed citizenship tests that are either under discussion or have been introduced in European countries such as the Netherlands, UK and Germany.

Education and training for active citizenship is one tool which can be used to maintain democracy and civil society, and one of the questions that this project has been asked is: to what extent is this effective? Thus indicators will be needed to measure not just education and training for active citizenship, but also the level of active citizenship in society, and to explore the correlation between the two.

How can active citizenship be defined?

In order to understand what indicators would be relevant to the topic of active citizenship it is necessary to define the field. The European Commission research project, Active citizenship for democracy, has created the following working definition for active citizenship:

"Participation in civil society, community and/or political life characterised by mutual respect and non-violence and in accordance with human rights and democracy."

Thus active citizenship is understood in a very broad sense, as the word "participation" suggests – ranging from cultural and political to environmental activities at local, regional, national, European and international levels. It includes new forms of active citizenship such as one-off issue politics and ethical consumption, as well as the more traditional formats of voting or membership of mainstream parties and NGOs. The limits of participation are defined in terms of its ethical boundaries.

Activities in which persons participate should support the community, and should not contravene principles of human rights and the rule of law. Participation in extremist groups that promote intolerance and violence would therefore not be included in this definition of active citizenship.

Examples of active citizenship might include the following:

- participation in European Voluntary Service: a young person volunteers abroad in an NGO to help save the environment;
- a local group of senior citizens decide that they would like to have a regular place to meet, and so they discuss with the town council how a community centre can be developed;
- a disabled person suffers discrimination at work, so she contacts the union and starts to campaign with the union to stop the discrimination.

Education and training for active citizenship in this context is defined within the Active citizenship for democracy project as:

> "Learning opportunities (formal, non-formal and informal) that occur at any stage of the life cycle that facilitate or encourage active citizenship."

Thus there are many possibilities for learning the relevant knowledge, skills, competencies, attitudes, values and beliefs for active citizenship throughout the whole spectrum of lifelong and lifewide learning.

Examples of education for active citizenship include, for example:

- a school that is governed through democratic principles, allowing the students, through such means as elected school councils, to influence the decision- making processes in the school;
- a youth club that facilitates young people to make changes to their local community – the young people learn to negotiate with the town council in order to have new sports facilities created;
- an adult attending a night course at an adult education centre on women in history learns the skills of critical reading and listening.

Work will be completed within this project to make precise the knowledge, skills, competencies, attitudes, values, beliefs and motivation required for active citizenship and the relationship with what is taught in learning opportunities on this matter.

Choosing the indicators

In this research project, we will be examining two types of indicators: those that measure active citizenship; and those that measure education and training for active citizenship. The basis for the development of indicators will be the key areas of policy interest outlined earlier in this chapter, the definitions described above, and research which has already been carried out in this field.

Indicators on active citizenship

The indicators that measure active citizenship will explore both traditional and new forms of participation. In the EC funded Regioplan study, indicators were proposed on active citizenship in the following areas: "voluntary work in organisations and networks, organising activities for the community, voting in elections and participating in political parties, interest group, peaceful protest and public debates"

(Weerd et al., 2005, p. 34). As the political emphasis and recent research trends focus more on new forms of participation and not only participation in the formal political sphere, we will need to try to find indicators that also reflect this alternative dimension, by exploring indicators on, for example, ethical consumption and cultural forms of participation.

Indicators on education and training for active citizenship

The indicators used to measure education and training for active citizenship will be divided into three types: input indicators; process indicators; and output indicators. The indicators that will be chosen will reflect all types of learning (formal, non-formal and informal learning opportunities). The input indicators will refer to content input, such the curriculum of a school or of teacher training (but see Lorna Roberts' chapter in this volume for some important caveats on the latter). For the indicators on process, data on the methods for teaching citizenship education should be used. For example, the Regioplan study (Weerd et al., 2005) suggested that an open climate for discussion is considered essential for schools to teach active citizenship. When examining the indicators on output, it is necessary to identify whether the knowledge, skills and competencies, attitudes, values and motivation to be able to participate in active citizenship have been achieved. Another dimension of education and training would be to explore data on teachers and trainers and to use data collected on training offers available on active citizenship education.

One recurring difficulty with the indicators on education and training is that the data which exists refers mostly to formal education. The focus for many international surveys is on the curriculum of schools, and the target population are usually students approaching the end of compulsory schooling. Since active citizenship is learned as much through non-formal and informal learning environments, it is difficult to obtain the full picture in relationship to out-of-school learning. A major task, therefore, will be to establish how indicators for these other contexts of learning can be developed, and how to collect the data relating to them. A further problem also exists in terms of age groups – much less information is available for the adult population, including young adults, than for students at schools.

This project is now in the process of establishing what will be the ideal indicators for education and training for active citizenship and for active citizenship in practice. The next step will be to map out what data exists in relationship to these ideal indicators. Where no data exists, then the research project will support the development of new surveys and add new questions within existing data collection processes with the intention of filling the data gaps. To follow the developments of this project, readers should visit the CRELL website: http://farmweb.jrc.cec.eu.int/Crell/.

Conclusion

Creating indicators for monitoring active citizenship and education and training for active citizenship is one method for evaluating policy developments directed towards increasing active and democratic participation across Europe. The research project Active citizenship for democracy will propose research-based indicators for monitoring progress towards the Lisbon objectives in this field. The decision on whether the indicators proposed will be adopted in the field of education will be the responsibility of the member states of the European Union. If indicators are used on this topic, it can provide a tool for citizens themselves to evaluate education policies aimed at increasing the level of active citizens and thus provide a

lever for good governance. The indicators could provide a resource to bring to attention any decreasing levels of active citizenship across Europe, and to highlight where policy needs to target improvement. They could also highlight countries or regions where active strategies to promote active citizenship are working well, and encourage the sharing of good practice between member states. Thus the results provided from the indicators would make a contribution to maintaining and developing democracy, civil society and social cohesion in Europe.

It is important to note, however, that indicators are only the first step to understanding what is happening across Europe on education for active citizenship. Further and more in-depth qualitative and quantitative research is always needed to provide a solid basis for explaining the results of the indicators, and to give a more precise evaluation of the policy strategies developed in education on the topic of active citizenship.

References

Allen, C. and Nielsen, J. (2002), *Summary report on Islamophobia in the EU after 11 September 2001*. Vienna: European Monitoring Centre on Racism and Xenophobia.

Audigier, F. (2000), "Basic concepts and core competencies for education for democratic citizenship". Strasbourg, Council of Europe. DGIV/EDU/CIT(2000)23.

Blanch, D. (2005), "Between the traditional and the postmodern: political disaffection and youth participation in Galicia", in Forbrig, J. (ed.), *Revisiting youth political participation*. Strasbourg: Council of Europe.

Birzea, C., Cecchini, M., Harrison, C., Krek, J. and Vedrana, S. (2005), *Tool for quality assurance of education for democratic citizenship in schools*. Strasbourg: Council of Europe.

Birzea, C. (2000), *Education for democratic citizenship: a lifelong learning perspective*. Strasbourg: Council of Europe.

Council of Europe (2003), "Experts on youth policy indicators – Third and concluding meeting". Strasbourg: Council of Europe.

Council of Europe (2006), *Education for democratic citizenship and the prevention of terrorism*. Strasbourg: Council of Europe.

European Commission (2006), "Staff working paper: progress towards the Lisbon objectives in education and training, report based on indicators and benchmarks". Brussels: European Commission.

European Council (2000), "Council conclusions of 24 March 2000 on a new strategic goal for the Union in order to strengthen employment, economic reform and social cohesion as part of a knowledge-based economy". Brussels: European Council.

Eurydice (2005), *Citizenship education at school in Europe*. Brussels: Eurydice.

Holford, J. and van der Veen, R. (2003), *Lifelong learning, governance and active citizenship in Europe*. Surrey: University of Surrey.

Kerr, D. (2003), "Citizenship education longitudinal study – First cross-sectional survey 2001-2002". London: DfES

Mutz, G. and Schwimmbeck, E. (2006), "Voluntary activities and civic learning: findings of a preparatory survey for a European case study", in Williamson, H. and

Hoskins, B. (eds.), *Charting the landscape of volunteering*. Strasbourg: Council of Europe.

Ogris, G. and Westphal, S. (2005), *Political participation of young people in Europe – Development of indicators for comparative research in the European Union* (EUYOUPART). Vienna: Institute for Social Research and Analysis.

Pleyers, G. (2005), "Young people and alter-globalisation: from disillusionment to a new culture of political participation", in Forbrig, J. (ed.), *Revisiting youth political participation*. Strasbourg: Council of Europe.

Social Watch (no date), "Development indicators" (online) (accessed 23 February 2006). Available at:
www.socialwatch.org/en/indicadoresDesarrollo/flash_content/index.html?lan=en&ind=A4.

Torney-Purta J., Lehmann, R., Oswald, H. and Schulz, W. (2001), *Citizenship and education in twenty-eight countries: civic knowledge and engagement at age fourteen*. Delft: Eburon.

Torney-Purta J., Schwille, J. and Amadeo, J.-A. (eds.) (1999), *Civic education across countries: twenty-four national case studies for the IEA civic education project*. Delft: Eburon.

Transparency International (2005), "Corruption Perceptions Index 2005" (online) (accessed 23 February 2006). Available at:
www.transparency.org/policy_and_research/surveys_indices/cpi/2005.

Veldhuis, R. (1997), "Education for democratic citizenship: dimensions of citizenship, core competences, variables and international activities". Strasbourg: Council of Europe.

Weerd, M., Gemmeke, M., Rigter, J. and van RiJ, C. (2005), "Indicators and options for monitoring active citizenship and citizenship education. Final report". Amsterdam: Regioplan Beleid-sonderzoek.

Williamson, H. and Hoskins, B. (eds.) (2006), "Charting the landscape of volunteering". Strasbourg: Council of Europe.

World Wildlife Fund (WWF) (2006), "Living Planet Report (online) (accessed 23 February 2006). Available at:
www.panda.org/news_facts/publications/key_publications/living_planet_report/index.cfm.

10. Kurdish women in Sweden: a feminist analysis of barriers to integration and strategies to overcome them

Amineh Kakabaveh

Introduction

In this chapter, I present my own contribution to research on issues of social exclusion: the testimony of myself and other Kurdish women refugees in Sweden, and an analysis of this experience from our standpoint. As Rachel Gorman shows in the case of disabled people (Chapter 13), and as the anti-racist, anti-sexist movement "Ni putes ni soumises" (www.niputesnisoumises.com) has also demonstrated, the voices of those who suffer exclusion is all too rarely heard in research or allowed to inform efforts for social inclusion. Our testimony, far from being "anecdotal", provides vital evidence from the perspective of those who live with disadvantage. Increasingly, we are also engaging with research and theoretical analyses, to make sense of our experiences and point to more effective strategies for inclusion. This chapter begins, then, with a brief account of my own history and of the situation of Kurdish women. I go on to analyse the contradictory situation and the barriers to integration that Kurdish women immigrants experience in Sweden, showing how race, nationality, gender, class and religion intersect to exclude them in sometimes brutal ways. I describe an initiative that Kurdish women have organised themselves to promote greater equality, and conclude that women in diaspora have specific and distinct needs that should be addressed in policy and practice – not just by initiatives directed at them, but by support for the initiatives they take themselves.

Kurdish women in diaspora

I have had lifetime commitment to issues of justice and equality. In all my adulthood, I have fought for human rights and gender equity. As a teenager, I was persecuted by Iran's Islamic regime because of my involvement with the Marxist Kurdish organisation, Komalah (Revolutionary Organisation of the Toilers of Kurdistan), and for disseminating political information among Kurdish youth. Komalah was the first political party in all four parts of Kurdistan (Iran, Iraq, Turkey and Syria) which took initiatives to address gender equality among *peshmergas*, the Kurdish freedom fighters. This was a daring and bold step if we consider the fact that gender relations in Kurdish society are organised on the basis of feudat religious-capitalist patriarchal power structures. Women and girls are treated as "half humans", whose lives are in the hands of their fathers, husbands or brothers. They are denied the freedoms that should be theirs according to the UN Declaration of Human Rights. I fled the suppression of the Islamic regime and joined the *peshmergas* at the age of 14. At that time Komalah was the only way out for thee persecuted girls and women, and I stayed on with them for six years.

Today, I live in Stockholm. I have been in Sweden since September 1992 when I arrived via Turkey as a refugee. I am a social welfare worker mainly working with families with children and youths in vulnerable situations. I have continued my political involvement within Komalah, and I am also involved in various voluntary organisations in Sweden who work towards equality and integration of newcomers. I am also a broadcaster for a community-based radio programme, in Kurdish, called Dengi Zhinan (Voice of Women Radio). As a social worker in Sweden, I encounter many children and youth who struggle with finding a secure place for themselves between the "homeland" and the "hostland." Already in the early stages of my stay in Sweden, I began to realise that patriarchy is also part of the structure of power in Sweden; that in modern Sweden women are oppressed systematically, too. I also realised that this patriarchy takes on a particular characteristic when it comes to women of a different origin. Even though migration increases some of the women's power resources, most women with non-Western backgrounds can be subjected to multiple levels of oppression: based on gender, race, class, ethnicity, sexuality, language and religion.

The lives of many immigrant women in Sweden are governed by the norms, values, culture and tradition of their countries of origin, in which women tend to be restricted to work in the home, and men are expected to be the breadwinner. I will even argue that in many cases the situation of women has noticeably worsened after moving to Sweden. It is not uncommon that youth from traditional patriarchal families experience many difficulties living in Sweden. Boys have a defined masculine role, in which they are expected to educate themselves and to be independent, while girls are raised to be obedient and submissive. Therefore, most girls live in isolation; mainly at home and do not get involved in socialising with their peers. Often, girls who take a step out into Swedish society and choose a life of their own are rejected by their community and become outcasts. According to Alexandra Ålund (1988), a dominant view of immigrant women is that they are passive victims of their surroundings, of patriarchal society structures and of their native culture. This complicates women's power resources and the possibility of using their power. Ålund believes that this view of immigrant women as help-needy victims is misleading. A more balanced debate is needed, one which views women as active creators of culture, and acknowledges women's ability to take action to resist and change traditional norms and values.

An anti-racist feminist analysis of barriers to integration in Sweden

In Sweden, research shows that women who have moved from countries in the Middle East to European countries have contributed to a power shift within the family, which has improved women's independent relationships to men and to their families (Hirdman, 1988; Darvishpour, 2003). In other words, the welfare state's numerous contributions strengthen a woman's autonomous status in the family. Even if she does not have a job, it is not the man who supports her, and therefore her position in the family changes in relation to home and the nation. The social democratic welfare system is built on different power structures, such as gender, class and ethnicity. The welfare model that exists in Sweden is one of the best in the Western world. Elements of this model, such as parental and social subsidies, have given women the possibility of being economically self-sufficient and independent of men. Well-developed childcare facilities are available for every child, which gives mothers the option of pursuing careers. The Swedish welfare state assists immigrant women and girls in finding ways to achieve freedom and rights that they themselves have long struggled for.

At the same time, there are also contradictions in this situation, so that immigrant women face numerous challenges. They are discriminated against partly because they are women and partly because they are "immigrant", since racist tendencies exist in all social systems (Dominelli, 1997). This can lead to disappointment and even to setbacks for those women who have migrated for the purpose of improving their social and economic status. Kurdish women refugees, who have fled persecution in their native country and sought protection in Sweden, can experience different types of trauma and be subjected to gender-related violence by the state's representatives as well as by close acquaintances, including fathers, brothers, other male relatives or male members of the community. However, they lack defence networks in Swedish society, often face language barriers to access support, and risk being ostracised by relatives and friends if they seek help outside the family. There is also the fear of deportation for women who report perpetrators or separate from their husbands before they have obtained permanent residency status.

Kurdish immigrant women's lives in Sweden, as I stated above, are still being governed by the patriarchal norms of their native country. In many cases the women's situation has even worsened as the power of their men has decreased, since the men still see themselves as the head of the family. Some women have been subjected to forced marriage, abuse, rape and so-called "honour" related violence. There is more discussion on this taking place in Sweden today as a result of many such crimes committed against Kurdish women, especially following the killings of Fadime and Pela. These two young women were murdered by the male members of their families: fathers, brothers, cousins and uncles were all implicated in these crimes.

Since these incidents, serious policy debates have started about the integration process and the social condition of Kurdish girls and women in Sweden (Mojab, 2004). Many journalists, politicians, scientists and private individuals from voluntary organisations have discussed the complexity of the problem from different perspectives. The media depict an image of Kurdish women as oppressed, uneducated and as not being respected by their families. This image is generalised all too often in public debates, while at the same time gender-related violence escapes criticism. Dominant Western ways of classifying other ethnic groups create a barrier to integration, and a barrier for women and girls to participate in rights that are supposed to exist in modern society (Brah, 1996). Mojab (2004) notes that the racist culturalisation of "honour killing" in Western countries ignores the fact that killing women is a universal phenomenon in patriarchal cultures in both East and West. This prevailing attitude in the public debate in Sweden about people from the Middle East is an expression of racism and nationalism. For example, in Sweden Muslim parents are allowed to deny their daughters the right to participate in co-educational activities such as school trips or swimming, under the banner of respect for cultural difference and diversity (Mojab, 2004).

There are different cultural and sub-cultural groups amongst the Kurds. Elements of both modernity and tradition can be found among them. As Mojab argues, what we should remember is that "... there is, in this culture, a century of ideas of gender equality and the struggle to achieve it" (Mojab, 2004, pp. 30-31). It is within the context of this history that a group of us decided to initiate a radio programme as a means of feminist consciousness raising among the Kurds living in Sweden. Let me tell you more about this initiative.

Voice of Women Radio: a Kurdish radio programme in Sweden

A group of Kurdish women volunteers started this Kurdish-language radio programme five years ago. The programme has gained support and has grown since then. We broadcast the programme, through the Internet, and thus make it available to Kurdish women in Iran, Iraq or anywhere in the world. Voice of Women Radio is a support and counselling programme for Kurdish women. We spread knowledge of and information on women's rights, on their responsibilities as new citizens in the Swedish society, and their role in their families. We try to engage with our listeners through radio discussions. We also try to reach out to Kurdish women through other means such as meetings and seminars on a variety of topics. This radio programme has been the only Kurdish media channel in the last five years that has addressed, from the point of view of women, questions such as equality, secularism, nationalism, human rights, democracy, integration, tradition and alternatives, and family-related matters such as child-raising and children's rights locally and internationally.

Our main goals are:

- to draw attention to women's issues in Sweden and discuss possible alternatives in addressing them;
- to raise women's consciousness about their bodies and sexuality, especially about their mental, psychological, and physical health and well-being;
- to create solidarity among women in order to break the sense of isolation and loneliness. Radio discussion is an important part of the programme time.

At the radio, we have come across a number of young women and girls who live under very hard conditions; many listeners call during the broadcast hours to seek help and support.

Since we have started broadcasting the programme live on the Internet, our audience has increased to about 25,000 listeners per month. Women who have migrated to Sweden with their husbands, or who have arrived later by other means, find themselves in a more vulnerable situation than women whose families have been in Sweden for a longer period of time. The first group of women is often totally dependent on their husbands. They may think that he has certain rights since he sponsored them and paid a high price to cover the cost of their trip and start a new life in a new country. Under these conditions, women have difficulties in making their own friends and social circles. Many hold on to old traditions and customs that support the view that the man has to protect the family's "honour" and integrity and that one should prevent divorce at all cost. Some of these women even hold on to traditions that are abandoned in their native country. This is a mechanism of survival in the new society where one's identity is being reformed as a hybrid of old and new values.

We at the Voice of Women Radio critically analyse the social processes which create and recreate segregation, "Otherness", racism and sexism. Our goal is to promote a feminist project on the basis of anti-racist feminism and feminist solidarity. We regularly invite international guests (to our radio show) to share their knowledge, research or experiences with our listeners. On several occasions, Dr Shahrzad Mojab, who is the Director of Women's and Gender Studies at the University of Toronto, has been our guest. Most recently, after she returned from a trip to Iraqi Kurdistan, we interviewed her about developments in the area after the US-led removal of Saddam Hussein. Another important guest has been Dr Jafar Hasanpoor of Karstad University. He has studied power structures within state-funded Kurdish immigrant organisations in Sweden, and found great injustices to the detriment of the female members. His research has contributed to questioning which organisations should receive state funding meant to promote integration and gender equality.

We have collaborated with women's organisations in Sweden as well as in other European countries. We have also worked with women's organisations in the Kurdish parts of Iran and Iraq. I visited Iraq in the autumn of 2002 and 2004, and met with many women working in NGOs or as volunteers. I also met women who were staying in women's shelters with their children. The lives of these women were in danger as they were considered to be violating the "honour" of their families. The punishment for that crime is death. We have saved a few women's lives through our collaborations with, for example, the Rewan Center in Sulaimani, in the Kurdish region of northern Iraq. I have filmed and interviewed a number of professional women who describe the living conditions of women and children. We have shown these films in Sweden and used them in seminars and conferences to raise Swedish public awareness of the situation in Kurdistan. Some of my observations on life in the Kurdish region have been reported in the Swedish media.

We have also participated in an international conference on "honour" related violence, which the Swedish Government arranged in December 2004. We have travelled to other countries and cities and have actively taken part in different conferences and seminars on gender relations and integration. We have been interviewed about these topics by different radio stations and the media in Sweden as well as other countries. We collaborate with non-governmental organisations (NGOs) in Sweden such as Save the Children Sweden, the Red Cross and various immigrant women's organisations. We celebrate 8 March, International Women's Day, by organising seminars, conferences and parties in collaboration with other women's organisations. We are active and are out demonstrating in support of many international causes. As I stated earlier, we do all this voluntarily, with no financial assistance from the Swedish Government. We fundraise by organising social gatherings where our patrons donate money to the station. We call such days "Radio Day".

We faced numerous challenges when we started the radio programme and other support programmes for women. Even many of our supporters thought that we would not be able to manage a radio programme. From the beginning, we received criticism from Kurdish men whom we knew and others who wished not to identify themselves. Some of these men were questioning our intentions and were suggesting that we would be of more help to women if we stayed at home. We were accused of being "men haters" with the intention of destroying family relations and informing women on how to sabotage or break up their family relationships. At one time, we were criticised for not having proper command of the Kurdish language and, thus, not being able to formulate and express ourselves. We confronted all criticism and, despite all the difficulties and opposition, we have continued our work to this day. What we have achieved is that most of those who challenged us are today our active listeners. We are the only Kurdish radio station that has successfully been able to discuss taboo subjects such as women and sexuality in public. Broadcasting on questions of democratic gender relations has enabled us to engage in rights-based debates, around integration and social inclusion as important aspects of life for immigrants who have fled from their native countries because of violations of these very rights. For instance, during public debates or referendums on different societal questions in Sweden, we thoroughly discuss the issues on the radio and encourage our listeners to take part actively in voting and making their voice heard. We also draw women's attention to their right to vote, and remind them that this basic right of citizenship is often violated under dictatorial regimes. The women's response has been positive, though slow. They need time to comprehend the process of democracy and exercise their rights.

Addressing social exclusion for refugees and immigrants in Sweden

The realities of social exclusion and marginalisation that prevail in society are not often brought into the light in public debate. All too often, the term "social exclusion" is used to promote the idea that more and more members of disadvantaged minorities should end up "on the side of" the majority society (Littlewood, 1999), and integration is viewed as a one-way process. But we need to pay attention to the fact that refugee and immigrant women experience diaspora in specific ways. Women with non-Nordic or non-European backgrounds are not presented as equals with Western women, nor are the common aspects of women's experiences properly recognised. Immigrant women are therefore treated as "different": not only as the "Other", but also classified along with the homogenised "Others" who together make up negative Western images of non-Western people. As Harding (1986) and Maynard (1994) note, culturally homogeneous generalisations about "a typical woman" obscure complex realities of women's oppression to the same degree as they prevent solidarity and more equal relations between women of different origins.

Integration of refugee communities and the struggle against women's oppression are both aspects of democracy and human rights. In order to further integration effectively, it is necessary to create a dialogue within society, and to create alternative strategies, including feminist approaches, in order to make changes happen. It is currently clear that more preventative work is needed in relation to male violence towards women and children. So far, "integration" has unfortunately been viewed as one dimensional. The "outsiders" are expected to integrate with established Swedish society, and the process is not seen as reciprocal. More than this, integration also has to be a mutual process supporting women as well as men. A first step by the Swedish and other Western governments would be to ensure that financial support is given not only to immigrants' organisations dominated by men, but also to autonomous women's organisations that are promoting women's rights and actively engaging women in democratic processes.

Acknowledgements

I would like to thank Dr Shahrzad Mojab of the Institute for Women's and Gender Studies at the University of Toronto for her helpful comments on a draft of this chapter.

References

Ålund, A. (1988), "The power of definitions: immigrant women and problem-centred ideologies", *Migration*, (4), pp. 37-55.

Brah, A. (1996), *Cartographies of diaspora: contesting identities*. London and New York: Routledge.

Dominelli, L. (1997), "International social development and social work: a feminist perspective", in Hokenstad, M.C. and Midgley, J. (eds.), *Issues in international social work: global challenges for a new century*. Washington: NASW Press.

Darvishpour, M. (2003), *Invandrarkvinnor som bryter mönstret: hur maktförskjutningen inom iranska familjer i Sverige påverkar relationen?* Stockholm: Almqvist & Wiksell International.

Harding, S.G. (1986), *The science question in feminism*. Ithaca: Cornell University Press.

Hirdman, Y. (1988), "Genussystemet – reflexioner kring kvinnors sociala underordning", *Kvinnovetenskaplig tidskrift*, (3), pp. 49-63.

Littlewood, P. (ed.) (1999), *Social exclusion in Europe*. Aldershot: Ashgate.

Maynard, M. (1994), "Race, gender and the concept of 'difference' in feminist thought", in Afshar, H. and Maynard, M. (eds.), *The dynamics of race and gender: some feminist interventions*. London: Taylor and Francis.

Mojab, S. (2004), "The particularity of 'honour' and the universality of 'killing': from early warning signs to feminist pedagogy", in Mojab, S. and Abdo, N. (eds.), *Violence in the name of honour: theoretical and political challenges*. Istanbul: Bilgi University Press.

11. Success stories? Roma university students overcoming social exclusion in Hungary

Anna Kende

Social exclusion of Roma in Europe

In countries where social disadvantage is compounded by cultural differences and prejudice, social exclusion appears in all areas of life, such as education, health or employment. Sociologists have tried to draw attention to the importance of schooling for the social integration of Roma (sometimes pejoratively referred to as "Gypsies") in Hungary for the past twenty to twenty-five years, but the school system still struggles to find solutions for discrimination and segregation. It is not accidental that one of the most important and challenging tasks of overcoming social exclusion in Hungary is to realise the educational integration of Roma children. From sociological research data and from the results of international assessment tests, such as PISA or PIRLS, we can assume that the Hungarian education system reinforces rather than reduces social disadvantage. A number of studies, for example, indicate that a Roma child in Hungary is three times more likely to attend a segregated special education class or school than a non-Roma child (Havas et al., 2002; Kende and Neményi, 2005; Luyten et al., 2005). Although there are multiple aspects of this issue, racism and anti-Roma attitudes can be pinpointed as key factors in the production and reproduction of the current situation. In her chapter in this book, Lorna Roberts makes clear that racism must be addressed first in order to achieve a socially just education for children of a minority ethnic background. Although she focuses on the role of teachers in countering racism, it is clear from her findings that teachers' practices can at best be only part of the solution, and that the educational opportunities of minority children cannot be dealt with without looking at the social processes through which racism come to exist.

The situation of Roma in Hungary, especially that of Roma youth within the education system, resembles their situation across central and eastern Europe. The size of the Roma minority, their socio-demographic situation, and their level of employment and education are all similar in these countries. These similarities are rooted in a common historical background and social history, in comparable educational systems, and in the cultural and social characteristics of Roma in these countries. However, the similarities extend to other western European countries, where we now witness the polarisation of society. More recent forms of poverty related to immigration and ethnic diversity bring new challenges to these countries, challenges similar to the issue of social inclusion of Roma in central and eastern Europe (Gallie and Paugam, 2002). Social class and ethnicity are inseparable in the context of social inclusion. Amineh Kakabaveh, in Chapter 10, points to the importance of analysing the intersection of multiple levels of oppression within the power structures of society, based on gender, race, class, ethnicity, sexuality, language and religion. The complexity of the situation of Roma cannot be reduced to cultural differences or economic problems. While the group of Roma people cannot be racially defined, as group membership is not biologically determined, but rather the result of self-categorisation based on family tradition, lifestyle, customs, appearance and language, as well as the result of external categorisation, it is true, however, that any attempt to generalise the situation of national and ethnic minorities in considering issues of cultural autonomy is misleading, as well as seeing the group merely as social class. It overlooks the most crucial differences between Roma vs. other minority groups in Hungary and in the east-central European region: discrimination based on perceived racial characteristics, and its consequences for social and economic integration, identity strategies and quality of life, as well as the internal diversity of an ethnically, economically, culturally and linguistically heterogeneous "racial" group. Therefore social policy should consider this in its attempts to overcome social exclusion.

A key priority in European policies for social inclusion – outlined in the European Commission White Paper on youth (European Commission, 2001) – is concerned with increasing the access of young people most at risk of social exclusion to lifelong learning opportunities, preventing early school leaving, and promoting a smooth transition from school to work. One of the common objectives of the European Council in fighting against social exclusion is to help the most vulnerable groups, including those experiencing particular integration problems (European Council, 2004). It follows from this objective, and from the context described above, that we must look at the prospects of Roma youth and focus on their educational opportunities. Understanding how their exclusion can be overcome is relevant not only in Hungary and other central and eastern European countries, but may be of importance in the fight against discrimination facing other minority ethnic groups elsewhere in Europe.

Studying the lifecourse of Roma university students

This chapter presents findings from a study of success factors for Roma youth who have become university students, conducted in the framework of a larger project on the political and human rights of Roma in Hungary, with the participation of several social science institutes of the Hungarian Academy of Sciences. The presence of Roma students at universities is minimal, from the Roma population, it is estimated that 0.02% attend, or attended higher education institutions. Our micro-level research, which used in-depth interviews with 20 university students participating in a programme for Roma youth, aimed to discover the characteristics of the lifecourses of young Roma university students. The programme, Romaversitas, in which they participate, offers scholarships, tutoring and a special training for their members to enhance both their academic performance and to help them develop a positive identification as Roma. The students who participated in our project are going to be the future Roma intellectuals of Hungary, in the footsteps of the few Roma adults who make up the present Roma intelligentsia (see definition of this term below). Their stories represent "success" stories: we tried to find out what made it possible for them to overcome marginalisation and social exclusion, to understand how they became agents for their own social inclusion, and to analyse the role of the family, peers, and schools in identity formation and educational advancement in this process (Kende, 2005).

As Bryony Hoskins suggests in her chapter, such qualitative studies can offer a valuable supplement to survey data on education, social mobility and the socio-economic and demographic situation of Roma. The lifecourses of a handful of university students are interesting because their cases are in many respects unique, and also because they set a positive example for other members of socially excluded groups. The very particularity of their experiences reveals the fine-grained knowledge needed to address complex policy problems (Rist, 1998), and a focus on factors related to resilience and success helps to avoid pathologising disadvantage (Werner and Smith, 1982). Their individual stories highlight some of the opportunities students of minority ethnic background have to overcome the multiple disadvantages and social exclusion they face within society. Although the stories describe individual strategies, it is extremely important not to overlook them: these students represent the ultimate goal of policy measures toward socially deprived, and especially Roma students. Both positive and negative experiences must be analysed to come to better policy measures: shared and individual experiences with families and schools, with prejudiced people and institutions, and with dilemmas of identity.

The group examined here occupies a special position among Roma in Hungary, just as they occupy a special position among young intellectuals and university students. We shall see that their strategies posed two challenges to simplistic notions of assimilation into majority ethnic society. Firstly, the social position of this group can be characterised as a form of social mobility, in which the acquisition of the new group membership does not require the renunciation of the old group membership. Secondly, the straightforward message of the programme – Romaversitas – in which they participate is that a university degree for a Roma student should not entail the denial of Roma identity, but rather create a new identity, that of the Roma intellectual.

Roma intelligentsia

The term "Roma intelligentsia" can be broadly defined as referring to individuals with a Roma identity who obtained a university degree. However, this broad definition does not address dilemmas related to the concept. While positive arguments for the relevance and significance of a minority elite group might stress its empowering effect for the entire minority group, the counter-argument might say that belonging to a minority elite group or being member of the minority intelligentsia is belittling for intellectuals of minority background. This dilemma is reflected in the identity strategies of our respondents.

The adult generation of educated Roma people predominantly chose two different identity strategies. They either attempted to assimilate to majority society, refusing to become members of the Roma elite and refusing to take on a Roma intelligentsia identity (Neményi, 1999). Their example therefore did little to alter the stereotype of Roma people being poor and uneducated. Alternatively, they participated in political activities, and identified themselves as the so-called Roma elite. Our interviewees had been pupils of teachers that belong to this second group: they received an education in which there was significant pressure on them to become

Roma intellectuals. Nevertheless, identification as Roma, Hungarian, intellectual or any combination of these is still a dilemma for them. The fact that there are so few Roma students at universities places great pressure on Roma students to become leaders or at least role models for Roma youth, to be agents in the fight against social exclusion, and to remain visible as Roma elite. However, as the teachers in Lorna Roberts' study found (see her chapter in this book), identifying as one or the other entails antagonistic responses from society creating great dilemmas in identity strategies.

The theoretical concept of a threatened identity can aid the understanding of the students' family background and their own identity strategies (Breakwell, 1986). Anti-Roma attitudes are very strong in Hungary, and the Roma are the most discriminated ethnic minority group (Erős and Fábián, 2002). As a result, the identity of Roma people in Hungary is psychologically threatened, as cultural otherness, discrimination, minority existence, and financial deprivation all contribute to negative self-esteem. Families show different ways of coping with threatened identities, ranging from attempts to assimilate to denial and withholding information on identity, from casually accepting the family's Roma identity and culture to suffering from isolation because of a Roma background (Erős, 2001).

Research sample and method

There were 12 men and eight women in our sample. Eight of them studied social sciences (sociology, social policy, social pedagogy), five were students of arts (fine arts or music), and seven studied other subjects ranging from agricultural engineering to psychology. This distinction is important as studying social sciences presumably entails a higher awareness of the situation of Roma, while arts is the area where success by members of the minority group has the most traditions, but all other subjects are disconnected from being Roma. (The interview excerpts indicate the interviewee's subject area in the above distinction.) They are half of all participants of the Romaversitas programme, whom we contacted via the head of the programme. Studying social sciences may bring a higher awareness of the identity issues of Roma students and possibly a better understanding of the situation of Roma in Hungary. Studying arts has always been the traditional way to succeed in life as a Roma, while studying any other subject means to excel in an area not connected to being Roma.

Eight students were born before 1980 and 12 after that date, which gives an indication of whether the respondents followed a more or less undisturbed path to university, or made detours in their life courses. As far as the Roma ethnic background is concerned, only four of them come from families who speak one of the Roma languages. There are three mixed families, with one Roma and one non-Roma parent, nine Hungarian Roma (they are also referred to as musicians or Romungro), two Vlach, one Boyash, and one person comes from a mixed Roma family, while four interviewees did not know exactly to which group their families belonged. We find differences in the standard of living: from extreme poverty and homelessness to an acceptable standard of living of, for example, merchants. The parents' level of education ranges from uncompleted primary education to university degrees in the case of three respondents. However, most of the parents of our respondents had no vocational or any other secondary training.

The interviews were semi-structured, and our respondents were asked to describe their family background, their early years, and their experiences in education from kindergarten to university. They talked about the influence of people and institutions, they told stories of discrimination, and described changes in identity formation, as well as their expectations for the future.

Typical lifecourse patterns

Despite the diversity of these stories, we identified some typical patterns in their lifecourses as far as family background, school career and external influences are concerned. These patterns allow for a categorisation of individual lifecourses, which is important from a policy point of view: for example, children with different socio-economic and demographic backgrounds face different problems during their school career, even if they belong to the same minority ethnic group. Children attending segregated and integrated schools do not experience social exclusion in the same way. Children from families that wish to assimilate have a different understanding of what it means to be a Roma or a Roma intellectual than those coming from families with strong ethnic identities. The patterns we identified in these lifecourses help us understand the prospects of Roma youth in higher education with different backgrounds and experiences. We identified three distinct typical life routes, which can be characterised as follows:

- Family support against a prejudiced society: this group is characterised by strong support from the family, and the significance of experiences of discrimination and prejudice. These students tended to live in areas and attended schools with no other Roma children around. They fell victim to the prejudiced attitudes of both peers and teachers. The parents of this group did not have degrees themselves, but supported the academic career of their children from the beginning.
- First generation intelligentsia: this group is characterised by difficulties created by an enormous discrepancy between family background and the wish to pursue education at a higher level. These students came from socially deprived areas, and attended schools with overwhelmingly Roma pupils, and occasionally schools or classes for mentally disabled children. The families did not support their children's ambitions to go on to higher education, because this option did not even occur to them, they would rather have seen their children engage in vocational training. Social exclusion was typical, but at the same time, support from the immediate surroundings, from the community, was strong. The presence of prejudice and discrimination was less apparent, but there was also a lack of prospect and purpose in life in general. These students were generally older, and had worked in manual occupations before they thought of getting a degree or even secondary-level education, and their entrance to university was enhanced by the support of NGOs.
- Second generation intellectuals: there was also a third group, consisting of only four people, three of them having parents with a university education, and a fourth one coming from a well-known family of musicians, becoming an educated musician himself. This third group indicates what the future may be for the children of first generation Roma intellectuals. All of them followed their parents' footsteps with respect to identity formation and field of interest.

There were still others who did not fit into any of these three categories. Their lifecourses defy technically rational explanation (cf. Hodkinson et al., 1996), and would more easily fit into a fairy tale, for example, the two students who came from extreme poverty and showed no promise, but still entered university very smoothly without the support of family, school teachers or non-governmental organisations (NGOs).

Main influences on the lifecourse

Family background

Students from the group with family support tended to describe their families as less deprived than members of the "first generation" group, among whom we find cases of extreme poverty. However, the financial status of the family did not clearly correlate with the three types of life route identified above.

> "My mother lived under difficult circumstances, she also lived in a Gypsy slum with my two sisters, but she did not have a house, but a hut made of plastic bags" (social sciences, female, 22 years old).

> "We stood halfway on the ladder. We did not have to struggle for a living. We could wash every day, we had food and we could afford schoolbooks as well" (arts, male, 23 years old).

Families' attempt to assimilate was most apparent among the group of interviewees from the "family supported" group. Their parents' generation could not possibly foresee any other strategy for success than to assimilate into Hungarian majority society and to deny their Roma background. Social mobility while retaining one's minority background, language and culture was not an option under the former socialist regime in Hungary. This strategy was only possible for those who were already somewhat better off financially than the majority of the Roma population and had a higher than primary education, namely they did not live the life of a "Gypsy" in the eyes of the majority society. Although in many ways successful, the identity strategy of assimilation is far from ideal, it is based on denial and detachment, and it is characterised by identification with a group which rejects the original group.

> "We did not live among Roma people. My family is Roma, my mother and father as well. But I was raised as an assimilant. At home, being Roma meant something bad, something you are going to suffer from. I learned that I was going to be different, I would have to prepare more in school, work harder. My father comes from a very poor family. I can see self-hatred in him. He is ashamed of being Roma" (other subject, female, 23 years old).

> "We spoke Hungarian at home. It was not a question, because it was clear that a child has to learn Hungarian, this is the language of the school. My father was Beash, my mother a mix of Boyash, Vlach and Romungro (Hungarian Roma). My mother spoke more languages. They spoke Beash with their parents. In fact this is what held the extended family together" (social sciences, male, 23 years old).

Some families built their identities on social exclusion and deprivation, having lost their traditional ties, and being unable to create new ones. They offered little of the cultural aspects of being Roma, and passed on the experience of deprivation to their children.

> "I think a Roma person does not have an identity. S/he cannot move in either direction. I received a Hungarian identity at home, but there is also Roma in it" (arts, male, 21 years old).

Quite different from these families we find families with a strong sense of cultural identity based on traditions and pride, even among families who did not speak any Roma languages, but maintained the tradition of music or other cultural customs. These two forms appeared in the "first generation" as well as in the "second generation" group, whose parents had made a conscious decision to maintain their identities.

> "My grandfather was a Hungarian Gypsy musician. He is a violin player. He was really famous, travelling everywhere in the country. He had a place in Miskolc" (arts, male, 27 years old).

We see that the original identity formation (that is, prior to university) of our respondents was strongly influenced by their parents' sense of belonging to a positively and negatively defined group. In this respect, people from the "family supported" group seemed the most vulnerable prior to university, as their childhood was mostly determined by trying to deny the original identity, or trying to live with it in a surrounding which considers only the negative aspects of it, including the attitudes of their own families.

Education

The two main influences on the lifecourses of our respondents were family and school. We find examples of segregation, integration and minority schooling, all of them seriously affecting the later life route and the path to higher education.

The "first generation" group predominantly attended segregated schools which offered a lower level of education for children of the poorest families. They lived in segregated areas, and had little contact with non-Roma people in and out of school in the first part of their lives. The prospect of further education did not occur in these schools.

> "It was in our neighbourhood that the small [compensatory] classes were introduced. Schools considered them as a way of getting extra funding. I ended up in one of those classes after having failed in biology. I think part of the problem was that my parents were unable to assert their rights. So we were the retarded kids, that is how I finished primary school" (social sciences, male, 27 years old).

Detours in education were cut short by the work of NGOs, whose activities focus on helping poor or poor Roma children in their educational career.

> "I have come across the advertisement of the Kurt Lewin foundation. I did not want to believe my eyes: they were looking for people who want to become sociologists, and they were looking for Gypsies. I called them to ask whether it was a problem that my secondary school scores were low and I was already 27 at the time. They said, no. I never wanted anything as badly as that. So I followed the courses, and I did everything I was told, I learned everything from the first letter to the last" (social sciences, female, 31 years old).

Within the segregated system, some teachers appear as role models, mostly because they gave children dignity:

> "In the second year of primary school, we received a teacher, a nice, honest woman. She taught us with such love and professional humbleness, that it should be taught somehow. She never made a distinction between Roma and non-Roma pupils. Public health authorities came to check whether we had lice. She always stood by us, and said this is a very clean head, very well washed,

> and this was so moving. I don't know why I am crying now ... She helped me a lot, she gave me extra tasks, she trusted me" (social sciences, male, 30 years old).

However, more often they appear as perpetrators of prejudiced acts and discrimination.

> "I had a teacher, a teacher of history, who was the first to really dislike me, to really make me feel that I was a Gypsy, and I knew he was a racist man. When I was absent, he asked the others, 'Where is that fat Gypsy boy from the corner?'"(social sciences, male, 27 years old).

We see, in the case of the two groups without a self-evident path to higher education that schools were a positive influence in the life of the "first generation" group, while they created obstacles for the "family supported" group. This seems a contradiction, suggesting that a segregated school offers more to a child, or that schools are friendlier to children with a non-supportive family background. However, it is important to remember that we were talking to university students, to those that had already achieved higher education despite their circumstances, and their stories show that this could not have happened without the support of individual teachers or organisations trying to help talented students from disadvantaged backgrounds. There is no doubt that the majority of students suffer from social exclusion in these schools and never manage to achieve what these students have, as it is suggested both by empirical research on segregated schools (Havas and Liskó, 2005), and by the extremely low number of Roma pupils in higher education. It was due to their own persistence, talent and the serendipitous fortune of coming across people who were willing to help that they managed to overcome the disadvantages embedded in their situations.

> "There was racism in school, but the teachers defended me. I went to them crying, that I am not going to stay here, but they talked to me, and my mother and father also told me that I shouldn't give up. I managed to finish the 5th grade, the 6th, and then I left for a six-year-school instead of staying for the full eight years" (other subject, male, 31 years old).

The "family supported" group attended schools that offered better education, but because they had fewer or no Roma peers in these schools, they suffered more from prejudiced attitudes. All interviewees had encountered discrimination, but the "family supported" group reported a higher incidence.

> "The catholic school, Szent Margit, did not want to accept me when I went with my mother. This was really obvious. I called the school and they said everything was alright, I should go in person. When I appeared with my mother, suddenly there was no place for me, they said my scores were after all not so good. And then my father went in – who does not look like a Gypsy – and I had a place" (other subject, female, 23 years old).

"I was alone as a Roma in the school. There were about 800 pupils and I was the only Roma. And I was reminded of this all the time. I came from a community where being Roma or not was not a question. They told me to go back to the trees and so on" (social sciences, male, 23 years old).

To conclude the main findings on education, at first glance the results are twofold and contain contradictory elements in connection with the role of the family and the actual school experiences. It is not surprising that only those families managed to facilitate children's educational advancement successfully who either attempted to assimilate into majority society and considered education the best means for the children to do that, or had a university degree themselves and the option of more freely choosing a Roma identity with it. Families strongly attached to Roma communities – either by traditions or by deprivation – had the most difficulty believing in and therefore contributing to children's educational success. However, it is precisely the children of parents with assimilating strategies and with strong aspirations for their children who experienced the most hostility and discrimination from peers and teachers in schools, for whom the earlier years of schools were made difficult by overt or covert racism directed toward them. Nevertheless, the fact that they remember their early years in school in much more negative terms than those who attended segregated institutions does not imply that their educational advancement was not better secured in these integrated schools. It is for this reason that difficulties and detours in their educational career are more closely connected to institutional forms of discrimination than the personal suffering of the individuals. Therefore the higher occurrence of prejudiced attitudes of peers and teachers could influence the "family supported" group to a lower extent than the institutional discrimination suffered by the "first generation" group in the friendlier atmosphere of segregated institutions.

Identifying as members of the Roma elite

The concept and role of the Roma intelligentsia were problematised during the interviews. Acquiring a university degree enhances one's chances of economic well-being, employment and self-realisation, but at the same time brings about a decision to be visible or invisible in the public eye, to support the social inclusion of people with similar difficulties, or to pursue one's own personal career. Students in social sciences feel most obliged to use their knowledge to enhance the social integration of Roma people, while others said that it is merely their example which should help future generations of Roma youths.

> "When I am finished with school, I would like to help an organisation every other week by giving art lessons. It is a little thing, but anyway I would try. To give this to disadvantaged children, not only to Roma children, but to any disadvantaged child" (arts, male, 23 years old).

> "I am never going to stop being a Roma intellectual. There are too few of us, we must help people" (social sciences, female, 21 years old).

The issues surrounding the concept of Roma intelligentsia do not only concern the tasks and roles of a Roma person with a university degree, but extend to the question of identity as well. For some, the new identity they gained by entering university and meeting other Roma students solved the problem of their threatened identities, from which they suffered all their childhood.

> "I attended the opening ceremony for those who were accepted for preparatory class, and then I felt some kind of an intellectual orgasm. I had never met so many clever Roma youngsters, it was such a wonderful feeling that there are after all people who want to do something, who are open-minded, who can get over the slum-romance" (social sciences, male, 30 years old).

> "I was really worried about Romaversitas, because I do not have Romani traditions, I did not speak the language, and I thought it would be embarrassing for me, because there are the real Gypsies and there is me. I was afraid to be excluded for not being a proper Roma, not knowing anything ... I am such an assimilant. But Romaversitas is a real treasure for me. It gave me a lot. My

> Roma identity is born, it was a difficult birth, but at last it is born" (other subject, female, 23 years old).

Others – either as a result of already having a firm sense of Roma identity from their family background, or by refusing to obtain this new Roma identity – did not consider themselves Roma intellectuals, but rather attempted to keep the two identities apart. The perceived antagonism in the categories of intellectual and Roma makes it difficult for some people to take on a Roma elite identity, as for them, elite group membership entails excluding oneself from the group of Roma people, who are predominantly poor and uneducated. For them, a dual identity is not possible. Although all of our respondents demonstrated agency in overcoming social exclusion, not all of them would choose to do it in public. Some refuse to be identified as Roma elite, and prefer to remain unnoticed while studying and working as a Roma intellectual.

> "I can't identify with being a Roma intellectual, it does not mean anything. I don't consider myself one. I am something else. I am simply an intellectual. And a Roma" (social sciences, female, 22 years old).

> "I don't want to be a Roma artist. I want to be an artist from a Roma background" (arts, male, 21 years old).

For the family supported group, the new Roma identity that the students acquired upon entering university changed the previously negative understanding of being Roma into a positive concept, and brought with it the discovery that "I am not alone!", that there are others who are similar. For the "first generation" group, university brought perhaps an even greater change, which included breaking away from their roots (be they traditional or assimilating). They always thought of themselves as far removed from Roma politicians or intellectuals, and they were well into their educational career before they realised that there was such a thing as a Roma intellectual identity. The discovery of this identity, and the fact that it is within their reach, became a decisive formative experience. It was only for the second generation group that a Roma intellectual identity was taken for granted; their identities and attitude towards their Roma ethnic background are characterised by stability.

These different understandings of Roma intellectual identity reflect problems with the concept of a minority elite. The fact that it brought a significant change in identity formation for both groups who come from families without (higher) education reflects the virtual absence or the invisibility of a Roma elite prior to this generation, as well as the perceived distance between their own lifecourses and those of their parents or people they knew before entering university. One must consider that most of these university students did not become just a little more educated than their families, but most of them have parents and relatives with only primary education, and who have worked all their lives as unskilled workers.

Conclusions

Our research points out that the difficulties a Roma youth faces in overcoming the educational gap are at least threefold. The degree to which these obstacles appear in the lifecourse varies for individual respondents, depending on the ways in which they experience the interaction of their class, ethnic or racial statues, including elements of prejudice, cultural and linguistic otherness and poverty. Nevertheless they can be identified as key issues in the interviews and elements of the marginalised situation of Roma in Hungary:

- they come across the difficulties of first generation intellectuals;
- they experience discrimination and prejudice in the course of the lifecourse;
- in connection with the above two, they come across complicated questions of identity and identification as Roma and as intellectuals.

The success of our respondents offers a valuable opportunity for policy makers to learn ways of effectively helping students of minority background to overcome social exclusion, as well as to understand the agency by which our respondents overcame their own social exclusion. Identifying both the difficulties and the successes within the typical patterns can offer guidelines for policy and practice on social inclusion.

Students coming from families who are demographically, culturally and economically not poor – not "typical" Roma – understand social exclusion mostly in terms of prejudice and threatened identity. In spite of their parents' lower level of education, they reach higher education because of their parents' attempt to assimilate and to offer their children a life that is "atypical" for Roma. Although in these individual cases, this approach seemed successful, it makes the group psychologically vulnerable, as it offers an identity defined only in negative terms, leaving little room for developing a positive self-concept. That is why inclusion policies do not consider assimilative strategies to be acceptable, and it also explains why our respondents attempted to create a new identity as Roma intellectuals to counter the negative identity strategies of their parents.

The main obstacles to success for children of the "first generation" group, that grew up in economically deprived, racially segregated neighbourhoods, are the low quality of the education they received and their lack of aspirations for the future. The interviewees from this group would not have reached higher education if it had not been for atypically humane, friendly and helpful individuals, or the help of NGOs. These people or NGOs became engines for the students' agency to overcome marginalisation. Although the diverse family backgrounds of the people in this group continued to influence their private identity strategies, they only affected their educational career to a lesser extent.

These success stories highlight the importance of the family background in cases where the family is capable of offering incentives to study in spite of a hostile school environment, and the importance of role models and civil organisations for those whose families could not provide such incentives. Most respondents found a new identity as Roma intellectuals after a long and hard process to arrive at a positively defined self-concept. Each story presents valuable examples of successfully overcoming, or rather successfully sublimating the obstacles created by social exclusion, economic deprivation and prejudice.

Policy makers throughout Europe therefore need to consider how they can assist minority ethnic families to support their children; how they can reduce personal and institutional racism and discrimination in schooling; and how they can support and enhance the impact of NGOs and of successful role models on the aspirations and life chances of minority ethnic youth.

References

Breakwell, G.M. (1986), *Coping with threatened identities*. London: Methuen.

Erős, F. (2001), *Az identitás labirintusai*. Budapest: Janus/Osiris.

Erős, F. and Fábián, Z. (2002), *Jelentés a 2002. májusi véleménykutatás eredményeiről*. Budapest: Tárki.

European Commission (2001), White Paper: "A new impetus for European youth" (online). Brussels: European Commission (accessed 10 January, 2006). Available at: http://europa.eu.int/comm/youth/whitepaper/download/whitepaper_en.pdf.

European Council (2004), "Joint report by the Commission and the Council on social inclusion" (online). Brussels: European Council (accessed 10 January, 2006). Available at:
http://europa.eu.int/comm/employment_social/soc-prot/soc-incl/joint_rep_en.htm.

Gallie, D. and Paugam, S. (2002), *Social precarity and social integration*. Report for the European Commission Directorate-General Employment, Eurobarometer 56.1, October 2002. Luxembourg: Office for Official Publications of the European Communities.

Havas, G., Kemény, I. and Liskó, I. (2002), *Cigány gyerekek az általános iskolában*. Budapest: OKI, Új Mandátum.

Havas, G. and Liskó, I. (2005), *Szegregáció a roma tanulók általános iskolai oktatásában*. Budapest: Oktatáskutató Intézet, Kutatás közben.

Hodkinson, P., Sparkes, A.C. and Hodkinson, H. (1996), *Triumphs and tears: young people, markets and the transition from school to work*. London: David Fulton.

Kende, A. (2005), "Értelmiségiként leszek roma és romaként leszek értelmiségi. Vizsgálat roma egyetemisták életútjáról.", in Neményi, M. and Szalai, J. (eds.), *Kisebbségek kisebbsége*. Budapest: Új Mandátum.

Kende, A. and Neményi, M. (2005), "A fogyatékossághoz vezető út", in Neményi, M. and Szalai, J. (eds.), *Kisebbségek kisebbsége*. Budapest: Új Mandátum.

Luyten, H., Scheerens, J., Visscher, A., Maslowski, R., Witziers, B. and Steen, R. (2005), "School factors related to quality and equity, results from PISA 2000" (online). Paris: OECD (accessed 10 January 2006). Available at:
www.pisa.oecd.org/dataoecd/15/20/34668095.pdf.

Neményi, M. (1999), *Csoportkép nőkkel*. Budapest: Új Mandátum.

Rist, R.C. (1998), "Influencing the policy process with qualitative research", in Denzin, N.K. and Lincoln, Y.S. (eds.), *Collecting and interpreting qualitative materials*. Thousand Oaks: Sage.

Werner, E.E. and Smith, R.S. (1982), *Vulnerable but invincible: a study of resilient children*. New York: McGraw-Hill.

12. Racialised identities: the experiences of minority ethnic trainee teachers

Lorna Roberts

introduction

> "... but in describing myself I would definitely say that I was Black. I would have to mention it some way and I don't know if that would be because I'd want to, but it's just because I'm so conscious of being different that I would have to say it anyway ..." (Evadney, a former trainee teacher).

Evadney, whom I quote above, was participating in a small-scale study which explored 19 Black and minority ethnic trainee teachers' experiences on a four-year teacher training programme in a British university. Talking about her own experiences as a pupil in a predominantly white school, and then as a student in higher education, her words do not just tell a private or unique story, but indicate how minority groups are marginalised. Evadney's experience is not unusual: we see echoes of it across Europe. In this book alone, Daniel Blanch, Amineh Kakabaveh and Anna Kende (Chapters 5, 10 and 11) also tell of the ways in which minority groups in Spain, Sweden and Hungary are positioned as "different" from the ethnic majority.

At the European level, we do not need research evidence to point to the disastrous consequences of social exclusion among minority ethnic youth. We have witnessed them over many years, from civil uprisings which took place across England in 1981, to those in the suburbs of Paris as this Youth Research Partnership seminar convened in late 2005. During this time, social inclusion has become a key focus for European policy, not least as a means to social cohesion. One of the top priorities outlined in the European Commission's (EC) draft joint report on social inclusion (2004) is to reduce poverty and social exclusion among immigrants and ethnic minorities. Member states have had to draw up national action plans to respond to this priority, alongside other common objectives for social inclusion. Within these policies, access to educational and employment opportunities is seen as crucial to meeting their goals.

This chapter examines one way in which these different strands of social inclusion policy – addressing ethnic minorities, education and employment – intersect in a particular way in England around initiatives to involve more minority ethnic students in teacher training. Although based on research in the English context, this can be seen as a case study with much broader relevance for understanding processes of social exclusion elsewhere. In his first term of office, UK Prime Minister Tony Blair declared the New Labour government's commitment to social inclusion. Education, and particularly teachers within it, was seen as playing a key role in creating a more inclusive society (Blair, 1998). However, almost ten years on, this vision of a meritocratic society is far from being achieved. Some Black and minority ethnic groups experience differential outcomes in education. African-Caribbean children are more likely to be excluded from school than white children. African-Caribbean girls are four times more likely to be permanently excluded, and African-Caribbean boys can, depending on location, be excluded as much as 15 times more than white boys, (Wright et al., 2005). Gillborn and Mirza (2000) highlight inequalities in educational attainment at the end of compulsory schooling among African-Caribbean, Pakistani and Bangladeshi young people. This has an impact on opportunities for youth education, labour and training markets and can increase the likelihood of social and economic exclusion in later life. Although minority ethnic groups are well represented in the undergraduate population of higher education as a whole, they are disproportionately more likely to be mature and are concentrated within the post-1992 universities (Home Office, 2005).

Some suggest that the difficulty with New Labour's educational policy lies in its contradictions and silences (Thrupp and Tomlinson, 2005). In this chapter, I will present the experiences of minority ethnic trainee teachers to illuminate the tensions which arise when dominant notions of teacher identity and teacher professionalism fail to take account of issues such as gender, "race" and ethnicity. In this situation, rather than being inducted into an inclusive profession, Black and minority ethnic trainees can often feel marginalised as a result of processes of Othering. Experiences of witting and unwitting discrimination can mean that Black and minority ethnic trainees' experience of training is qualitatively different to that of their majority ethnic peers. Reasons for withdrawal are complex; racism alone is not always the sole contributing factor; however, evidence suggests that perceptions of racism can compound difficulties experienced during training and strengthen the trainees' resolve to withdraw (Basit et al., 2004, 2006). Statistics from the Training and Development Agency for Schools (TDA) (no date, a) show that 23.8% of minority ethnic trainees did not qualify compared to 10.3% of their majority ethnic peers. Minority ethnic withdrawal from training programmes totalled 6.6% compared to 3.8% of the majority ethnic group and those yet to complete number 9.4% compared to 3.9% of the majority ethnic group.

Drawing on qualitative data from four research projects spanning a period from 1999 to 2005, involving 74 participants, I explore how the trainees are racialised in their daily encounters with their majority ethnic peers, pupils and colleagues, and suggest implications for policy and practice in combating racial discrimination.

increasing the numbers of minority ethnic teachers

In the UK there has been a long-standing concern about the recruitment and retention of minority ethnic teachers, related to the belief that a more diverse teaching force would help to create a more socially just society. Increasing the number of minority ethnic teachers has been viewed as one way to improve the experience of minority ethnic pupils and raise their aspirations and achievement. The absence of Black and minority ethnic teachers is seen as a waste of talent to education and society as a whole (Neophytou and Ali, 2000).

Other contributors to this book such as Anna Kende (Chapter 11) and Christiane Weis (Chapter 15) suggest ways in which the education system may contribute to, rather than mitigate, educational disadvantage for young people from minority groups. In the UK, the educational attainment of some Black and minority ethnic groups has given cause for concern (Gillborn and Mirza, 2000; Pathak, 2000). In particular, African-Caribbean, Bangladeshi and Pakistani boys appear to do less well. The role of institutional racism within the education system and society as a whole in producing low attainment and disaffection among minority ethnic young people has long been acknowledged. In 1981, for example, a Department of Education and Science (DES) interim report identified racism as the cause of underachievement among minority ethnic pupils. The report recommended an increase in the numbers of minority ethnic teachers to ensure equal opportunities across the service, a call that has been repeated in subsequent policy documents over twenty-five years, (Department of Education and Science, 1985; Home Office, 2005).

Schools are seen as a vital conduit for promoting understanding of different cultural groups and improving racial harmony (Commission for Racial Equality, 1999). The perceived benefits of having a representative teaching force include not only providing "role models" (Department of Education and Science, 1985; Home Office, 2001), but also "reflecting the racial composition of the society in which [children] are growing up" (Haynes, 1988, in Jones et al., 1996, p. 34) and promoting equality of opportunity and social justice (Neophytou, 2000). Minority ethnic teachers are arguably "better able to combat some of the debilitating effects of in-school racism" (Jones et al., 1996, p. 34) and "work as advocates for minority ethnic students and raise their expectations in ways which are less available to white teachers" (Maguire et al., 1997, p. 1, see also Osler, 1994; Gillborn and Gipps, 1996). Additionally, minority ethnic teachers, as Black professionals in interactions with white students and parents, can be powerful agents for change, and contribute to the promotion of racial equality within society (Tomlinson, 1990). Minority ethnic teachers could also enhance the effective functioning of majority ethnic children in a multicultural world (Basit et al., forthcoming). This should lead to a greater understanding between different communities thus creating less segregation and more cohesion.

In its strategy to increase race equality and community cohesion (Home Office, 2005; Training and Development Agency for Schools, no date, b), the Labour Government have set a target to increase the number of minority ethnic recruits to the teaching profession from 7% to 9% by November 2006 and to maintain this level over the next three years. Although there is evidence that the numbers of minority ethnic trainees entering the teaching profession have increased (Home Office, 2005; Training and Development Agency for schools, no date, b), teaching continues to be a predominantly white occupation. National statistical data on ethnicity of teachers in British schools are not currently available as schools have only recently been advised to undertake ethnic monitoring of staff. In 1991, Brar (1991) estimated that 2.3% of teachers in British schools were from a minority ethnic group. More recently, Ross (2001) estimated the national figure to be approximately 5%.

Minority ethnic trainees' experiences of training: the case of Marcia

These data are taken from a study examining the transition of final year primary trainee teachers to qualified teacher status. Some sixteen trainees participated in the study. Marcia and Brenda were the only two minority ethnic participants. All trainees were interviewed at the beginning of the final year of training and towards the end of training. A smaller sample of trainees were followed in their first teaching post; they were interviewed in the early stages of their teaching career and towards the end of the first year of teaching. Marcia did not explicitly discuss her ethnicity in our first two encounters, however, by comparing and contrasting the ways in which she talked about herself, it is possible to explore processes of racialisation and how trainees come to experience themselves as different. In our first interview in the early stages of her final year of training, Marcia discussed her teacher identity. She spoke about her third-year school placement experience in an ethnically mixed school:

> "... you are two different people, my style is individual. I have not come across a teacher yet who I can ... share and really say, 'Well, wow! This is something else.' And I feel that that's what I have got ... I don't think people do see me as what you would call a normal teacher; when I go in there, those children are learning. The objectives are achieved, I am doing everything that I need to be doing as a teacher, but there is something about what I do in that classroom that is different ... my presence, the way I am, the way I come across, it's totally different, and having to work in what may be a normal classroom teacher's way of doing things is really stifling. Oh my soul, I don't know, it's taking me away. It's taking all my values and who I am and what I want to be and what I want to bring in the classroom ... it's keeping that down."

On the surface the struggle to fit into another teacher's shoes is not untypical; other trainees have spoken about the difficulty of trying to conform in order to satisfy the training requirements. However, Marcia's account does not appear to be simply about taking over someone else's class. She seemed to be positioning herself outside the teaching community to which she was seeking entry. The separation is marked by the "wow" factor she believed she possessed. Her practices were in tune with what should be done, but it was her "presence", "the way [she] is and comes across" that marked her out as different. I wonder what meaning to attach to Marcia's notion of presence? What marked her presence as different to that of the classroom teacher's? She was also different because she believed that she would not be perceived as a "normal" teacher. Marcia made a distinction in her definition of what she understood normal to be. The meaning depended on whether one was positioned as pupil or professional colleague. So from the pupils' point of view, Marcia believed "you have to be professional". But:

> "At the end of the day I am human and I want my children to know I am human. You know, they will know that my role in that classroom is to teach them, that's what I am there for I'm the teacher but in the same breadth ... I also want them to know that I am human, I am a normal person, OK I am here to teach you, but I am a normal person. Because teachers are often seen not to be normal."

So teachers are not "normal" people from the pupils' point of view. According to Marcia, children do not perceive teachers as normal because they "see the teachers as ... not having a clue about where they're coming from ... or not really understanding". There is a hierarchical relationship – "it's like they're the teacher and we're the pupils ..." and "they don't see this, they don't see a relationship there or a real link between that".

Considering "normal" from the teaching community's point of view, Marcia did not think she was the "ideal view of what a teacher should be actually in the eyes of some people". When pressed to explain what "the ideal view" entailed, she stated:

"Prim and proper, I don't know, middle class, and I don't know, I don't think I am their idea of a teacher, but I know I am a good one anyway." She felt there was:

"... a particular way that you've got to look and you've got to act and if you don't sort of fit into that ... it's very hard to define it, but if you don't fit into that category there, you are seen as strange because even now – 'Oh! You're training to be a teacher?' ... It's like ... and I can't explain it, but the feeling's there."

Despite her perceptions of not really belonging to the teaching community, Marcia felt at home in her classroom and the wider community: "When I'm with the children ... well, me and the children, it's separate, but in a wider sense" she did not fit in. Marcia's connection to the wider community is illustrated when she spoke about the relationship with her pupils' parents:

"... me and the parents just seem to bond. I seem to spark up relationships with parents. Before I know, parents are crying on my shoulder you know, we are able to talk to each other like we are humans at the end of the day, they are not afraid to approach me. And the way I am with them, my attitude toward them, I'm really relaxed ... I'm not acting in any way to make them feel threatened or that I am better than them, do you understand me?"

Marcia again invoked the notion of "human" which seemed to be in opposition to "teacher". To be human implies an ethic of care where individuals are able to connect socially and emotionally. Placing the concepts of human and teacher in opposition, Marcia seemed to be suggesting that teachers are disconnected from pupils and the community. Marcia too, was disconnected from the wider school community, she certainly did not relate to colleagues in the way she did with the pupils and parents. Further evidence of this polarisation can be seen in the following data taken from our third interview. Marcia had now qualified, and was working in a predominantly white school where she also completed her final placement. For the first time she made an explicit reference to her Blackness:

"I feel they're very wary of me ... I'm the only Black teacher here and to them maybe ... I look about 22 ... so it's ... not sussed me out and ... a colleague of mine commented ... that sometimes I come across as being very business-like because I'll come in, in the morning ... this is my job, I come in, in the morning and I'll bring my bag down and what-not and ... maybe I won't write a message of the day, I'll just be ... I'll just get on, I'll be marking and what-not, so maybe they've found me ... not like other teachers that they know."

Taking account of Marcia's depiction of what it is to be human, this description of her professional conduct positions her as less "human". Gone is the sense of emotional attachment. The significance of this begins to unfold further in the final extract. After completing her final placement in this school, her father encouraged her to accept an offer of employment:

"He said 'It doesn't matter, you go there and you show them, you know, there are your type of people out there' ... but it's different ... I've got different expectations and values and what-not, and morals going up here, whereas down there I felt ... there was ... I felt there was a moral running through between us all ... I don't know, it's weird ... You know where I'm coming from and I know where you're coming from and so we bond straight away ... whereas when you don't know where somebody's coming from you can't bond ... I don't think you can bond, and if you do bond I think it's only on a superficial level ...."

"... well up here, even more so that word professionalism is over me, because I come to work and I do my job. I'm here to teach and it's like I'm doing the best job I can whereas may ... maybe down there I g[o]t more involved, I'd get more emotionally ... emotionally attached."

The data point to a complex picture of identity. Marcia's identity is intersected by "race", class and gender; her account of transition perhaps signals the way professional identity is shaped by this matrix. It is striking to note the way in which the school locales are positioned by Marcia and her father: "there", "out there", "down there", "up here". These phrases could signify geographical location, but they also point to the hierarchical class/'race' relationships. Implicit in this is the suggestion of boundaries, knowing one's place: who is able to go where (Sibley 1995). "Out there" places Marcia and her previous placement school on the periphery, outside, marginal: positioning Marcia, her previous school's pupils and their parents as "them" as opposed to "us" on the inside. In advising Marcia to "go there", her father was encouraging her to transgress the boundary, to counter dominant perceptions of who can teach. However, it is not just about technical delivery: there are "expectations", "values" and "morals". Marcia defined "morals" as "an understanding". Are current conceptions of teacher identity and professionalism degendered, deraced, disembedded and decontextualised? Does such understanding allow for difference and diversity? How is it that Marcia and her father come to locate themselves as "out there" or "down there"? This brings me back to the opening quote from Evadney, a trainee teacher (now qualified) who was so aware of her difference that she felt it necessary to identify that which marked her out as different. What are the processes that enact difference? I now turn to a wider data source from other studies which focused specifically on the experiences of minority ethnic trainees.

"Them and us"

The following data are taken from three projects. One was a small-scale investigation looking specifically at issues relating to the recruitment and retention of minority ethnic trainees (Roberts et al., 2002). The second was an externally funded national project exploring reasons why minority ethnic trainees left their initial teacher training programmes (Basit et al., 2004). The final project involved three higher education institutions and examined support mechanisms for minority ethnic trainees experiencing racism on school placements (Basit et al., 2005).

Trainees' accounts show ways in which Black and minority ethnic trainees are made both visible and invisible. For instance, Fatima described a situation in her placement school where she was partnered with a white trainee (some initial teacher training programmes place trainees in schools in pairs during school experience blocks):

"I think the teachers may not realise that they're doing this, it's that implicit that ... when they are addressing us as students they sort of .... They'll look at my friend ... even though they're addressing the both of us, they'll make eye contact with her rather than me and maybe talk to her rather than addressing the both of us ...."

Similarly, Shakeela found that "most of the time ... maybe it was natural for them to go and start speaking to my partner".

Unlike France, where the *hijab* (headscarf) is banned in schools, teachers and pupils are allowed to wear headscarves in England. But, at the same time, a headscarf is a strong marker of difference which makes trainees highly visible. Shakeela chose not to wear her headscarf in new situations believing this would make her more approachable, but "the moment I go home, I change into my own clothes, because that's how I feel more comfortable". Fatima, on the other hand, did wear her headscarf:

> "... when I go into school I don't have to just fight the usual thing that any other student going into the placement would be fighting ... I have to break through a lot of those stereotypes and sort of prejudices" (Fatima).

Stereotyping appeared to be a phenomenon that occurred amongst the ethnic majority. Yvonne commented:

> "I don't think a lot of people are as aware as they need to be when they go into classrooms. I do believe there are perceptions, everybody has stereotypes and a lot of them aren't meant ... Although a lot of people try not to conform to them, it's in the media and everywhere around us. There are those stereotypes going on and it's really hard to break them."

Yvonne was very aware that as a Black student, "when you go somewhere, you might be the only Black". She and Ravinda found that they had to continually account for who they were:

> "... You almost have to explain everything and explain the fact that you're different" (Yvonne).

> "Wherever I go I do find that I have to explain what I am, who I am, what I'm about to dispel myths and stereotypical images that people tend to have" (Ravinda).

Fatima and her friends were frequently singled out for "always being together". She commented that other students sit together with their friends, "but it's not apparent because there are so many more of them and there's less of us, they can basically notice that we're together".

Just as the headscarf marked difference, the evidence suggests that physical features became the trainee's sole defining factor. Describing her entrance to her placement, Tracy commented, "When I walked in you could just cut the atmosphere with a knife". Maureen explained, "I think they'll look at me and think I'm Black before they even notice my ability". For this reason Maureen was keen to be seen as a teacher rather than as an "Afro-Caribbean teacher":

> "I don't think that they'd have that respect for me as a teacher. ... they won't see me as the teacher that I am and I want them to see me as a teacher. Because then I'll have the same status as everybody else. If they see me as an Afro-Caribbean teacher, they'll probably nit pick and find some faults ...."

Andrea, a practising teacher, highlighted the difficulties minority ethnic teachers might have in gaining an authoritative presence:

> "It's hard for the kids to take you seriously. I mean I'm young and I'm Black ... I don't know if the kids thought it was a joke, it was like 'Oh yes miss, touch,' and all that as if I was some sort of rap artist on TV – that's the way Black people are perceived ... It's hard to see you in a postion of authority when they are not used to that. You can be made to feel that way as well."

Despite feelings of discomfort, Audrey, a newly qualified teacher, and unemployed woman of African-Caribbean descent, believed it important that she had been placed in predominantly white schools during her training. She felt she had not experienced any racism in school, but nevertheless, spoke about the pupils' curiosity: they wanted to know why she spoke such good English. Audrey believed she could make a positive contribution in terms of countering the negative assumptions and beliefs pupils may have, and that she had indeed made a positive contribution to the school.

Many trainees who have experienced discrimination are determined to bring about change. Some enter the profession to specifically address issues related to Black and minority ethnic pupils, and want these pupils to see them as role models. Maureen, for instance, who wanted the majority ethnic pupils to see her as a teacher, also wanted the Black and minority ethnic pupils to see her as "an Afro-Caribbean teacher," to raise their aspirations.

However, placing Black and minority ethnic trainees in the position of role models imposes an additional burden on these students – a responsibility which their majority ethnic peers do not have to shoulder. Moreover, the assumption that Black and minority ethnic teachers will deal with issues relating to Black and minority ethnic pupils and their parents allows the institution to abrogate its responsibility, shifting it squarely onto the shoulders of the individual. Carrington et al., (2001) found that not all Black and minority ethnic trainees want to be seen as role models. Indeed, their evidence suggests that some of these trainees experienced difficulties when placed in multi-ethnic schools. For example, in some cases black and minority ethnic pupils did not recognise the minority ethnic teacher's authority. In other cases minority ethnic pupils confided their difficulties to minority ethnic teachers, ascribing them power when, in effect, they may have had limited or no influence.

The data presented here give a particularly negative picture of minority ethnic trainee teachers' experiences. This is perhaps inevitable, given the nature of some of the projects from which the data were drawn. These focused specifically on reasons for Black and minority ethnic trainee teachers' attrition rates and on experiences of racism. It should be stressed that not all minority ethnic trainees have such a negative experience, indeed there are examples of individuals whose personal agency enable them to overcome the obstacles presented here. It would be valuable to examine these successful cases to identify factors which contribute to more positive outcomes, as Anna Kende has done in her study of successful Roma students in Hungary (Chapter 11).

However, we should be wary of trying to find "recipe" solutions for what is a very complex set of phenomena. The research has shown that minority ethnic groups are not homogenous: there are differences within and across groups. The recruitment and retention of teachers is a general issue within the UK and not just specific to minority ethnic groups. Various strategies have been adopted by member states to eradicate xenophobia and racism. Despite equal opportunities legislation within the UK, minority ethnic groups still encounter varying degrees of racism in their everyday lives as this data demonstrates. My fellow contributors to this volume also point to the enduring nature of discriminatory practices in education. The move to create a more diverse teaching profession marks a positive step towards realising systemic change; however, it is clear that the mere presence of minority ethnic teachers will have limited impact on racist attitudes within society as a whole.

The issues arising from the research projects which generated these data are very complex, and limited space does not allow for a detailed discussion here. They have, however, already been debated within *Resituating culture* (Titley, 2004), a collection of papers from a previous seminar in the Youth Research Partnership. Its contributors highlight the interplay between race, gender, class, sexuality and disability and discuss inherent difficulties with notions of citizenship, culture and multiculturalism. O'Cinneide (2004), for example, argues that claims to neutrality and universality can in fact support discriminatory practices rather than alleviate them. We need to critically engage with these concepts, if we are to deepen our understanding and find practical solutions.

Working towards a genuinely transformative education?

Pauline, who left her initial teacher training course stated in no uncertain terms:

> "We all know that we are living in a society that is institutionally racist, it just comes out and some of them don't even realise that they are so racist. They have this superiority complex where they feel that Black people just can't live up to the same standard. They expect more from Black people than a white person."

Here Pauline is presenting a view that has also been developed through critical race theory literature (Ladson-Billings, 2004; Ladson-Billings and Tate, 1995); namely that racism is so ingrained within the fabric of society that it has become a "normal" fact of life. It is so much part of the everyday practices that it is imperceptible to the white majority, yet most perceptible to those who suffer its effects. "Race" and ethnicity "operate on the surface and in the deep structures of our world" and are "part of the way the world operates" (Knowles, 2003, p. 2).

In 1999, the Macpherson report into the police handling of the investigation of the murder of Stephen Lawrence, a young African-Caribbean man, acknowledged the existence of institutional racism, and made a series of recommendations to counter such discrimination. However, in 2003, the then Home Secretary David Blunkett dismissed the concept:

> "I think the slogan created a year or two ago about institutional racism missed the point. It's not the structures created in the past but the processes to change structures in the future and it is individuals at all levels who do that" (cited in Cole, 2004, p. 35).

Perhaps here lies the problem. Is racism perpetuated structurally, or is it promulgated by the individual? Knowles (2003) presents a persuasive argument that in order to understand the operation of "race", we need to understand the interplay between its structural manifestation and its enactment at the level of the individual.

Lentin's (2004) analysis of the weaknesses inherent in the notion of culture and human rights as means of tackling racism in society points to the need to acknowledge "the structuring effects of racism upon our national societies" (p. 100). We can see this in operation through educational provision. Consider the examples of Roma children in Hungary (see Anna Kende's Chapter 11),and of the educational curriculum in Luxembourg (see Christiane Weis' Chapter 15). Here pupils are disadvantaged by the nature of the curriculum or establishment they attend and the language of instruction.

In England, many minority ethnic trainees experience difficulties in predominantly white schools in locales with a very small minority ethnic population or none at all. Here pupils have limited or no contact with minority ethnic groups, and can have negative stereotypical views about minority groups. Wilkins (2001) conducted a research project to explore majority ethnic trainee teachers' attitudes. He argues that if teachers are to counter racism through their teaching they will need an understanding of the social processes that foster and reinforce racism. All teachers need to be prepared to teach and prepare pupils for life in diverse societies.

Perhaps it is time to turn the focus away from minority ethnic groups and shift towards problematising the majority ethnic population:

> "(Whiteness) issues from a perspective that privileges a certain black experience of racism and insists that racism is primarily a white, not a black, problem. In this story, whiteness is the new white man's (and woman's) burden, their first task is to recognise and then to help lift its oppressive yoke by acknowledging its function as a badge of racial exclusion and privilege" (Cohen, 1997, in Knowles, 2003, p. 175).

Rather than relying on Black and minority ethnic individuals to be powerful agents for change or to advocate on behalf of Black and minority ethnic communities, attention should be diverted to systems and practices which foster and maintain exclusion and privilege. It is unlikely that discriminatory practices will be effectively eradicated, if attention is not paid to the "structuring effects". For this reason the critiques raised in *Resituating culture*, should be heeded, and positive action should be taken to address racism:

- issues of diversity need to permeate the curriculum;
- positive action is required to eliminate structural discrimination;
- steps should be taken to ensure that minority ethnic trainees are supported when they encounter discrimination;
- all teachers should be prepared to teach and prepare pupils for life in diverse societies;
- equality policies need to be monitored and regularly reviewed to ensure movement from the level of rhetoric to practice.

At the same time, we need to recognise that different nation states bring different histories and movement of populations. All of this will configure the way in which racism plays out, and how it can be addressed. Systems need to be in place to support individual actions, there has to be accountability, and care needs to be taken that strategies do not become divisive. Above all, the responsibility for structural change should not be passed off onto the shoulders of those individuals who suffer most from structural inequities. Without all of these measures, and without a full awareness of how racism is fostered, expressed and experienced, well-meaning policies to address social exclusion of minority ethnic groups may (to adapt Howard Williamson's phrase) continue missing the target by dint of missing the point.

Acknowledgements

I gratefully acknowledge funding provided by the Teacher Training Agency (now the Training and Development Agency for Schools), Multiverse, the Economic and Social Research Council and Manchester Metropolitan University which made it possible to undertake the projects from which the data are drawn. I also thank my colleagues, Dr Tehmina Basit, Dr Olwen McNamara, Ann Kenward, Professor Bruce Carrington, Professor Meg Maguire, Professor Derek Woodrow, Professor Tony Brown and Professor Ian Stronach who worked with me and supported me during the course of the projects. I would also like to acknowledge the late Gill Hatch whose drive facilitated the Recruitment and Retention projects.

References

Basit, T.N., Kenward, A. and Roberts, L. (2005), "Tackling racism on school placements: final report to Multiverse" (online). Available at: www.multiverse.ac.uk/viewArticle.aspx?categoryId=11933&taggingType=3&contentId=1187.

Basit, T.N., McNamara, O., Roberts, L., Carrington, B., Maguire, M. and Woodrow, D. (forthcoming), "'The bar is slightly higher': the perception of racism in teacher education", *Cambridge Journal of Education*.

Basit, T.N., Roberts, L., McNamara, O., Carrington, B., Maguire, M. and Woodrow, D. (2006), "Did they jump or were they pushed? Reasons why minority ethnic trainees withdraw from initial teacher training courses", *British Educational Research Journal*, 32(3), pp. 387-410.

Basit, T.N., Roberts, L., McNamara, O., Carrington, B., Maguire, M., Woodrow, D. and Stronach, I. (2004), "Reasons why minority ethnic trainees withdraw from initial teacher training courses". Report submitted to the Teacher Training Agency.

Blair, T. (1998), "Forging an inclusive society", *The Times Educational Supplement*, 11 September.

Brar, H.S. (1991), "Unequal opportunities: the recruitment, selection and promotion prospects for black teachers", *Evaluation and Research in Education*, 5, pp. 35-47.

Carrington, B., Bonnett, A., Demaine, J., Hall, I., Nayak, A., Short, G., Skelton, C., Smith, F. and Tomlin, R. (2001), *Ethnicity and the professional socialisation of teachers*: report submitted to the Teacher Training Agency.

Cole, M. (2004), "'Brutal and stinking' and 'difficult to handle': the historical and contemporary manifestations of racialisation, institutional racism, and schooling in Britain", *Race, Ethnicity and Education*, 7(1), pp. 35-56.

Commission for Racial Equality (1999), *Learning for all: national standards for racial equality in schools in England and Wales*. London: Commission for Racial Equality.

Department of Education and Science (1981), *West Indian children in our schools*. Cmnd. 8273. London: HMSO (the Rampton Report).

Department of Education and Science (1985), *Education for all: final report of the committee of inquiry into the education of children from ethnic minority groups*. Cmnd. 9453. London: HMSO (the Swann Report).

European Commission (2004), "Draft joint report on social inclusion". Available at: http://europa.eu.int/comm/employment_social/soc-prot/soc-incl/Joint_rep_en/htm.

Gillborn, D. and Gipps, C. (1996), *Recent research on the achievements of ethnic minority pupils, Office for Standards in Education review of research*. London: HMSO.

Gillborn, D. and Mirza, H.S. (2000), *Educational inequality: mapping race, class and gender: a synthesis of research evidence*. London: Office for Standards in Education.

Gordon, J. (2000), *The colour of teaching*. Buckingham: Open University Press.

Home Office (2001), *Community cohesion*. London: HMSO (the Cantle Report).

Home Office (2005), "Improving opportunity, strengthening society: the government's strategy to increase race equality and community cohesion" (online) (accessed 17 January 2005). Available at: www.homeoffice.gov.uk.

Jones, C., Maguire, M. and Watson, B. (1996), "First impressions: issues of race in school-based teacher education", *Multicultural Teaching*, 15(1), pp. 34-38.

Knowles, C. (2003), *Race and social analysis*. London, Thousand Oaks, New Delhi: Sage Publications.

Ladson-Billings, G. (2004), "Just what is critical race theory and what's it doing in a nice field like education?", in Ladson-Billings, G. and Gillborn, D. (eds.), *Multicultural education*. London, New York: RoutledgeFalmer.

Ladson-Billings, G. and Tate, W. (1995), "Toward a critical race theory of education", *Teachers College Record*, 97, pp. 47-68.

Lentin, A. (2004), "The problem of culture and human rights in response to racism", in Titley, G. (ed.), *Resituating culture*. Strasbourg: Council of Europe Publishing.

Macpherson, W. (1999), *The Stephen Lawrence inquiry: report of an inquiry by Sir William Macpherson of Cluny*, Cm4262-1. London: The Stationary Office.

Maguire, M., Jones, C. and Watson, B. (1997), "An investigation into the school experience of ethnic minority student teachers". Economic and Social Research Council project (R000221772) final report.

Neophytou, M. and Ali, S. (2000), "How far have we come? Issues of ethnicity in initial teacher training". Paper presented at the Annual Conference of the British Educational Research Association, University of Cardiff, September.

O'Cinneide, C. (2004), "Citizen and multiculturalism: equality, rights and diversity in contemporary Europe", in Titley, G. (ed), *Resituating culture*. Strasbourg: Council of Europe Publishing, pp. 43-55.

Osler, A. (1994), "Education for democracy and equality: the experiences, values and attitudes of ethnic minority student teachers", *European Journal of Intercultural Studies*, 5, pp. 23-37.

Pathak, S. (2000), *Race research for the future: ethnicity in education, and the labour market*. Nottingham: Department for Education and Employment Publications.

Roberts, L., McNamara, O., Basit, T.N. and Hatch, G. (2002), "'It's like black people are still aliens': retention of minority ethnic student teachers". Paper presented at the Annual Conference of the British Educational Research Association, University of Exeter, September.

Ross, A. (2001), "Towards a representative profession: teachers from the ethnic minorities". Paper presented to the Seminar on the Future of the Teaching Profession, Institute for Public Policy Research, London, 11 December.

Sibley, D. (1995), *Geographies of exclusion; society and difference in the west*. London: Routledge.

Teacher Training Agency (TTA) (2003), "Record numbers, record quality in teacher recruitment achieved" (online). Press release, 9 November. Available at: www.tda.gov.uk/about/mediarelations/2003/20031109.aspx?keywords=press+release+2003.

Thrupp, M. and Tomlinson, S. (2005), "Introduction: education policy, social justice and 'complex hope'", *British Educational Research Journal*, 31(5), pp. 549-556.

Titley, G. (ed.) (2004), *Resituating culture*. Strasbourg: Council of Europe Publishing.

Tomlinson, S. (1990), *Multicultural education in white schools*. London: Batsford Press.

Training and Development Agency for Schools (no date, a), "Frequently asked questions on policy and practice" (online) (accessed 27 June 2006). Available at: www.tda.gov.uk/partners/quality/ittprogsinitiatives/diversesociety/policy.aspx.

Training and Development Agency for Schools (no date, b), "Recruitment targets and supporting funding" (online) (accessed 27 June 2006). Available at: www.tda.gov.uk/partners/quality/ittprogsinitiatives/diversesociety/targets-funding.aspx?keywords=recruitment+targets.

Wilkins, C. (2001), "Student teachers and attitudes towards 'race': the role of citizenship education in addressing racism through the curriculum", *Westminster Studies in Education*, 24(1), pp. 7-21.

Wright, C., Standen, P., John, G., German. G. and Patel, T. (2005), "School exclusion and transition into adulthood in African-Caribbean communities" (online). York: Joseph Rowntree Foundation (accessed 23 September 2005). Available at: www.jrf.org.uk/knowledge/findings/socialpolicy/0435.asp.

13. Social exclusion or alienation? Understanding disability oppression

Rachel Gorman

introduction

People with disabilities often find themselves segregated from places and activities to which others have taken-for-granted access. At the same time, their daily lives can be heavily regulated by social and health services, and they may be politically and economically disenfranchised as a result. This situation exists despite government policies of integration and greater public awareness about disability as a human rights issue in a number of countries in Europe, as well in Canada where I live and work. It might seem important, then, to ensure that the experiences of disabled people are central to discussions about social exclusion, and that their needs are taken into account in plans to enhance social inclusion.

But how helpful are notions of social exclusion and inclusion in understanding (and therefore combating) the problems that disabled people face? How effective has recent legislation against disability discrimination been? And how might we understand and respond better to lived experiences of disability, in ways that significantly improve those lives? This chapter tries to answer such questions. It is centred on evidence drawn from one case study in my doctoral research on cultural performances in which disabled artists in Canada, who are also disability rights activists, portrayed their life histories (Gorman, 2005). I begin by asking questions about whether social exclusion and inclusion are the most helpful ways to think about disability, and then explain how particular approaches to research can highlight some of the invisible issues that need to be tackled. I then present the story of one disabled artist, Spirit Synott, which illustrates these issues very clearly. In particular, it shows how legislation on access to buildings – intended to promote "inclusion" for disabled people – can have counter-productive effects, and exclude them further still. The next section of the chapter discusses the deeper understanding of disability oppression, as a process of objectification and alienation, which we can gain from Synott's story, and I end by outlining some of the implications of this very different way of thinking for policy and practice in this field.

Social exclusion or disability oppression?

More than any other concept, "inclusion" has emerged as the organising principle for disability activism, studies and culture of the past decade, yet its meaning is all too rarely defined. This shift in the way of conceptualising disability has two major aspects on which we need to reflect.

First, "inclusion" tends to be defined (often implicitly) in a circular way, as "not exclusion". In this way, the rhetoric of inclusion "masks a reality of increasing division" (Preston-Shoot, 2001, p. 302). As a result, disability activists themselves have focused more on disability as a social construction or category, as a product principally of negative ideas and attitudes, and less on defining and theorising the material abuses that are associated with disability, such as physical or emotional violence and poverty. Second, over the past decade, the notion of "social exclusion" has become part of the discourse of global capitalist restructuring. It has come to refer to entire populations who have been organised out of the global labour market, or who are outside it and yet are targeted for incorporation into capitalist relations of production and distribution (see, for example, Organisation for Economic Co-operation and Development, 2000).

In a convergence between these two discourses, the goal of inclusion of people with disabilities has come to include the twin demands of consumer choice and labour market access. On the one hand, disabled people are viewed only as needing services and as being unable to perform work. All too often, even critical voices, whose goal is to question and challenge the level of choice disabled people are afforded in their daily lives, talk about them in terms of "clients" who deserve better service, rather than citizens who have rights (Johnson, 1998). On the other hand, many influential disability theorists argue that people with disabilities will never be able to compete in a capitalist labour market, and that changing capitalist relations of production is essential in the struggle for an inclusive society (Abberley, 1999; Barnes, 2003; Gleeson, 1999). Paradoxically, this fatalistic view treats the structures of society that exclude disabled people as abstract and inevitable forces – ones which transcend history, are an essential feature of human experience and are impermeable to resistance.

De facto, then, the notion of "exclusion" has come to supplant that of disability oppression in related policy and theory. But the problem with trying to understand disability oppression through the lens of "exclusion" is that this obscures the power relations, social actors and material practices which produce that oppression. "Social exclusion" is such a general concept that it is effectively meaningless. Before moving on to present Spirit Synott's story of her encounters with disability discrimination and oppression, it is important first to explain the methods behind the research, and the theoretical approach that can help us understand the evidence it produced.

Studying disability oppression

In my research with disability artists and activists, I wanted to examine how the concept of "inclusion" – as a vague, ill-defined set of demands for overcoming the "exclusion" of disabled people – works to organise the way we think about disability. The relational and reflexive method of social analysis that I developed draws on a radical view of agency, and on the use of stories as a starting point for analysing social relations (Bannerji, 1995). It also draws on Smith's (1997) method of explicating from a particular standpoint how people are involved in the relations or regimes of ruling that organise their experience. Relations of ruling are independent from people's individual intentions, but these regimes are not equally removed from everyone's lives. There are interests of certain groups at work – these are the groups that Smith (1997) refers to as the collectivities whose standpoint is objectified and imposed onto others. These are the ideas that I put to work on texts by artist-activists with whom I have worked on cultural performances, in the hope of revealing the social relations of disability. At the same time, I also wanted to keep in sight the social relations that mediate how each story is put forward in the public sphere.

I chose to ground my discussion of disability oppression in stories that have been intentionally produced by artist-activists with a view to having them performed in public and/or read as texts. These consciously produced texts constitute a form of witnessing (similar to the accounts in Chapter 10, by Amineh Kakabaveh), since the author's intention is to reveal or highlight social relations in order to develop people's consciousness about those relations. Analysing the active process of developing these scripts, and revealing the social relations in which this process happened, enabled me to analyse how the concept of "exclusion" obscures the social relations of disability oppression.

Such a method has to engage in detailed analysis of a few specific stories, rather than developing an aggregate of many different ones. Because political struggle – in this case, the struggle for disability rights – arises in particular and specific contexts, it is impossible to convey the political content of a story when it is combined into an aggregate with other stories. For this reason, all of the stories I analysed in my study are interconnected in two important and inseparable ways. First, all of the artist-activists were working in the same context in terms of time, place, and political and cultural "scene". Second, these stories, as conscious interventions, reveal aspects of our collective understanding of disability oppression, and our collective ideas about how to end it. Here, I only have space to present just one of them – but the method used allows even a single case to provide a point of entry into the way that disability oppression is enacted in discriminatory practices, however unwitting or unintentional they may be, and the relations of ruling that shape that enactment.

Organising exclusion: "lifts and stairs"

A major issue for disabled people is their exclusion from buildings, and measures to address this are often central to legislation against disability discrimination. Here, I want to explain how exclusion from buildings is a process rather than a one-off event that occurs when the building is first constructed, or a recurring event when a person arrives at a building but cannot enter it. The social relations by which inaccessible buildings are created begin to unfold before a person approaches the building, and continue to unfold after she has left. Spirit Synott's story "Lifts and stairs" (Synott, 2000) reveals that a space can be rendered inaccessible through a process not of physical obstruction, but of obstructing the human relations through which a person would otherwise gain access to that space.

Synott's story describes her encounters with the social relations surrounding her access to buildings, and how these relations unfold across time and geographical location.

> "I never went to a special public school – I was always the only one with a disability. I went to a high school that specialised in the arts – visual art theatre arts, fine arts, graphic art and commercial arts. It was an incredible school – and it was not accessible when I went there. I was able to walk short distances until I was 17, so I used to bring my wheelchair with me to school and the students would carry it up and down stairs for me. I lost the use of my right leg

> when I was 17, so after that the students and the staff carried me up and down the stairs. Almost twenty years later, the school is now accessible.
>
> It was the art director who was instrumental in getting me into that school. He said 'We've got a football team, we can handle you!' I've kept in touch with several of the teachers over the years, and they're all very supportive. I recently went back and talked to the art director. Now he says he thinks that what they did back then was ludicrous, and that they never should have carried me up and down the stairs."

This part of the story reveals a contradiction between what is "accessible" as a code or set of regulations, and what is accessible in a human or active sense. The art director refers to new regulations or standards that would prevent the staff from allowing Synott to be carried into an inaccessible building; while in the past it was friendships with athletes that she could rely on to get her into the building. Students carrying her up and down means that the responsibility is spread over many people. This is a very different than making it the responsibility of the teacher. If one person did it all the time it could lead to back strain, and if the teacher is absent that day she would not be able to get inside. This excerpt is also an account of a change in consciousness the art director had as a result of changes that had taken place between the time Synott had been a student there and her visit twenty years later.

In the following excerpt, Synott shows how "obvious", simple, or logical solutions become impossible because of the ruling relations that were in place before Synott arrived at art college, and the new regulations that were created as she tried to change the situation:

> "After high school, I worked for several years before enrolling in a fine art and design college. It was here that I had a draining and unresolved struggle over the inaccessibility of the school. Unlike my high school experience, the administration refused any obvious, simple or logical solutions to the problem of access. The student gallery and the cafeteria were both inaccessible to me. They had special seminars with guest speakers talking about how to market your work, how to copyright your work, how to get legal advice, and how to get affiliated with galleries – all of the things that an artist really needs to know. These were always held in a completely inaccessible area. I went to the student services department on several occasions to make them aware of my situation. I even suggested that their audiovisual department students could videotape the seminars, and they said no.
>
> In fact I finally filed my complaint with the Human Rights Commission because they wouldn't issue me a key to the hydraulic freight lift that I used to get into the building. I had to wait for someone to come and get me. Later they put a buzzer system in and hired students to come and activate the lift – but they were never available. They actually preferred to pay another student to activate the lift rather than allow me free access in and out of the building. Their rationale was that if something screwed up they would have someone to fire."

Despite Synott's creativity and advanced skills in self-advocacy, a complicated set of rules are referred to as the "object" that is keeping her out of the building.

An important point in this excerpt is that another student is paid to operate the lift instead of Synott. As the ruling relations governing Synott's coming-and-going increase, so, it seems, does the work involved in negotiating the space. As the person whose coming-and-going is being organised by these ruling relations continues to try to access the space (instead of dropping out of school and staying home), this additional work of negotiating the space has to become increasingly organised. If Synott had to wait for an administrative worker to check randomly to see if she was waiting to use the lift, it would be impossible to follow her class schedule with any consistency. In order to ensure that someone who uses the lift can get into the building in a regular fashion (that is, without waiting for administrative staff with a key to pass by randomly), then it has to become someone's responsibility to check the lift regularly, or answer the buzzer, or meet Synott before her classes start. Of course, this arrangement precludes Synott from behaving like other students and choosing when she wants to attend and when she wants to come late to class.

If the college human resources staff hire another (presumably able-bodied) student paid to carry a key that Synott is not allowed to carry, this can certainly be seen as an indication that the human resources workers do not see the disabled student as competent to use the elevator, even if she is physically able to do so. However, the decision to hire someone to carry the key has more to do with insurance guidelines. Having an employee carry the key means there will be someone to fire if something goes wrong.

All of this implies an additional set of work activities. Administrative staff must interpret building codes and policy, and write new procedures in order to address the lift situation. Any fellow students, who may have been helping Synott informally, must be instructed to desist. Human resources managers have to hire someone to operate the lift. This turn of events ensures that an offer to carry Synott up the stairs will be seen as an act of rebellion rather than a logical solution to a mundane problem, which is to ensure that a 95 pound woman can get up one flight of stairs to her art class.

Understanding disability oppression: a process of alienation and objectification

Synott's story shows how the altering or obstructing of human relations has consequence both for people's (in)ability to move through space, and also for people's consciousness about disability. The possibility of casual helping is removed, and these more spontaneous human relations are reconfigured as labour relations. Furthermore, when most social spaces are segregated, and some are inaccessible, it appears as though the "original" state of the built environment is inaccessible, and that demands for accessible spaces are demands to modify a pre-existing social matrix. "Social exclusion" (as far as building accessibility goes) can therefore more helpfully be thought of as a process of alienation, through which people's labour brings about objectified relations of ruling. Some of this terminology may seem unfamiliar, but it is worth making the effort to think them through. It helps us to gain a deeper understanding of these seemingly simple everyday exclusions. It also helps us to understand how some of the most common ways of thinking about and responding to disability oppression fail to address the root of the problem.

In the non-Marxist usage, "objectification" and "alienation" connote processes that happen to a person in an oppressed group. The process of alienation is located where the effect is felt. For example, disability rights activist and author James Charlton (2000) asks us to consider the sign "Elevators for freight and handicapped only – please use stairs" as an example of the dehumanisation, objectification and alienation of people with disabilities. In the Marxist use of these terms, however, objectification and alienation are different things, which may come about through the same process. Objectification is the process by which human labour is concretised into a product, while alienation describes the separation of human beings from their own "species nature", from other human beings and from the natural environment. When human labour results in the concretisation of social relations, then the process involves both objectification and alienation (Boal, 1985; Ollman, 1971; Postone, 1996). In this way, when helping a disabled person is turned into a form of labour, rather than an act of human solidarity, the human element disappears; the labour involved becomes an independent object alien to the helper; and that labour then becomes a power that confronts her (cf. Ollman, 1971).

In Synott's story, not only are the new procedures brought about through labour, but the resulting situation now requires even more labour than was needed before. These interactions are mediated by legal and insurance regulations similar to ones that Synott's high school art director was concerned about.

I argue, therefore, that these ways in which the social category "disability" is mediated mean that we should understand it as an expression of class struggle. There is a struggle over the definition of needs, as seen in Synott's (2000) story. People struggle for democratic control (in the case of groups) or autonomy (in the case of individual services) over the social structures that regulate how their needs are defined and met. There is also a struggle over revealing the forms of consciousness and the structures that mediate people's everyday lives. This struggle is both submerged in, and represented by, the binary concept of social exclusion/inclusion.

Some activists have described disability-related services as a process of commodification of people with disabilities. Judith Snow has argued that people become the raw material before the therapy is performed, and are the modified product at the end. The therapist expends her labour power to transform the raw material (pretherapy person) to the product (therapised person), and the surplus of that labour power is appropriated by the organisation that collects the fees for the service (Snow and Gorman, 1997).

Many authors writing during the neo-liberal political climate of the 1990s have observed that the expansion of capital means that more and more dimensions of human activity can be performed for profit (for example, see Rikowski, 1998, on the deepening of capitalist relations in education). From the perspective of the person receiving the services, it may be useful to understand this process as one of alienation. Whether or not the service is provided for profit does not have a direct correlation with whether the recipients of the services have control over them. Considering the historical context of institutional violence against disabled people, it is important to recognise the role of state-provided services in the capitalist mode of production.

Like other commodities that are produced within capitalist social relations, these services are distributed on the basis of profit and scarcity. These services are not produced in order to meet needs, but for profit. These profits are achieved in part through the professionalisation of therapists and other health service providers. In Europe, North America and Australasia, public health care is dismantled and privatised, while the health infrastructure in specific parts of Latin America, Asia and Africa is destroyed through low- and high-intensity warfare and imperialist expansion, while pharmaceutical industries grow and internationalise.

"Exclusion" is therefore a very partial way of understanding the collective location of people with disabilities within the universe of capitalist social relations – and in this way, "social exclusion" can be considered to be an ideology. Two interrelated aspects of ideology are both applicable to the way the word "exclusion" functions in the discourse around disability. "Exclusion" is both a partial understanding of social relations based on the appearance of these social relations, and a concept that masks contradictions that are inherent in these social relations. When we think about "exclusion", we imagine structural forces that must cause this exclusion; indeed, much disability-ßstudies literature and many activist organisations refer to "barriers". However, as we think through the story I have included here, or as activists try to identify and "remove" these barriers, we see that the oppression that people are experiencing does not disappear when a ramp is installed.

It is important to distinguish between the understanding that certain power relations are built into and of the very fabric of our social organisations, and the belief that these power relations are inevitable, therefore transhistorical and essential to human nature. This fatalism arises from the appearance of ableist social relations in every facet of our society. A belief in the permanence of disability oppression also leads us to ignore the resistance to these relations, or leads us to explain the resistance we observe as being part and parcel of disability. As some of the other stories in my study showed, "non-compliance" to treatment can be explained by those working with disabled people simply as a further symptom or attribute of a disorder or disability (see also Pupavac, 2001).

Conceptualising disability as social exclusion ultimately places the contradiction at the individual level:

- whether it is the attitude of the person discriminating, or the attitude of the person discriminated against (for example, a person who has not yet acquired the social/employment skills required for integrating into society, and/or has not yet become "empowered" enough to advocate for services to help her/himself cope);

- or whether it is a structural barrier that a "non-normal" body cannot navigate (for example, when wheelchair-users cannot get into a building, this exclusion is experienced one-by-one; or an individual's inability to afford an assistive device that will help them participate in their workplace or community).

If we take a political economy approach, we might think about disability in terms of structural unemployment and conclude that "disability" is the category of individuals who are less employable and are therefore unemployed. A slightly different conclusion might be that people can work; however, they are not usually needed in capitalist relations of production, except during the rare times when near-full employment happens.

"Inclusion" functions, then as a class ideology, in that it is a partial way of understanding disability oppression; and in that it represents a set of beliefs about class and group goals. Articulated demands for "inclusion" may be good for certain segments of the larger political grouping at certain times, however, we must continue to ask ourselves who benefits from disability politics, both in its organisation and its demands.

implications for support work and inclusive education for disabled people

Synott's story highlights the processes of rendering a space inaccessible, of obstructing spontaneous human interactions, and of reconfiguring these interactions as caregiving and/or labour relations. Furthermore, this process erases each person's unique set of needs and abilities and replaces individuality with a "wheelchair icon" identity. In this way, what was accessible through human relations is rendered inaccessible through adherence to policy guidelines. Unless they are organised in a democratic way, the processes of creating formal accessibility often render buildings less accessible than they were before the process began.

Coming to see this process of formalising the labour required to negotiate regulations, and coming to see the role that these regulations play in diminishing opportunities for human interaction, both have implications for how we understand support work and inclusive education. Based on Synott's account of her educational experiences, it seems that instead of looking to a future in which an inclusive society encourages less regulated human interaction, we are looking to a past in which human interactions have become progressively more complicated. It is this less regulated human interaction that inclusion activists as divergent as radical Judith Snow (2001) and philanthropist Jean Vanier (1998) argue is missing in our society. Despite their very different political analyses, and very different visions for an "inclusive society", both would argue that we need to pursue these human interactions in order to create a better society, for people with disabilities and non-disabled people alike.

The ruling relations of building procedures that Synott describes are made through human labour, and are not easily unmade – they form the objectified social relations that Smith (1997) describes, they become the "virtual consciousness" that replaces embodied experience. In terms of activism, it is not our strategy to try to unmake these relations of ruling, only to argue for more or different policies and procedures. Indeed, the ruling relations Synott describes refer to building codes that have actually resulted from struggles for building access. She also turns to the Human Rights Commission for recourse.

The distinction between Marxist and non-Marxist ways of thinking about this process is important, because the two different conceptualisations can lead to very different strategies for social change. Conceptualising alienation as a process that takes place between individuals implies that there is a person doing the alienating, and a person being alienated. Strategies might include education for the individuals who do alienating things, and empowerment for the individuals who have been alienated.

This education may help, in that it may bring the staff to join the struggle for human rights, or it may encourage them to reorganise their work (insofar as they can do so) in order to find solutions for the problem. But if we understand alienation to be a process that only takes place in the immediate relations between two people, we may have a different response to the story than if we understand it in terms of relations of ruling. Unless we take the time to deconstruct it, someone listening to this story might simply conclude that the staff and administration have no regard for disabled people. In the situation described above, the options for the staff are very limited, and involve either developing a personal relationship with Synott and giving her a copy of the key as a favour, and/or ignoring fire regulations. In any case, the staff risk being reprimanded.

Here, I argue that the process of objectification and alienation are reproduced through, but do not originate in the interactions between the individuals in the present tense of the story. Rather the relations of ruling that mediate this situation were produced in earlier interactions in different sites. In other words, even if the individuals working at the school had absolutely no intention of alienating Synott, they brought about her alienation through their labour of administering the school.

In such a situation, sensitivity training and other kinds of workshops aimed at changing staff or administration attitudes may not have much of a practical impact when individual choices are bounded by regulations. Training aimed at altering individual attitudes can do little to change a situation in which the intentions of individuals are mediated by relations of ruling. This is not to imply that these individuals cannot choose to act or find ways to change their work relations. Rather, I am pointing out that these changes would more effectively be brought about through learning to rewrite policy and organise political coalitions, as well as learning how to have a better attitude.

References

Abberley, P. (1987), "The concept of oppression and the development of a social theory of disability", *Disability, Handicap and Society*, 2(1), pp. 5-19.

Bannerji, H. (1995), *Thinking through: essays on feminism, Marxism and anti-racism*. Toronto: Women's Press.

Barnes, C. (2003), "Disability, the organization of work, and the need for change", statement to the Economic Co-operation and Development Conference on Transforming Disability into Ability, 6 March (online) (accessed 23 April 2003). Available at:
www.leeds.ac.uk/disability-studies/archiveuk.

Boal, A. (1985), *Theatre of the oppressed*. New York: Theatre Communications Group.

Charlton, J. (2000), *Nothing about us without us*. Berkeley and Los Angeles: University of California Press.

Gleeson, B. (1999), *Geographies of disability*. London and New York: Routledge.

Gorman, R. (2005), "Class consciousness, disability and social exclusion: a relational/reflexive analysis of disability culture". Unpublished Ph.D. thesis, University of Toronto.

Johnson, K. (1998), "Deinstitutionalisation: the management of rights", *Disability & Society*, 13(3), pp. 375-387.

Ollman, B. (1971), *Alienation: Marx's conception of man in capitalist society*. London and New York: Cambridge University Press.

Organisation for Economic Co-operation and Development (OECD) (2000), *Overcoming exclusion through adult learning*. Paris: OECD Publications Service.

Postone, M. (1996), *Time, labor and social domination: a reinterpretation of Marx's critical theory*. New York: Cambridge University Press.

Preston-Shoot, M. (2001), "Editorial", *Social Work Education*, 20(3), pp. 301-302.

Pupavac, V. (2001), "Therapeutic governance: psycho-social intervention and trauma risk management", *Disasters*, 25(4), pp. 358-372.

Rikowski, G. (1998), "Only charybdis: the learning society through idealism", in Ranson, S. (ed.), *Inside the learning society*. London: Cassell Education.

Smith, D.E. (1997), "From the margins: women's standpoint as a method of inquiry in the social sciences", *Gender, Technology and Development*, 1(1), pp. 113-135.

Snow, J. (2001), "Personal assistance: What it is and what it is not". Toronto: Unpublished manuscript.

Snow, J. and Gorman, R. (1997), "Disability, identity and class". Unpublished manuscript, Department of Adult Education, OISE, University of Toronto.

Synott, S. (2000), "Lifts and stairs", adapted for the Things we didn't learn in school soundtrack. Premiered at Oakham House, Toronto: Mayworks Festival of Working People and the Arts, 5 May.

Vanier, J. (1998), *Becoming human*. Toronto: Anansi Press.

Waring, M. (1999), *Counting for nothing: what men value and what women are worth*, 2nd edn. Toronto: University of Toronto Press.

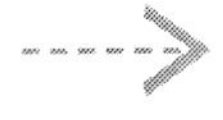

14. Social inclusion, young people and sexual health: what are the links?

Kate Philip, Janet Shucksmith, Janet Tucker and Edwin van Teijlingen

Introduction

This chapter uses findings from the independent evaluation of Healthy Respect, a Scottish Demonstration project on teenage sexual health (Tucker et al., 2005) to examine the ways in which attempts to improve young people's sexual health can be construed as a way of promoting social inclusion. In particular the paper asks whether Healthy Respect's multi-agency approach to the provision of health education and sexual health services allowed the project to be more inclusive than would have been the case where service was provided within separate professional groups. This approach is in line with the strategy developed by the Council of Europe's European Committee for Social Cohesion in 2000 and revised in 2004 and is also coherent with the Europeen Convention on Human Rights (Council of Europe, 1998) in attempting to work with rather than on young people. Findings from this longitudinal evaluation hold implications for the training of professionals and for empowerment of vulnerable groups.

The term "social inclusion" has become a key element of EU and UK Government strategies to tackle inequality (Alexiadou, 2002). Within the UK it has been used to underpin the aims of the government in improving the health and welfare of the population, lifting children and families out of poverty and contributing to the development of social capital. The term is useful in drawing attention to how poverty combines with a range of inequalities to prevent individuals from participating fully in the wider society but it remains a contested term subject to a range of interpretations. Since these questions are well rehearsed in the overview chapter in this book by Howard Williamson, we focus our discussion on an exploration of links between exclusion and poor sexual health before examining the questions outlined above.

What are the linkages between social inclusion and sexual health?

A wealth of social research has consistently pointed to enduring links between social inequality and health and to how interactions between different forms of inequality combine to reinforce the exclusion of particular groups. The Economic and Social Research Council (ESRC) Health Variations programme demonstrated the impact of these linkages in influencing trajectories throughout the lifecourse

(Graham, 2000). This recognition led the UK Government to initiate the Social Exclusion Unit (SEU) in England which reviewed research, policy and practice on key aspects of social exclusion. Coles (2000) has noted how their reports on truancy and social exclusion, homelessness and communities represented a new approach from government in highlighting the impact on youth. The reports on teenage pregnancy (SEU, 1999a) and Bridging the Gap (SEU, 1999b), a study of young people not in training, education or employment (NEET), focused on the cumulative impact of exclusion on the youth population. Thus young people who were already marginalised, such as those within the care system, were more likely to fail or be excluded from school, to become involved in crime, to experience mental health problems, to experience poor sexual health, homelessness and to be isolated from the mainstream.

How is sexual health implicated in this story of the connection between social exclusion and health? It is clear that social exclusion experienced in childhood is an indicator of poor future sexual health. Thus being brought up in care is a strong predictor of future teenage pregnancy (Corlyon and Maguire, 1999). But poor sexual health frequently leads to further exclusion: low levels of educational achievement, with all the consequences of this for employment and subsequent earnings, are common outcomes for young women who experience early pregnancy. Within Scotland, the improvement of teenage sexual health was identified as one of four targets for a more socially inclusive society (Scottish Office, 1999) and as one element of attempts to promote social inclusion within the UK. Central to this has been the statistic that the UK has the highest teenage pregnancy rate in western Europe, currently five times that of the Netherlands, double that of Germany and triple that of France (Goveas, 2005). Similarly the increase in sexually transmitted infections among the youth population has raised anxiety among health professionals.

Clearly, we are only beginning to understand about the complexity and variety of young people's own understandings and beliefs about sexuality and sexual health. A growing body of empirical work has shown that sexual behaviours take place within a set of cultural and gendered practices in which the power to negotiate is highly uneven (Thomson and Scott, 1990). These findings suggest that service design and delivery has to take account of the diversity of experience and expertise among the youth population. Important gaps exist in our knowledge about how vulnerable young people negotiate the challenges that face them in dealing with sexual health. Little evidence is available about the active involvement of young people in strategies designed to improve sexual health or to tackle social exclusion. Better understanding of these issues may enhance our understanding of how young people can exercise their rights to participation within other contexts such as employment, family life and participation in civil society.

Sexual health interventions: educating for inclusion?

Schools are viewed as a central mechanism for reaching the majority of young people but they can also reinforce exclusion (see, for example, Chapter 15 by Christiane Weis). Nevertheless schools offer a broad base for the provision of information on sexual health within an educational framework. Within the UK they have been criticised as having met with little success and as being riven with contradictions in their aims, frameworks and value base (Rolston et al., 2005). Teachers have frequently complained about being ill-prepared and supported for this role while young people have also consistently criticised school-based education. Many have reported a reluctance to view teachers in general as credible or reliable sources of advice and information on these topics (Sex Education Forum, 1999; Measor, 2004). However, some evidence suggests that young people see schools as legitimate settings in which they should be able to learn about sexual health and sexuality (Rolston et al., 2005).

It is equally clear from research findings that in seeking advice or services, young people have largely avoided traditional health services (Shucksmith and Hendry, 1998). A number of reasons can be outlined. Firstly, many services are highly medicalised which some groups find intimidating and fear that staff are likely to be judgemental and unable to take a holistic view of their needs (Meyrick and Swann, 1998). Few such services have marketed themselves to young people and have rarely seen the need to make concessions to the needs of young people in general, far less those of vulnerable groups. Moreover most are described as "family planning", which can discourage many young men and women who are lacking in confidence, and who fear they may encounter adults from their family at the clinic or who may have little desire to plan a family at this stage of their lives. Access is often problematic for those in peripheral estates and rural areas (Glasier, 2000).

By contrast, agencies that do provide dedicated services to young people have been more popular, and studies of such initiatives have provided useful insights into how other services could become more "young person friendly" (Redman et al., 1997; Brook, 1998). Successful services have been defined by young people as likely to offer confidentiality, friendly and non-judgemental staff and a setting which is relaxed, sensitive to the needs of different groups and unlikely to cause embarrassment (Burtney, 2000).

The new social inclusion agendas have placed schools and health services at the centre of policy development on the assumption that this provides an opportunity to develop both universal and targeted approaches or, in the jargon, to offer "joined up" solutions (Swann et al., 2003). School-based sex and relationships education (SRE) was identified as a crucial mechanism for the promotion of positive approaches to sexual health and for equipping young people to make informed decisions. Onsite services managed and run alongside such programmes were viewed as supplementing this and as having potential to reach out to those young people who have traditionally been excluded, or excluded themselves, from mainstream sexual health education (Scottish Executive, 2000). A partnership approach drawing in a range of expertise and support could further engage communities and young people themselves in the processes.

For these reasons, the Scottish Executive initiated a four-year demonstration project which set out to improve the sexual health of young people in Lothian. We now consider some dimensions of these approaches in relation to teenage sexual health and social inclusion before going on to examine how these developed in the work of the Healthy Respect demonstration project.

integrated multi-agency approaches to social inclusion

The benefits of partnership approaches in tackling social exclusion have been well rehearsed but the advantages in relation to efforts to improve young people's sexual health have been less evident. This is due, in part, to a lack of rigorously evaluated work in this field. In this section we highlight some of the potential benefits and challenges of partnership approaches before considering how this developed within the Healthy Respect demonstration project.

Partnership can offer a synergy of effort whereby the collective extends the capacity of those previously working in isolated departmental "silos". In relation to sexual health, this can be particularly useful in building a holistic approach and an environment in which "educational", "caring" and "health" agendas complement each other within an overall social model of health. It enables issues previously viewed as peripheral to the core work of an individual agency to assume a more central focus and engender more flexibility. Awareness of the needs of hitherto "hidden" groups is more visible within a partnership where different perspectives and experiences are shared.

The involvement of voluntary sector groups at strategic levels can lend credibility to their work. Thus agencies such as Rape Crisis and Lesbian, Gay, Bisexual and Transgender Youth (LGBT Youth) relished the opportunity to join the Healthy Respect partnership, seeing this as a gateway to disseminating their messages more extensively, and opening up debates at more senior levels.

Partnership approaches can foster the potential for "one door services" which are user friendly and accessible to young people. In this way the needs of different groups can be accommodated more readily in contrast to the "revolving" door experience of being referred from one agency to another, a common complaint of young people in seeking help. Related to this is the potential for localised generic services to be developed in ways which enable young people to "test out" on less sensitive topics, prior to trusting the service to deal with their issue on their own terms. These may also empower young people to select support by providing both a menu of services and access to different approaches when, for example, youth workers, school nurses and teachers work together.

Partnership approaches can offer targeted support for young people who may be at risk through sexual activity but who are alienated from school provision. A health drop-in worker who also provides sexual health education may be a valuable "bridge" between school and services. Moreover the mix of skills and a generic approach has the potential to validate educational frameworks which engender active participation and dialogue (see Chapter 13 by Rachel Gorman; also Chisholm and Hoskins, 2005). But partnership working in itself implies a continuity of approach in developing services that are accessible, embedded in local cultures and which are sustainable (Milbourne et al., 2003). Where agencies perceive their involvement as a marginal element of their work they may be reluctant to engage in more fundamental shifts in their mode of working (Berkeley and Ross, 2003).

Power relationships between partners inevitably influence the extent of partnership working (Milbourne et al., 2003). Although there is a strong push for the voluntary sector to be included, the advantages for small organisations may be double edged: it can offer a platform to raise the profile of the agency, to promote the work more widely and to bring their experience to a wider constituency; but it may reinforce their subordinate position, and drain already scarce resources in attending meetings and planning. Furthermore, partnership working is time consuming in "getting partners round the table" to develop a shared vision, and smaller agencies may lack the capacity for staff to take on such a role (Easen et al., 2000). For all partners, the early stages of partnership can be difficult in demanding new approaches which may challenge taken-for-granted practices. In a field as contentious as teenage sexual health, this can be even more problematic, as partners often work in disparate fields with different professional frameworks and lines of accountability.

At a professional level, clashes between different organisational and disciplinary cultures may arise from different perspectives on what integrated working means. Within large hierarchical organisations, some professional groups may be protective of their own expertise as educators or service providers and fail to recognise others as competent in the field (Shucksmith et al., 2005). Some groups may simply see themselves as operating their existing service "in the community" rather than at their clinic base and be reluctant to extend their remit to developing their skills in working with young people. At a managerial level, little time may be allocated to enable such staff to meet with others, plan or review activity.

The potential for young people themselves to be actively involved as stakeholders in partnership work implies even more fundamental shifts in professional discourses and perspectives. Barriers include a lack of consensus over the competence of young people; an absence of structures which support young people to participate in partnership working; a lack of understanding of the rights of young people to take part; and importantly, a reluctance to develop mechanisms for supporting them to exercise what rights they do have. Nevertheless work on children's rights has highlighted ways in which young people can become more central to these processes (Franklin, 2004).

An example of multi-agency working

In this section we explore an example of a partnership approach through the work of Healthy Respect. This project aimed to work towards improving the sexual health of young people in Lothian and was funded initially for four years by the Scottish Executive. It set out to:

> "Promote positive good health and relationships, to reduce the level of teenage pregnancies and to prevent the spread of STIs (Sexually Transmitted Infections) among young people in Lothian" (Lothian Health, 2000, p. 2).

The overall initiative aimed to promote good interpersonal relationships and respect for self, develop a climate in which sex and sexuality could be discussed openly without embarrassment, encourage responsible attitudes on the part of young people and discourage coercive and manipulative behaviour.

The demonstration project brought together a number of different agencies and organisations to support 19 component strands under the leadership of Lothian National Health Service Board. In this respect it was a strategic partnership with representation from health services, local authority education departments and the voluntary sector. At (field) working levels, delivery partnerships were also developed, and these form the basis of the discussion in this paper. These partnerships set out to

- link services and education to address needs at both universal and targeted levels;
- set the scene for example by devising comprehensive guidelines.

The mechanism for this was the work of the 19 strands (see Table 1). The majority of these components were involved in work in schools: these included the Sexual Health and Relationships Education (SHARE) work, Getting the Message Across, the LGBT project, Work with Young Men and the Parents project. In addition the Chlamydia project produced a video for use in schools and supported some drop-in work, and Rape Crisis educated professionals to be more responsive to young

people who experienced abuse. It is important to note that many of the projects began from different starting points and orientations.

- The overall evaluation was designed and undertaken by an interdisciplinary team of researchers from the University of Aberdeen. This was a multilevel evaluation which included both quantitative and qualitative elements (see Tucker et al., 2004 for a summary of the overall report). A comparative quasi-experimental study of population based sexual health behaviour and outcomes took place before and after the intervention.
- This paper draws on findings from the qualitative evaluation study. This included a series of case studies of a selection of ten component projects (highlighted in bold in Table 1). The case studies included analysis of self-audit data, repeated semi-structured interviews with project staff and Healthy Respect management, group discussions and interviews with young users and parents, observation and analysis of documentary evidence.

Table 1 – 19 component projects of Healthy Respect *with the 10 selected case studies (in bold)*

Improving contraceptive services in abortion services
Young people with specific needs
(a) Looked after and accommodated young people
(b) Getting the message across at Caledonia Youth
Chlamydia testing
Emergency contraception and chlamydia testing
Sexual health promotion in further education colleges
Lesbian, gay, bisexual and transgender (LGBT) work
Sexual health and relationships education (SHARE) in the school setting
a) Edinburgh City
b) West Lothian
c) School nurses
d) Inreach/outreach work
e) East Lothian
f) Mid Lothian
Confidentiality and child protection
Developing and supporting the role of parents
Young men's sexual health
Young women who have experienced sexual abuse or coercion
Creating affirmative cultures
Cross-cutting all: Developing young people's involvement

How did partnership work develop in the case of Healthy Respect?

As with many such strategic partnerships, Healthy Respect originated in order to bid for resources in response to the call for funding applications. By contrast, the subsequent process of becoming a working partnership was generally agreed by participants to take up a considerable amount of time, resource and energy over the life of the demonstration project.

Translating the initiative into a delivery partnership took place through the development of projects at school and community levels. Some areas were already working on sexual health in partnership and were able to embark more quickly on their task. However, across the project overall, the status of the representatives on the partnership varied considerably. For example, local education managers sat on the partnership but had limited remits over the work in schools where head teachers were responsible. In some practice settings, partnership working was in place, in others, these partnerships only developed towards the end of the demonstration project while in others, partnership working broke down. Overall this element of the work took considerable time. For example, agreements over confidentiality guidelines for work with young people were not reached until after the completion of the demonstration project.

At a fieldwork level, partnership working was viewed as an essential mechanism for linking both targeted and universal approaches. Central to this approach was the introduction of the SHARE sex education package into a sample of schools. SHARE is a package targeted at teachers which includes an extensive training programme based on educational theory and research evidence about the behaviour of young people (Wight and Abraham, 2000). The programme had previously been piloted in several schools in the Lothian area and was subject to a randomised control trial and process evaluation which reported in 2002 (Wight et al., 2002).

Multidisciplinary training was undertaken with a range of professionals prior to implementation of the programme in 10 secondary schools in the four local authority areas of Lothian. Drop-in services were initiated alongside to provide information, advice and services in tandem with the programme. Overall this aimed to offer an integrated package with a universal approach through the school-based programme and a targeted approach through the drop-ins. The drop-in work was envisaged as attracting those less likely to be receptive to the SHARE work.

The SHARE training was successful in bringing together a range of professionals who gave positive feedback about the benefits of the multi-agency training. Teachers, especially, valued the high quality training and the opportunity to work alongside other professionals. However, the implementation of SHARE in schools was uneven and the extent of multi-agency working was dependent on individual school. Thus the drop-ins offered more scope to develop partnership working by drawing on the expertise of a wider range of staff.

The drop-ins set out to provide generic health services including sexual health advice and information in stylish and imaginative ways. In setting up these services a number of challenges were encountered and these illustrate some important underlying difficulties that bedevilled the partnership approach. For example, drop-in services based in schools were not permitted to provide contraception unlike those based in the community. This was despite repeated findings from consultations that young people wanted such services to be provided. Unsurprisingly, the non-school-based dedicated services were more heavily used than those based on school premises. One of the most successful services was operated by a SHARE trained outreach family-planning nurse who already worked in the existing young people's health centre adjacent to the school. The nurse was well known to young people and was identified by name to the researcher as "reliable" by young people interviewed for the study. The drop-ins therefore offered some potential to respond to locally identified needs.

Involving the local community became an important feature of the preparation for the opening of the drop-ins. In one public housing neighbourhood, considerable effort went into convincing the management committee of a community centre to house the drop-in service. Imaginative efforts to inform young people and parents about the services were also deployed: drop-in workers attended school assemblies and organised one-off sessions in youth work settings and Healthy Respect leaflets were distributed to schools, community groups and parents. In another area an extensive consultation was undertaken with both parents and young people over the proposed services. While this work aimed to downplay hostile media coverage and action by evangelical groups, it boosted enthusiasm and brought parents into the partnership from the outset.

Attempts to involve young people actively in planning and managing the services were less well thought through. For example, staff at one drop-in had invited a group of young women to design a room for the service, but their offering was seen as "too girly", and staff subsequently continued with their own design. This gave out mixed messages about the role of the young people. In another setting professionals sought donations from firms, and a stylish design was devised with young people consulted as it developed. However, neither of these services drew young people into the management of the service beyond this consultative element.

It could be argued that the heavy focus on in-school education and provision drew attention away from the demands of targeting and working with excluded young people. For example, one community based drop-in was so successful in attracting young people to its weekly session that the youth work and nursing staff were overwhelmed by the sheer numbers. The final straw for the nurses involved in the drop-in was the boisterous behaviour of one group of young men who were seen as behaving in an "inappropriate" way which was likely to "scare off" older teenagers. As a result, this group of boys was banned from the service. This incident demonstrated a need for better understanding of the challenges of working with vulnerable young people, for all staff to be "skilled up" in youth work methods and for adequate support to be in place. Despite an assumption that young men were a key target group, little consideration was given to how best to deal with this group, which frequently included a range of maturity and of experience. In another setting, the drop-in service was suspended as a result of young people making inappropriate statements about the nature of the project which staff feared would attract adverse media coverage. The participation at strategic level of community education and youth workers might have helped to bolster a more positive environment, where links could be made between the actions of the young people and broader themes of exclusion (see also Chapter 8 by Andreas Walther).

The uneven staffing and management arrangements of the drop-in services clearly influenced the capacity of workers to deal with young people. Unlike the teaching staff, all development workers were on short-term contracts, and the predictably high turnover of staff further inhibited the development of the services. This had negative implications for building up relationships with young people, an aspect that has received considerable attention in the academic literature but less in the practice of social inclusion. Little support was available for those working with vulnerable young people in informal settings, in enlisting participation or in dealing with uncertain situations. Thus, while school nurses and health visitors expressed confidence about working in one-to-one consultations, few felt equipped to deal with the uncertainties of working in community settings with vulnerable young people.

Despite this, interviews with users of the drop-ins demonstrated that several staff made and sustained good relationships with client groups. Where drop-in staff were known and trusted by young people, they were seen not only as reliable sources of advice on sexual health, but also as capable of helping on a variety of mental and emotional issues, either by dealing with it themselves or referring on. This cut across professional boundaries, with young people in the user groups identifying individual outreach workers, school nurses and development workers as reliable and trustworthy.

One example of sustained work with vulnerable young people took the form of a fortnightly session for young gay men in a rural area. Particular problems existed for this group in accessing help and support – even attending the group meetings constituted some risk to maintaining anonymity. Although this was not a conventional drop-in, it offered similar services. The group designed their programme alongside a development worker and were involved in all aspects of this small-scale initiative. Numerous obstacles were put in their way: newspapers and bus companies refused to publicise the initiative, lack of co-operation from key agencies meant posters were sometimes hidden in offices or ripped off walls and the group was forced to meet in a series of inadequate premises. Despite these challenges, the group thrived and it was mainstreamed at the end of the demonstration project. The support from the demonstration project ensured credibility for the group and provided encouragement and advice for the setting up of similar groups in other areas. It is unlikely that this would have been the case without the support of the partnership and the demonstration project.

SHARE and linked drop-ins did provide a low threshold service that attracted young people. However, the time lag between the SHARE delivery and the inception of the drop-ins meant that some of these benefits were lost. In addition, the uneven staffing and management of the drop-in services resulted in variable opening hours, modes of operation, staffing and target groups. Appropriate premises proved elusive in several areas and opening times were rarely planned in relation to the needs of users. Clearly, the fieldwork partnership working was inadequately supported at a strategic level, since many of the problems arose from poor communication over ownership, design, staffing arrangements and managerial constraints.

Young people's participation

The presence of drop-ins was an important step forward in acknowledging the need for a diversity of services and some imaginative attempts were made to engage with young people. However, less evidence has been gleaned about how young people could become active participants in the processes of devising and managing services. Where partnership work was most successful it was highly localised and dependent on key staff rather than leverage from the initiative. The opportunities to capitalise on the demonstration project to develop bold experiments in working with young people was largely lost, in part because key agencies with skills in informal education were not included in the strategic partnership. Debate about how to involve young people was also missing, as partners struggled to negotiate the cultural differences and priorities in defining their own roles within the demonstration project. However, where parents and young people were involved, it strengthened the partnership work.

Perhaps the expectations of partnership were unrealistically high when we consider the extent of the cultural shifts that are implied in this multi-agency approach within the UK. Extending this to engage actively with young people poses further challenges, and suggests the need for radical rethinking about how young people are conceptualised and understood within professional discourses.

Key findings

In many respects, the work of the demonstration project highlighted the difficulties in developing partnerships that reach out and include vulnerable young people. It is clear that the heavy emphasis on work in schools may have drawn attention away from the challenges of working in non-school settings. The key role of strategic partnerships in underpinning such work, and in supporting fragile initiatives was strongly underlined. This is important in illuminating potential and real barriers to effective partnership working beyond sexual health.

Raising awareness can also increase the temperature of debates in a highly contested area. The implications of joint working for professional confidence and expertise are brought into sharp focus in working on sexual health. Bringing previously taboo issues into public policy and debate and involving representatives of activist groups served to broaden understanding and to focus on how to address prejudice at strategic and fieldwork levels (see Amineh Kakabaveh's analysis of similar issues for Kurdish women in Chapter 10).

The demonstration project facilitated some sharing of approaches and methods which enabled health and education workers to extend their own skills and to cascade these to others. However, much of the experience is too sporadic, localised and uneven for generalisations to be made. More analysis at strategic level of the complexity and processes of social exclusion would have strengthened the value of the shared learning.

Most disappointing was the lack of evidence of ways that young people could actively participate other than as users of services. This is clearly acknowledged by the partners and provides important lessons for further work in combating exclusion. The most useful legacy of the intervention was in making services accessible within a holistic attempt to deliver sex and relationships education. These hold important clues for developing strategies for informal learning. Building up a reputation as a reliable and confidential service which meets the diverse needs of young people within their communities requires strong support from stakeholders. This needs to be underpinned by continuing and reflexive articulation between education, training and dedicated service delivery.

The approach built on localised partnerships which set out to enhance and increase service provision and contributed to the development of national and local strategic action plans. It brought together key agencies of public health, clinical health and local authorities into a sustained partnership. Partnership was extended to the voluntary sector and although small in scale, these component projects benefited used this to provide a new platform for the issues on which they worked. In turn Healthy Respect benefited from their networks with local communities or specific population groups to promote an inclusive approach.

implications for European-level policies and practice

Research has confirmed clear interactions between poor sexual health and the processes of social exclusion. Increases in sexually transmitted infections, sexual abuse and exploitation, violence against young women, gender inequalities and risks of homophobic attacks hold clear implications for poor sexual health and for exclusion from the mainstream in relation to employment, successful family life and active citizenship (SEU, 1999). Poor sexual health disrupts educational and training opportunities for many young people and this in turn pushes them into further exclusion. Furthermore, this may reinforce a sense of fatalism about the potential of future generations to break through barriers to inclusion.

Healthy Respect was initiated by the health section of the Scottish Executive with the aim of tackling social exclusion by improving sexual health with a more flexible approach than that offered by existing school and service provision and by adopting a multi-agency approach. By blending a universal approach in schools with a targeted approach to disadvantaged groups, the initiative aimed to overcome traditional barriers to work in this field. Despite being sponsored by government, Healthy Respect did not succeed in developing high-level strategic partnerships which could support the work horizontally and vertically. The lack of interaction between education and health policy-making bodies, particularly at the outset, undermined much of the good intention.

Such partnerships at European levels could play a vital role in providing support to national and regional interventions. Recognition of the need to build social policy which takes account of the needs of vulnerable young people, of the cultural and social contexts in which they are making their transitions to adulthood and the value of strong links between inclusive approaches to employment, participation and active citizenship have been strongly made and, arguably, implicitly promote a holistic approach (Call for papers, Research Seminar on Social Inclusion and Young People: a research seminar to inform policy and practice, August 2005). However, this needs to be embedded within formal and informal educational and health domains in order to ensure coherent strategic work can be developed within sustainable frameworks.

A recent call by the Commission of the European Communities to the Council, the European Economic and Social Committee and the Committee of the Regions offers an approach which implicitly encompasses the improvement of sexual health in aiming:

> "to give priority, under the social inclusion strategy to improving the situation for the most vulnerable young people and to initiatives to prevent educational failure as a contribution to the European Youth Pact" (European Commission, 2006, p. 3).

Elsewhere in this document, reference is made to the need for an increasing role for health promotion and disease prevention policies. However, this document focuses on the elderly, and makes little reference to how this would be applied with young people. Similarly, little connection is made between this approach and efforts to take a long-term perspective on promoting social cohesion and eliminating gaps between rich and poor,

> "The perspective of sustainability places the long-term dimensions of social protection and social inclusion policies firmly in the policy frame, giving added impetus to focus on child poverty, through which poverty and exclusion pass

> from generation to generation and Europe's future human resources are diminished" (ibid., p. 6)

It goes on to reinforce the value of partnership working:

> "One of the key policy messages to emerge from work under the OMC is that policy making and delivery bears fruit if all actors, branches and levels of government work together and suggests that this has been evident in the NAPS work on mainstreaming social inclusion" (ibid., p. 7).

However, strategies which link the improvement of the sexual health of young people with efforts to enhance social exclusion are not explicit in policy documents at European levels. It is important for this to be remedied since the intervention reported in this chapter has demonstrated that tackling social exclusion by improving sexual health has potential to enhance the capacity of young people themselves. Positive aspects of good sexual health include enhanced respect for relationships with partners and others, better understanding of concepts of sharing and consideration for others, improved communication and negotiation skills and critical reflection on stereotypical assumptions. In sum this implies more potential for a sense of agency in dealing with social relationships and an understanding of the social forces that shape and underpin intimate behaviour. Importantly, it can illuminate links between social stereotypes and gender roles and help to challenge discriminatory practices. By opening up discussion about homophobic bullying, sexual harassment and violence, spaces can be created for more active engagement between young people and their social worlds.

References

Alexiadou, N. (2002), "Social inclusion and social exclusion in England: tensions in education policy", *Journal of Education Policy*, 17(1), pp. 71-86.

Berkeley, D. and Ross, D. (2003), "Strategies for improving the sexual health of young people", *Culture, Health and Sexuality*, 5(1), pp. 71-86.

Brook Clinic (1998), *Someone with a smile would be your best bet ... What young people want from sex advice services*. London: Brook Advisory Service.

Burtney, E. (2000), "Briefing paper on teenage sexuality in Scotland". Edinburgh: Health Education Board for Scotland.

Chisholm, L. and Hoskins, B. (2005), "Introduction: tracks and tools for trading up in non-formal learning", in Chisholm, L. and Hoskins, B. (eds.), *Trading up: potential and performance in non-formal learning*. Strasbourg: Council of Europe Publishing.

Coles, R. (2000), *Joined-up youth research, policy and practice*. Leicester: Youth Work Press.

Corlyon, J. and Maguire, C. (1999), *Pregnancy and parenthood: the views of young people in public care*. London: National Children's Bureau.

Council of Europe (1998), Convention for the Protection of Human Rights and Fundamental Freedoms as amended by Protocol No. 11 (online). Strasbourg: Council of Europe (accessed 28 January 2006). Available at: http://conventions.coe.int/treaty/en/Treaties/html/005.htm.

European Commission (2006), "Joint report on social protection and social inclusion" (online). Brussels: European Commission (accessed 28 September 2006).

Available at:
www.lex.unict.it/eurolabor/en/documentation/com/2006/com(2006)62en.pdf#search=%22COM%202006%2062%20Final%22.

Franklin, B. (1995), "Introduction", in Franklin, B. (ed.), *The handbook of children's rights*. London: Routledge.

Glazier, A. (2002), "Sexual health services for young people. Report of teenage sexuality in Scotland Deliberative Seminar on Young People and Sexual Health". Edinburgh: Health Education Board for Scotland.

Goveas, A. (2005), "Confusion over strategy's effect", *Children Now*, 20-26 July.

Hendry, L.B., Shucksmith, J. and Philip, K. (1995), *Educating for health: school and community approaches with adolescents*. London: Cassells.

Measor, L. (2004), *Young people's views of sex education: education, attitudes and behaviour*. London: Routledge

Milbourne, L., Macrae, S. and Maguire, M. (2003), "Collaborative solutions or new policy problems: exploring multi-agency partnerships in education and health work", *Journal of Education Policy*, 18(1), pp. 19-35.

Redman, J., Goudie, H. and Taylor, K. (1997), "Angus young people's health project: making health services more appropriate and accessible", *Health Education*, 2, pp. 65-71.

Rolston, B., Shubotz, D. and Simpson, A. (2005), "Sex education in Northern Ireland schools: a critical evaluation", *Sex Education*, 5(3), pp. 217-235.

Scottish Office (1999), "Towards a healthier Scotland: a White Paper on health". Edinburgh: The Stationery Office.

Shucksmith, J. and Hendry, L.B. (1998), *Health issues and adolescents: growing up and speaking out*. London: Routledge.

Shucksmith, J., Philip, K. and Spratt, J. (2005), "Young people's mental health and well-being in schools: final report to Scottish Executive". Edinburgh: Scottish Executive Education Department, Pupil Support Division.

Social Exclusion Unit (1999a), *Teenage pregnancy*. London: The Stationery Office.

Social Exclusion Unit (1999b), *Bridging the gap*. London: The Stationery Office.

Swann, C., Bowe, K., McCormick, G. and Kosmin, M. (2003), *Teenage pregnancy and parenthood: a review of reviews. Evidence briefing*. London: Health Development Agency.

Thomson, R. and Scott, S. (1990), "Researching sexuality in the light of HIV/Aids". WRAP Paper 5. London: Tufnell Press.

Tucker, J., van Teijlingen, E., Shucksmith, J., Philip, K., Penney, G. and Immamura, M. (2005), "External evaluation of healthy respect, a national health demonstration project. Final report to the Chief Scientist Office". Aberdeen: University of Aberdeen.

Wight, D. and Abraham, C. (2000), "From psycho-social theory to sustainable classroom practice: developing a research-based teacher delivered sex education programme", *Health Education Research*, 15(1), pp. 25-38

Wight, D. and Buston, K. (2003), "Meeting needs but not changing goals: evaluation of in-service teacher training for sex education", *Oxford Review of Education*, 29(4), pp. 521-543.

Wight, D., Raab, G., Henderson, M., Abraham, C., Buston, K., Hart, G. and Scott, S. (2002), "Limits of teacher delivered sex education: interim behavioural outcomes from randomised trial", *British Medical Journal*, 32(4), pp. 1-6.

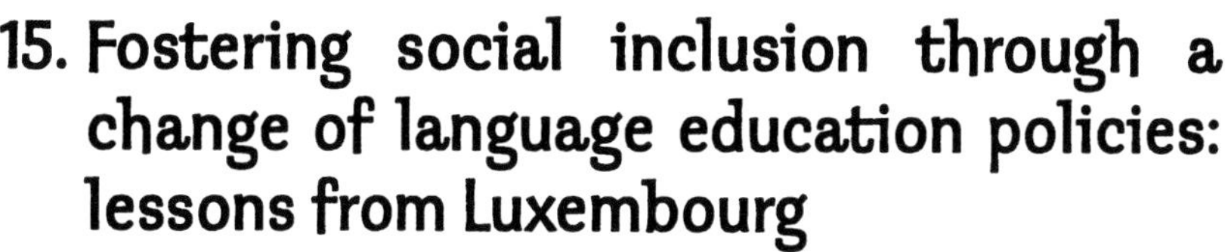

15. Fostering social inclusion through a change of language education policies: lessons from Luxembourg

Christiane Weis

introduction

In the joint report on social inclusion by the European Commission and the Council of the European Union, assessing the related national action plans of all member states, one of the challenges signalled was to tackle poverty and social exclusion faced by young people. Young people deprived of skills (for example, early school-leavers with no qualifications) are particularly at risk of social exclusion. In this context, one of the key priorities was to "implement a concerted effort to prevent early school leaving and to promote smooth transition from school to work".

The Grand Duchy of Luxembourg has put particular emphasis on planning measures to promote the social inclusion of young people under 25 by preventing school failure and loss of employment, as well as specific measures for young people in situations of distress. Given the complex language situation in Luxembourg (described in greater detail below), specific policy initiatives have been taken to address the risks of social exclusion that language can pose for young people. In collaboration with the Centre d'Études sur la Situation des Jeunes en Europe (CESIJE: Study Centre on the Situation of Young People in Europe), the Ministère de l'Éducation nationale et de la Formation professionnelle (MENFP: Ministry for National Education and Vocational Training) has enlisted the help of the Council of Europe in establishing an educational language policy profile (Council of Europe Language Policy Division, 2004). This profile will make it possible to describe the status of language education in Luxembourg. It should also help identify the steps or reforms required to improve the language and communication skills of Luxembourgish youth, while ensuring that language requirements do not become a barrier to gaining a qualification.

There are two parts to the scheme defined by the Council of Europe. Firstly, CESIJE, mandated by the ministry, issued a report illustrating the complexity of the language situation in Luxembourg. After having received the report, the Council of Europe experts spent a week in the Grand Duchy. During their stay, they were able to visit schools and meet some of the staff concerned. Following this visit, the group reporter worked closely with the other experts to produce an expert report summarising their comments and giving their point of view on the language situation in

Luxembourg (Goullier et al., 2005). The experts' observations and propositions were discussed during a round table meeting in December 2005. Following this round table, the group of experts then wrote the country profile (Goullier et al., 2006), which was jointly published by the Luxembourg Government and the Council of Europe in the spring of 2006. This profile presents the experts' observations and analysis of the situation, and gives suggestions as to how the ministry should orient its policy.

This chapter draws on a larger study of educational language policies in Luxembourg (Berg and Weis, 2005), focusing on the first stage of the process described above. Its aim is to analyse the impact of language education policies on the social inclusion process of young people. In the first part, I describe the heterogeneous composition of Luxembourg's society and sketch its complex language situation. The second part analyses how the school system copes with plurilingualism and the problems it generates. In the final section, I will try to identify and explore strategies for improving the system in a sustainable way, in particular by developing a language education policy agenda that furthers the social inclusion of young people. Given the increasingly multicultural nature of communities across Europe, these conclusions are likely to have wider relevance beyond Luxembourg itself (see, for example, Chapters 10 and 11 by Amineh Kakabaveh and Anna Kende in this book).

Methodologically, the analysis presented here rests on an epistemological optimism, respecting social actors' own interpretations; mirroring and mapping discourses and situations; developing visions from the existing status quo; and contributing to the co-construction of political agendas (cf. Milmeister and Williamson, 2006). The main data used were documentary, such as research reports, policy documents, newspaper and journal articles. In the process of data analysis, academic literature was not automatically assigned a higher status than other statements concerning the country's language situation.

The heterogeneity of Luxembourg society and its impact on language usage

Luxembourg's population has been steadily growing since the start of the 20th century: in 2001, the population was 439 500 inhabitants (compared to 234 600 in 1900, 314 900 in 1960 and 384 400 in 1991). Population expansion is mainly the result of immigration, the number of nationals having risen only slightly. One of the major characteristics of Luxembourg society is therefore its increasing heterogeneity. In relation to its size, it has an extremely international population, with a high proportion of foreigners. In 2001, foreign nationals accounted for 36.9% of the general population, and in 2004, this was estimated by the Service central de la Statistique et des Études économiques (STATEC, the Central Service for Statistics and Studies in Economics) to have risen to 38.6% (STATEC, 2004). Immigrants come mainly from other European countries, particularly Portugal, Italy and then the bordering countries of France, Belgium and Germany, and finally from the ex-Yugoslavian countries. The high level of diversity gives rise to a certain number of questions concerning cultural integration. Major changes in the usage and status of the different languages in use are already clearly visible, notably in the workplace, where foreign workers – both residents and borderers (namely, those living near the border and crossing it to work) – can be found in large numbers, a presence which has risen steeply since the 1990s. According to STATEC, in 2004 the workforce consisted of 33.4% Luxembourg nationals, 27.2% foreign residents and 39.4% borderers (from France, Belgium and Germany).

> "Half of the labour force is foreign, this figure including both foreigners living in Luxembourg and the borderers, the *frontaliers*, *Grenzgänger*, who daily commute to Luxembourg across the borders from one of the neighbouring countries, France, Belgium or Germany. This inevitably has a significant influence on the use of languages as communication, especially in the working place and in commerce" (Hansen-Pauly, 2002, p. 147).

The complex language situation of a multilingual[1] country

The language situation in Luxembourg is rather complex, as three languages, French, German and Luxembourgish, are commonly in use. Unlike Switzerland and Belgium, no linguistic regions have been defined. The inhabitants generally speak several languages and in daily communication, different languages co-exist side by side. In addition, the languages preferred for oral and written communication are not necessarily the same. Finally, with immigration and the opening of the economy, the languages spoken by immigrants, particularly Portuguese, Italian and the international languages (notably English), have become widespread and are gradually being adapted to their new environment.

Some authors develop the image of a parallel between linguistic and social hierarchies. Gilbert Trausch explains that in Luxembourg, the three languages are superimposed hierarchically in a pyramid shape with, from the base to the top, Luxembourgish, German and finally French (Trausch, 1986, p. 10). Claudia Hartmann-Hirsch (1998) found that Luxembourg's society is characterised by strong foreign representation at both extremes of the social ladder. She used the image of the pyramid to represent society. The pyramid shape also reflects language organisation in Luxembourg. The everyday French spoken with migrants forms the base of the pyramid, then comes Luxembourgish, then German, and finally a standardised "upper class" French (and to a lesser extent English) which, in Luxembourg, have legitimate language status. Although it is evident that a link exists between inequality and social status on the one hand and differentiation of communication practices on the other, it is nonetheless difficult to reduce these systems systematically to a simple mirror image of each other. Variations of these languages exist and their status can change, depending on the context or situation in which they are used. Models that tend to oversimplify the situation have only a limited value for the coherent development of an educational language policy. They are often the result of the tension inherent in the language situation in Luxembourg, where migrants are necessarily confronted with choices to be made and rendered official. They are also sometimes obliged to calculate the relative benefits of learning or using one language as opposed to another (Tonnar-Meyer, 2003).[2]

1. I use the terms "plurilingualism" and "multilingualism" as they are defined by the Council of Europe: multilingualism refers to the presence of several languages in a given geographical area and plurilingualism refers to a person's competence, the repertoire of languages that he or she uses to communicate.
2. "Defined in this way, plurilingualism is a characteristic of every speaker: it is not relevant only to officially multilingual countries, i.e. situations in which the multilingual nature of society is recognised and identified as such (federal structures, regions with a special linguistic status, urban environments)" (Beacco and Byram, 2003, p. 67).

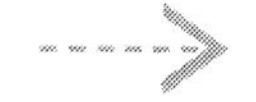

However, the status of a language is often complex: it may change rapidly, be deployed in paradoxical ways, and be viewed differently in different communities and situations. One interesting example is French, the status of which has changed dramatically in the course of the last century: from being the distinctive sign of the upper social strata, of the city-dwelling worthies, it has become the primary means of communication between Luxembourg nationals and non-Luxembourgers. In addition, as it has become the primary working language in many socio-professional categories, particularly amongst blue-collar workers, it has lost its elite nature and become a popular language (Tonnar-Meyer, 2003, p. 81). Given the communication practices that emerged owing to the strong presence of migrants and borderers, the use of French as an oral language has become widespread. It is much more commonly used than Luxembourgish for shopping, in restaurants and in cafés (Fehlen et al., 1998, p. 36).

To provide insight into how plurilingualism is perceived on a daily basis, I will describe language usage in two daily situations, in the family and in the workplace. Most families use their mother tongue at home (Fehlen et al., 1998). Luxembourger parents generally speak Luxembourgish to their children. By the same token, Portuguese parents will speak Portuguese to their children and are generally proud to transmit their linguistic heritage to them (Beirao, 1999, p. 97); almost 80% of Portuguese immigrants consider that learning Portuguese is important (Dubajic, 2002, p. 387).

The situation is different in the economic arena, where there is growing linguistic diversity owing to the strong presence of foreigners (residents and borderers). Analysis of language usage shows that French is most in demand, followed by German, English and Luxembourgish. There are, however, sector-related differences (Piroth and Fehlen, 2000). The labour market has indeed become internationalised, but segmentation into external and internal sectors has also developed in parallel. For the "more protected" sectors, often characterised by a strong national presence, knowledge of the three working languages of the country is often a prerequisite, thus restricting access of foreigners to these sectors. For the "less protected" companies, which employ a high proportion of foreign workers and therefore often have a more international outlook, Luxembourgish and the traditional trilingualism are less important. Finally, the demands of the company's different suppliers and clients – not generally restricted here by reference to specific norms, as would be the case in an officially monolingual country – necessarily influence the reality of economic communication. It is evident, for example, that the rise of the services industry in today's era of globalisation particularly promotes the use of English. As companies now not only conduct their business at a local level, but also extend beyond national frontiers and operate in the international markets, they no longer insist strongly that their employees have the language skills traditionally and officially expected in Luxembourg (Weitzel, 2002).

It is nonetheless difficult to draw conclusions concerning socio-cultural practice as regards use of languages in the workplace. Primarily, mastery of a language can, of course, form part of the individual's cultural and social capital. But it appears clear that there is no regulatory norm that unequivocally determines language use. Various mechanisms, such as differences between socially unequal groups, labour market structure and economic function, combine to give shape to the vague and complex landscape with which we are confronted.

In conclusion, it can be said that, in Luxembourg, mastery of several languages is the norm, as is switching easily and frequently from one to another. Generally speaking, Luxembourgers will adapt their language to the person with whom they are speaking: that is, they do not wait for the foreigner to speak to them in their language. Faced with this situation, one gets the impression that neither French, nor German nor even Luxembourgish can be fully considered to be mother tongues. Perhaps plurilingualism could be regarded as the hidden mother tongue of many Luxembourgers and Luxembourg residents.

The role of languages in the educational system

Without a doubt, most language learning takes place in school. The educational system reflects the multilingual situation of Luxembourg society. German, French and Luxembourgish are mandatory.

"Today, an average 50% of a child's time at school will be spent learning languages (both general and technical sections)" (Boisseau, 2003, p. 4).

Languages effectively play a very important role throughout schooling: this role is twofold. When looking at the position of languages in Luxembourg's educational system, two different aspects must be taken into account. On the one hand, languages are scholastic disciplines, and are as much a part of the school curriculum as any other subject. On the other hand, languages are used as vehicles for learning (and communication), and allow pupils to acquire other knowledge.

Luxembourgish only plays an important role in pre-school teaching and in early education. This is particularly important for children of immigrants who often encounter Luxembourgish for the first time at *maternelle* (kindergarten). Luxembourgish is considered to be a necessary prerequisite for a successful school career. In fact, a good knowledge of Luxembourgish can be considered to open the door towards learning German (Maurer-Hetto et al., 2003).

Second languages are introduced at primary school. Children learn to read and write in German. German is not simply the language of literacy, it is also used when teaching a certain number of other subjects. While Luxembourgish only plays a minor role at primary school, French lessons begin in second year.

Beyond the primary level, education in Luxembourg is divided into two sections, general secondary education (SE) and technical secondary education (TSE). (Despite the fact that the ministry has organised a series of valorisation campaigns for the technical secondary education, general secondary education is still regarded as the section leading to better diplomas and job opportunities (Fehlen, 1994).) German and French lessons are continued at this level, while English is taught from the second year of secondary education. It has a rather unusual status, given that it is considered to be the first foreign language taught in Luxembourg's educational system. As far as teaching of non-linguistic subjects is concerned, there are differences between the general and technical secondary education sections: in SE, German is the teaching language for the first three years, followed by French. In TSE, the whole curriculum is taught in German.

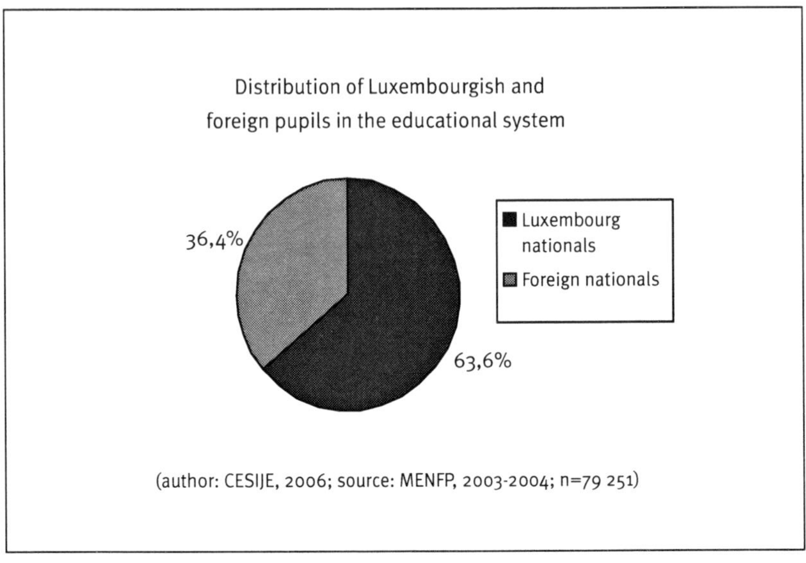

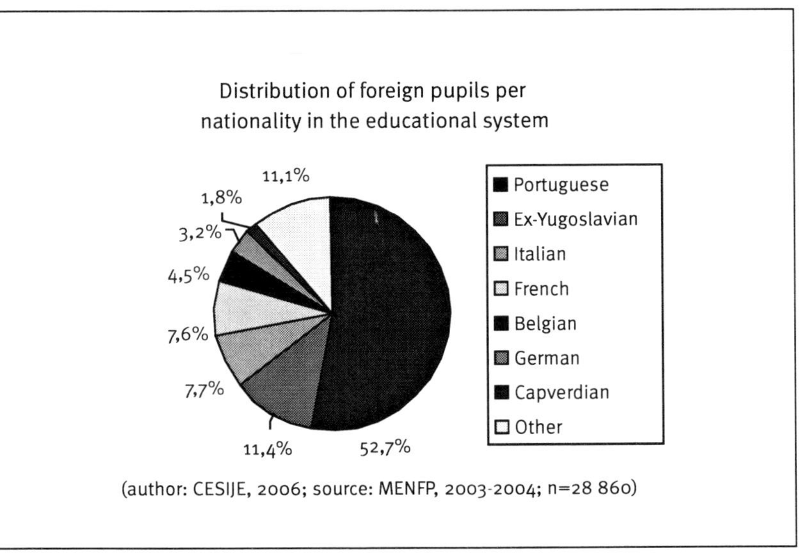

With its heterogeneous composition, the school population reflects closely the structure of Luxembourg society. The analysis of the distribution of pupils per nationality shows that 63.6% of pupils are Luxembourg nationals and 36.4% foreign nationals (school year 2003-04). Of the foreign nationals, the Portuguese form the largest group, accounting for 52.7%. This group is followed by pupils of ex-Yugoslavian origin (11.4%), Italians (7.7%), French (7.6%), Belgians (4.5%), Germans (3.2%) and Capverdians (1.8%) (Lanners et al., 2005, p. 19).

The foreigner-national ratio is not the same throughout the educational system. This is most evident in post-primary teaching, where clear differences can be observed from one section to another. In technical secondary education, foreigners account for 37.9% of the population versus 16.5% in general secondary education.

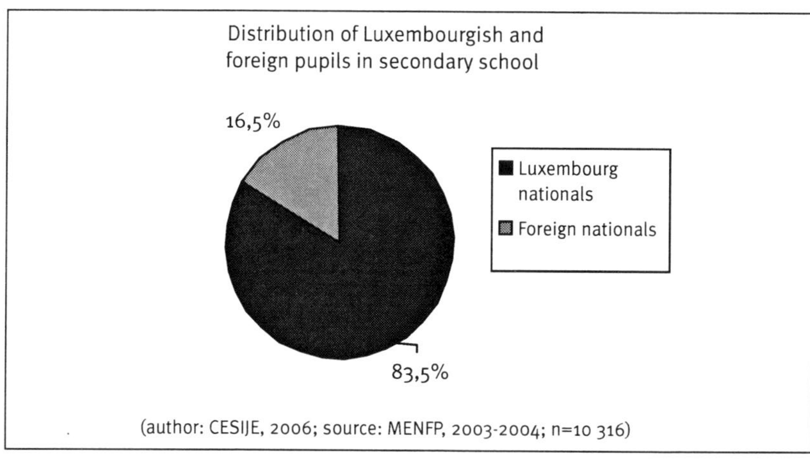

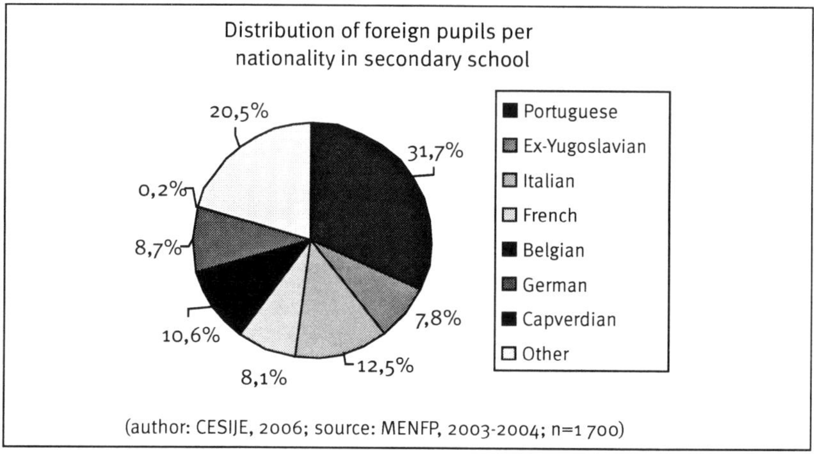

In general secondary education, Portuguese are the majority group of foreign pupils with 31.7%, followed by Italians (12.5%), Belgians (10.6%), Germans (8.7%), French (8.1%), ex-Yugoslavians (7.8%) and Capverdians (0.2%) (Lanners et al., 2005, p. 47).

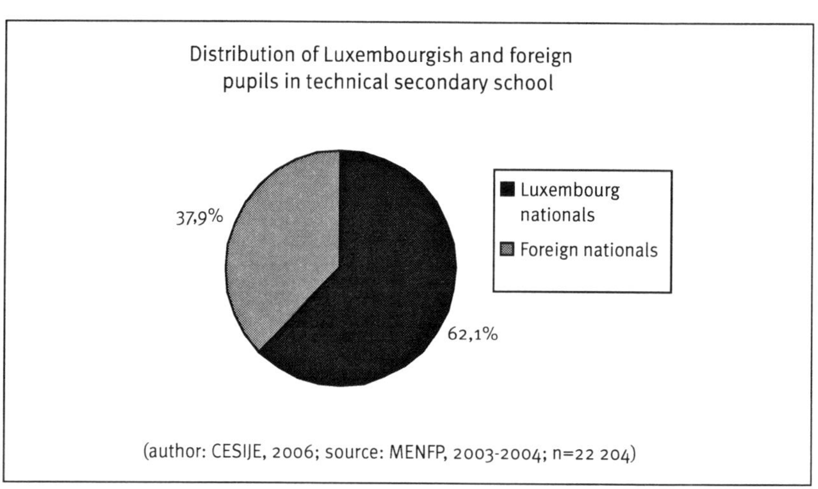

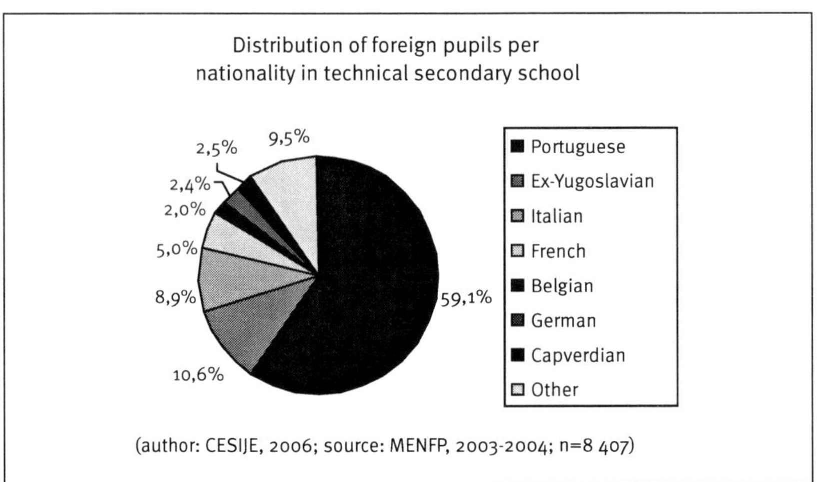

(author: CESIJE, 2006; source: MENFP, 2003-2004; n=8 407)

The foreign population present in technical secondary education can be divided as follows: the Portuguese who are again the majority group (59.1%), followed by nationals from ex-Yugoslavia (10.6%), Italians (8.9%), French (5%), Germans (2.4%), Capverdians (2.5%) and Belgians (2%) (Lanners et al., 2005, p. 55).

The marginal position of Luxembourgish in the educational system

Strangely enough, the national language of Luxembourg, "Lëtzebuergesch" or Luxembourgish, is the poor relative in the educational system.

"We are one of the few countries in which the national language plays such a minimal role in education: there is only one Luxembourgish lesson a week in primary school and even less in secondary education. In contrast, the other languages account for almost 50% of time spent in the classroom" (Tonnar-Meyer, 2003, p. 83).

As a result, Luxembourgish is only rarely used as anything other than an oral language. The average Luxembourgish reader only has a vague idea of the spelling and grammar of the language he speaks, although these have been clearly defined. Even "educated" Luxembourgers holding important positions in their country's society do not necessarily have a particularly good knowledge of the national language. On the contrary, in the media they often express themselves using a linguistic mix that owes much to French, sometimes with some German or English thrown in for good measure, and one that is painful to the ears of those who hold Luxembourgish dear.

Luxembourg's educational system and children of immigrant origin

Many foreign children, as mentioned above, are present in Luxembourg's educational system (36.4%). This non-Luxembourger population mainly consists of children speaking one of the Romance languages (52.7% Portuguese, 7.7% Italian, 7.6% French, 4.5% Belgian-French, 1.8% Capverdian = ~ 74%). Besides these Romance language-speaking children, two other populations are also important: the ex-Yugoslavians (11.4%) and the Germans (3.2%).

Learning Luxembourgish has always been of vital importance for foreign children. Before early education (for 3-year-olds) was started, these children often first encountered the national language in kindergarten (at age 4). One of the major problems was that the children never fully mastered the language and, even after two years of pre-school learning, had considerably fallen behind their Luxembourger counterparts.

> "In the following school years, a 'scissor' effect can be seen, in that what may start out as a slight delay in learning is gradually accentuated and leads almost inevitably to academic failure" (Martin, 1995, p. 33).

The creation of "early education" was a decisive step towards remedying this situation. The primary aim of early education was to enable these children to learn Luxembourgish by bringing them into daily contact with their Luxembourger counterparts (Folscheid et al., 2004). However, studies show that, despite these measures, foreign children do not reach the same level in Luxembourgish as mother tongue pupils. They may have a good command of Luxembourgish but it does not equal the mastery of a mother tongue, which is necessary to access the German language easily.

Furthermore, in Luxembourg's educational system, the native Romance language speakers are disadvantaged compared to their Luxembourgish-speaking counterparts.

> "This is due to the fact that the two foreign languages, German and French, are not taught at the same speed" (Martin, 1995, p. 31).

German is taught and expected to be learnt much faster than French. This primary school curriculum is ideally adapted to pupils who have Luxembourgish as their mother tongue, since Luxembourgish lays a basis for learning German. For them, giving precedence to German as the language of learning can be considered to lighten the burden of the subjects to be learnt. However, it penalises Romance language-speaking children (Beirao, 1997), for whom German is much more difficult. Recourse to French would therefore appear to be preferable for the children of many immigrants (Martin, 1995, p. 32). In addition, such children also have to learn the language of their forebears, which means that they are often confronted with four languages (German, French, Luxembourgish and their own mother tongue).

> "It is therefore not at all surprising that a high proportion of immigrant children fail at languages right from the start of their school career" (Martin, 1995, p. 31).

These problems are particularly accentuated at two stages in the educational system: the first years of primary school, and the passage into secondary education (Berg and Thoss, 1996). Teaching reading and writing in German slows down the acquisition of the language itself, and is an impediment to the development of cognitive and communication skills in the children. It can sometimes be an insurmountable barrier for Romance language-speaking children. The problem is even greater when one considers that the difficulties encountered in primary school will continue into and worsen at secondary school.

> "For these children, the problems will continue into secondary education; owing to their failings in German, they will not have access to the prestigious classes in secondary education where French is the major teaching language" (Fehlen, 1997b, p. 40).

These problems are difficult to overcome, particularly since it would be unthinkable to abandon the trilingualism that characterises Luxembourg's educational system. For a certain time, there was much debate about the possibility of teaching reading

and writing in French. One of the main criticisms levelled at this idea was that it might create two categories of learners with very disparate language skills. This could result in the formation of two distinct linguistic communities (Fayot, 2001).

Steps taken

As we have seen, the children of immigrants are often victims of Luxembourg's educational system. As a result, the MENFP has developed a series of measures intended to promote the integration of children while preserving their cultural identity. The integration measures particularly of interest here concern the creation of classes in which the teaching language is French, that is where all subjects are taught in French, and of "integration classes" where German or French are taught using intensive methods. In technical secondary education, induction classes have been set up. These are open to pupils who have not been through Luxembourg's educational system. After the induction class, the pupils follow the curriculum in a language immersion class which will subsequently enable them to join the mainstream system.

Other steps have been taken over recent years: efforts have been made to inform non-native-speaking parents and heighten their awareness through information meetings and exchanges. Information sheets intended for parents have been translated into several languages (Portuguese, English, Serbo-Croat and Albanian). In addition, intercultural mediators play an important role in the communication between teacher and parent (MENFP, 2005).

However, can all these measures effectively resolve the problems encountered by Luxembourg's educational system?

> "We must nevertheless ask ourselves whether offering more numerous and diverse French-speaking courses is the long-term answer to the problem of integration of children of immigrants in Luxembourg's educational system. It appears idealistic to recommend splitting in two all the existing courses in Luxembourg" (Martin, 1995, p. 44).

Demographic changes must also be taken into consideration in this equation: the immigrant population is no longer exclusively Romance language-speaking, many now come from the east, particularly from the Balkans. Of course, for such children lessons in French would in no way be an advantage.

Challenges for Luxembourg's educational system

Luxembourg's educational system faces a double challenge: it must not impede the integration of foreigners by erecting insurmountable linguistic barriers, but on the other hand it must continue to guarantee standards of excellence for pupils that will allow them to meet with success in Luxembourg's labour market. The system has not always been able to rise to this double challenge and the perverse effects of an educational system based on plurilingualism have appeared:

> "... the fact that multilingual teaching takes its toll particularly in primary school must not be ignored. If it appears that, for those at the top, learning foreign languages is a means of communicational and cultural qualification, at the other end of the scale, it becomes a means of academic selection, and even exclusion and social reproduction" (Berg and Thoss, 1996, p. 88).

Along with mathematics, languages are a cause of academic failure for many pupils. German is the first "means" by which Romance language-speaking pupils are isolated in the educational system, particularly during the transition from primary to secondary education. Next comes French, the language of prestige, which is a cause of failure for Luxembourger pupils from less culturally privileged families (Fehlen, 1997). Success in Luxembourg's educational system is reserved for an elite the system has a tendency to reproduce. While plurilingualism has been fully embraced by this elite, it can make life difficult for those who do not share their mastery of the official languages. Take for example a Portuguese immigrant family: speaking a regional dialect and having suffered the trauma of their inability to communicate on their arrival in the country, the parents have learnt only the basics of French. At school, their child could very well be penalised if asked to learn Luxembourgish, German and French in a very short time span. The dynamic and communicative teaching methods, with a sort of didactic violence, will force the child into expressing himself in a new language too quickly, and may in the long run damage his or her communication skills. Mastery of foreign languages therefore becomes an element of social distinction:

> "That languages should be used to differentiate but also as a source of intellectual and cultural enrichment: such is the vision that has predominated and predominates still. This view supposes major sacrifices on the part of children and is particularly favourable to the elites" (Trausch, 1986, p. 20).

Over and above the problems related to language learning, the individual's social background continues to have a significant impact on academic success. Academic and social success is neither entirely nor primarily dictated by educational policy. In this context it is interesting to note that parents play a crucial role in Luxembourg's educational system (Davis, 1994, p. 109). They must assist their children with their homework. However, expectations and motivations differ considerably from one social class to another. Besides, unemployment, accommodation, health and other problems often prevent parents from managing their child's education in satisfactory conditions. This is true for both immigrant parents and Luxembourg nationals encountering the same type of difficulties. Ensuring that all children have an equal chance for success is therefore a national challenge that must be taken up by Luxembourg's society as a whole: it goes far beyond the bounds of the educational system which, without assistance, will not be able to guarantee equal opportunities for all (Hartmann-Hirsch, 1994).

Conclusions

Multilingualism in Luxembourg is related to the country's history. Recognising this in no way means to be struck by some kind of sociological blindness (see criticism from Fehlen, 2006), since multilingualism is also an economic and cultural necessity. For people living in Luxembourg, multilingualism is a rich opportunity, but is also an obligation and can be seen as a double-edged sword. It is an extraordinary resource, while at the same time it can constitute a source of academic failure and social exclusion. For some, plurilingualism will be an enriching experience, adding to their cultural capital and allowing them to communicate and participate in the cultural life of several countries. For others, it can be a stigma, the actual trigger of a "negative career". It will be a breeding ground for "semi-lingualism", preventing the acquisition of language skills and leading to illiteracy. It could also severely hinder language development in the children and adolescents concerned, and may also impair their mental health and social success. In the Luxembourgish school system a certain number of pupils are, so to speak, inside school but outside learning.

It is therefore one of the factors which is shaping what may eventually become a two-speed educational system and which could both enrich and detract from Luxembourg society. To date, the educational system has not acted as a coherent whole. It has become clear that the debate on languages may cause segregation by establishing social groups based on language skills. This could happen particularly in a society which, faced with poorly managed complexity, will not develop the social reflexivity required to formulate appropriate questions or knowledge to deal with this complexity, based notably on empirical evidence. And indeed, current national curricula no longer reflect the reality of communication in an open and culturally diverse society and must undergo radical change. Plurilingualism can be maintained through a public policy that is adapted to the new economic and social realities, while its negative effects should be minimised and its advantages made available to the greatest number possible.

Defining the profile of a future educational language policy is a major element in an innovative social inclusion strategy whose aim is to promote the continuing prosperity of the urban area centred around Luxembourg, through enhanced competitiveness. It is therefore an important task which could have an impact on the future of the country, and requires synergistic and coherent input from a variety of sectors. In general, it appears important that educational language policy should be compatible with the general economic and cultural framework, and that it should fall within the scope of sustainable social development. In order to define the next steps, there is a need for greater knowledge of the language situation in Luxembourg and the Grande Région (composed of the Saarland, the Rhineland-Palatinate, the Lorraine, Luxembourg and the Wallonia, consisting of the French community and the German-speaking community of Belgium), and of its social implications. Developing general and more specific policies for Luxembourg's educational system, and monitoring their implementation via a transparent and reliable evaluation system, able to cope with the complexity of the situation in Luxembourg, would appear to be the primary areas for didactic and methodological work. In relation to this, the initial training and continuing professional development of teachers obviously has a role to play (although Lorna Roberts warns of the danger of overemphasising teachers' power to effect change in Chapter 12).

The Luxembourgish situation is certainly not a unique one. The kind of language problems described above have to be faced by foreign pupils in many other countries as well. Europe having always been multilingual, as it is now and will remain in the future, migration and language problems are issues with which Europe as a whole will have to deal in coming years. Measures implemented in the Luxembourgish context could be a contribution to a common European language policy. According to the Council of Europe, the development of plurilingualism is essential for increased and more effective intercultural understanding, international co-operation, mobility and employment opportunities. The Council's activities in the domain of language policy aim at promoting plurilingualism and pluriculturalism among European citizens. Furthermore, languages are indispensable to participate in active citizenship. The education system should therefore enable each resident to become a citizen and to participate in the democratic and cultural life of his/her country.

"All languages for all" is certainly a maximalist, unrealistic slogan, but it is also the concise, jubilant expression of a viable educational project (education for plurilingualism as valuing and developing everyone's linguistic repertoire) and the identification of a consensual value (education for plurilingual awareness as education in linguistic tolerance) that are both constituents of democratic citizenship in Europe." (Beacco and Byram, 2003, p. 29)

References

Beacco, J.-C. and Byram, M. (2003), "Guide for the development of language education policies in Europe. From linguistic diversity to plurilingual education". Strasbourg: Council of Europe Language Policy Division.

Beirao, D. (1999), *Les Portugais du Luxembourg. Des familles racontent leur vie*. Paris: L'Harmattan.

Berg, C. (2003), "The role of grounded theory and collaborative research", *Reading Research Quarterly*, 38(1), pp. 105-111.

Berg, C. and Thoss, R. (1996), "Une situation de multilinguisme. Le cas du Luxembourg", *Revue internationale d'éducation*, 9, pp. 79-90.

Berg, C. and Weis, C. (2005), *Sociologie de l'enseignement des langues dans un environnement multilingue. Rapport national en vue de l'élaboration du profil des politiques linguistiques éducatives luxembourgeoises*. Luxembourg: Ministère de l'Éducation nationale et de la Formation professionnelle (MENFP)/ Centre d'Études sur la Situation des Jeunes en Europe (CESIJE).

Boisseau, M. (2003), *A propos ... des langues*. Luxembourg: service information et presse du gouvernement du Grand-Duché de Luxembourg.

Chambre des députés (2004), "Débat d'orientation sur la politique d'immigration. Rapport de la commission spéciale 'immigration'". Luxembourg: Service central des imprimés de l'État.

Council of Europe Language Policy Division (2004), "Languages, diversity, citizenship. language education policy profile. Guidelines and procedures". DGIV/EDU/LANG (2002) 1 Rev. 5 (online). Strasbourg: Council of Europe Language Policy Division (accessed 29 September 2006). Available at: www.coe.int/t/dg4/linguistic/Source/GuidelinesPol_EN.pdf.

Davis, K.A. (1994), *Language planning in multilingual contexts. Policies, communities and schools in Luxembourg*. Philadelphia: John Benjamins Publishing Company.

Dubajic, N. (2002), "Les relations aux autres dans une société multiculturelle", in Legrand, M. (ed.), *Les valeurs au Luxembourg – portrait d'une société au tournant du 3e millénaire*. Luxembourg: Éditions St Paul.

Ewen, N. (2005), "L'illettrisme en actes", *Forum*, 246, pp. 34-37.

Fayot, B. (2001), "Pour une politique des langues au Luxembourg", *Luxemburger Wort*, 27, p. 11.

Fehlen, F. (1994), "Die portugiesischen Schüler. Eine statistische Beschreibung ihrer Chancen im Sekundarunterricht", *Forum*, 156, pp. 19-27.

Fehlen, F. (1997a), "De l'importance économique du luxembourgeois", *Forum*, 177, pp. 31-36.

Fehlen, F. (1997b), "Parlez français, s.v.p.!", *Forum*, 177, pp. 37-41.

Fehlen, F. (2006), "Le rapport du Cesije sur l'enseignement des langues. Un guide pour la 'jungle des langues'", *Lëtzebuerger Land*, 53(2), pp. 14-15.

Fehlen, F., Piroth, I. and Schmit, C. (1998), "Les langues au Luxembourg", in Estgen, P. (ed.), *Le sondage "Baleine". Une étude sociologique sur les trajectoires migratoires, les langues et la vie associative au Luxembourg*. Luxembourg: Service Socio-Pastoral Intercommunautaire (SESOPI) Centre intercommunautaire.

Folscheid, M., Pirsch, F. and Botzler, U. (2004), "Integrationssprache Luxemburgisch". Raus aus dem Abseits. *Télécran*, 8, pp. 24-29.

Goedert, J. (2006), "English, here we come ...", *Lëtzebuerger Land*, 53(4), p. 15.

Goullier, F., Cavalli, M., Maradan, O., Perez, C. and Thalgott, P. (October 2005), "Rapport du groupe d'experts: Grand-Duché de Luxembourg. Profil des politiques linguistiques éducatives". Strasbourg: Council of Europe Language Policy Division.

Goullier, F., Cavalli, M., Maradan, O., Perez, C. and Thalgott, P. (2006), "Profil de la politique linguistique éducative. Grand-Duché de Luxembourg". Strasbourg/Luxembourg: Council of Europe Language Policy Division/MENFP.

Hansen-Pauly, M.-A. (2002), "The languages of literature as a reflection of social realities and traditions in Luxemburg", in Schmeling, M. and Schmitz-Emans, M. (eds.), *Multilinguale Literatur im 20. Jahrhundert*. Würzburg: Verlag Königshausen & Neumann.

Hartmann-Hirsch, C. (1994), "Les exclus de l'enseignement", *Forum*, 156, pp. 27-32.

Hartmann-Hirsch, C. (1998), "Affirmer le rôle du luxembourgeois", *Lëtzebuerger Land*, 51, pp. 10-11.

Lanners, M., Boehm, B., Freiberg, M., Levy, J., Origer, M.-P., Unsen, M. and Vallado, D. (2005), *Les chiffres clés de l'éducation nationale. Statistiques et indicateurs. Année scolaire 2003-2004*. Luxembourg: Service de Coordination de la Recherche et de l'Innovation Pédagogiques et Technologiques(SCRIPT)/MENFP.

Martin, R. (1995), "Prévention de l'échec scolaire et de la marginalisation des jeunes dans la période de transition de l'école à la vie adulte et professionnelle – Étude de la politique et des pratiques au Grand-Duché de Luxembourg". Luxembourg: Centre d'études de populations, de pauvreté et de politiques socio-économiques.

Maurer-Hetto, M.-P., Wirth, A., Burton, R., Heinen, S., Mertens, P., Roth-Dury, E. and Steffgen, G. (2003), *Description et évaluation de la lecture à la fin de l'enseignement primaire*. Luxembourg: SCRIPT/MENFP.

Milmeister, M. and Williamson, H. (eds.) (2006), *Dialogues and networks. organising exchanges between youth field actors*. Esch-sur-Alzette/Luxembourg: Editions PHI (ScientiPHIc, Youth Research Monographs, vol. 2).

Ministère de l'Éducation nationale et de la Formation professionnelle (MENFP) (2005), *Rapport d'activité 2004*. Luxembourg: MENFP.

Piroth, I. and Fehlen, F. (2000), *Les langues dans les offres d'emploi du Luxemburger Wort (1984-1999)*. Luxembourg: Centre de recherche public Gabriel Lippmann – Cellule STADE.

Service central de la Statistique et des Études économiques (STATEC) (2004), *Annuaire statistique du Luxembourg*. Luxembourg: STATEC.

Tonnar-Meyer, C. (2003), "Lëtzebuergesch als Integratiounsfacteur am ëffentlechen Enseignement", in Melusina Conseil (ed.), *Actes du cycle de conférences. Lëtzebuergesch: quo vadis?* Luxembourg: Imprimerie Victor Buck.

Trausch, G. (1986), "La situation du français au Luxembourg: une prééminence précaire dans un pays d'expression trilingue", in Arend, C., Fantini, E., Heinen, S., Melan, F., Obertin, M. and Reding, P. (eds.), *Le français à l'école primaire.* Luxembourg: MENFP.

Weber, J.-J. (2006), "Le rapport du Cesije sur l'enseignement. Le dit et le non-dit", *Lëtzebuerger Land*, 53(3), p. 15.

Weitzel, V. (2002), "Le statut du luxembourgeois (et ses pratiques orales et écrites)", in Melusina Conseil (ed.), *Actes du cycle de conférences. Lëtzebuergesch: quo vadis?* Luxembourg: Imprimerie Victor Buck.

APPENDIX I

Report of the European Youth Research Partnership Seminar on Social inclusion and Young People: executive summary

Helen Colley, Bryony Hoskins, Teodora Parveva and Philipp Boetzelen

1. Both the Council of Europe and the European Commission regard social inclusion as a central policy goal, essential to social cohesion. Increasingly, employment and economic growth are seen as crucial to achieving this goal. Participation in civil society is also regarded as an important element, especially for the youth sector.
2. Despite more than a decade of policy attention to the problem of social exclusion, polarisation between the life chances of different groups of young people is increasing. It is spatially concentrated in some regions and neighbourhoods, linked to social class. It is also racialised, gendered and related to other inequalities such as disability. Some young people in Europe feel unable to influence mainstream political processes, and withdraw from conventional political participation.
3. A generic, top-down definition of "social exclusion" is not adequate to represent the whole picture. Researchers are concerned that the vagueness of the term can obscure the many different ways in which exclusion is manifested. Its meanings should acknowledge the multiple dimensions, cumulative combinations, and effects over time and generations of specific forms of disadvantage. Adequate resources are necessary to combat exclusion across this spectrum, to avoid setting marginalised groups in competition with each other, with the risk that some become more deeply excluded and alienated.
4. Economic poverty is a prime cause of social exclusion, although it invariably combines with other social and cultural factors. It is more widespread and more severe among young people than is generally acknowledged. It is also a recurrent experience for many. In contrast with the mid-20th century, when they were less at risk than other groups, young people are now among those most vulnerable to poverty in Europe. Welfare systems designed in that earlier period are inadequate to meet young people's needs today. Moreover, in many countries, young people's eligibility for welfare payments is more restricted than for previous generations, exacerbating their deprivation.
5. Many young Europeans affected by poverty are in some form of education, training and employment. While a lack of job opportunities causes social exclusion for young people, so too do jobs with poor conditions and low wages, low-

quality training opportunities, and stereotyping and discrimination on the basis of race, gender, class and disability. It can be difficult, even with financial incentives, to engage employers in breaking the cycle of exclusion for young people from disadvantaged communities. Activation policies directed solely at young people cannot address these problems, and should be combined with adequate funding for education and training, and active labour market policies directed at employers.

6. European lifelong learning policies have emphasised the need for new policy strategies, including new pedagogies, to create more effective and inclusive forms of learning, but little progress has as yet been made with regard to pedagogy. Recent advances in the theory of learning as a process of situated, social participation offer significant potential for creating more inclusive vocational education and training for young people, if resourced for further research and development. The attention to informal aspects of learning in this approach also indicates new opportunities for the youth sector to contribute to this sphere of young people's learning.

7. Policies directed at supporting young people's transitions (to adulthood and from school to work) are less effective if based on outdated assumptions that these transitions are linear. "Yo-yo" transitions in and out of independence or formal systems of education, training and employment are increasingly common. Young people encounter barriers due to systems that are insufficiently flexible to provide multiple points of re-entry. Policy measures for disadvantaged youth have a greater effect when they form part of a co-ordinated and integrated youth strategy that can address the de-standardisation of youth transitions and varied constellations of disadvantage across countries.

8. Despite the growing breadth of opportunities for young people, these are not equally available to all. In some countries, there is a trend towards restricting individual autonomy in youth transitions. Participatory approaches, which focus on the strengths of young people rather than their deficits, and which offer a real choice of transition options and the possibility of step-by-step engagement, are more likely to mediate successfully between systemic and subjective interests.

9. Racism, xenophobia, and gender-related discrimination and violence are major contributing factors to social exclusion. Evidence suggests that they are endemic in the education system, and that attempts to challenge them on an individual basis are ineffective without broader efforts to eradicate institutional discrimination. Attention also needs to be paid to the barriers they present to equitable labour market access.

10. Some policies intended to promote social inclusion have had unintended, counterproductive consequences, reinforcing rather than reducing social exclusion, and imposing negatively stereotyped identities on some young people. Common factors appear to be: a failure to involve disadvantaged youth in devising and revising policies for inclusion; insufficient attention to empowering excluded youth; and individualised responses inappropriate for tackling forms of exclusion that are systematised and/or structural. Social exclusion is the consequence of a political economy in which some groups secure privilege and exert power at the expense of others, however unwittingly, and policy attention needs to be directed to mitigating such practices (for example, institutional racism).

11. Longer term, holistic initiatives, which account for the complex and lengthy transitions required by the most vulnerable young people, are more helpful than expectations of rapid results. Critical to such interventions are the quality of young people's relationships with practitioners, and the credibility and relevance of what is on offer to them through systems of personal support, social provision, and education, training and employment. Respecting young people's confidentiality, and avoiding stigmatisation, are also crucial to establishing this trust.
12. Multi-agency strategies for social inclusion may be more effective than single-agency initiatives. Early evidence from such approaches suggest that they offer a more holistic response to young people's needs, and maximise the effective use of local resources and the sharing of good practice. However, they require substantial time and funding, and champions at senior management level, to overcome inter-professional boundaries and ethical conflicts, "initiative fatigue", the uncertainty of short-term funding, and user-dependency. While they often have a positive focus on developing local social capital, this should not be treated as a substitute for state funding to support disadvantaged young people.
13. Some effective transformations for socially excluded young people have been produced by the self-organisation of marginalised groups to empower themselves, protest publicly against discrimination and exclusion, and take more direct forms of political action. In some cases, such movements have been highly successful in engaging with policy makers to promote positive change.
14. Given the limitations of a single seminar, there are important issues relating to social inclusion and young people that are not addressed here. Vocational education and guidance is one of the most significant, and its absence reflects a need to support more research in this area. However, a wealth of evidence about the importance of career guidance, especially in relation to the relaunched Lisbon Strategy for growth and jobs, is provided by the recent international policy reviews published by the OECD and by CEDEFOP.
15. Open and productive dialogue between researchers, policy makers and practitioners is vital in this important area of concern. Policy makers and practitioners need to take account of the full range of evidence in planning and implementing initiatives, while research training should include building the capacity to engage effectively with policy and practice.
16. Further research is needed at all levels from local to European to determine more fully the extent, variety, causes and consequences of social exclusion for young people, and to develop effective measures and flexible pathways with multiple entry points to help young people out of social exclusion. Investigation of subjective, local and particular experiences of social exclusion is essential alongside large-scale investigation of trends.

APPENDiX ii

Recommendations from the European Youth Research Partnership Seminar on Social inclusion and Young People

1. Further research should be funded at local, regional, national and European levels to determine more fully:

- the extent of social exclusion for young people;
- the variety of its manifestations (including those which are less visible, or recurrent);
- the range of causes of social exclusion and their compound effects;
- longer-term consequences of social exclusion for young people;
- effective measures to prevent young people becoming socially excluded;
- flexible pathways with multiple entry points to help young people out of social exclusion.

2. More comprehensive research data and analyses are needed to inform better-calibrated policies that can address varied forms of social exclusion and new factors or causes. Research methods should be developed to reveal the compound effects of different contributing factors, long-term exclusion, relative poverty, and recurrent episodes of poverty and exclusion. There is a need for both large-scale quantitative survey evidence of trends, and smaller-scale qualitative evidence of young people's subjective experiences of social exclusion.
3. Authoritarian strategies towards socially excluded young people are economically costly, and may be counterproductive. Social inclusion policies should pursue opportunity-focused strategies, not only in terms of learning and employment, but also by providing constructive leisure and volunteer activities, and opportunities for civic and political participation at local, national and European levels. These have to be open to all and indicators should be developed to measure progress in this regard.
4. Prejudice, stereotyping, discrimination and violence on the basis of ethnicity, gender, social class, disability and sexual orientation are major causes of social exclusion. Policy initiatives should challenge these barriers within "mainstream" society, in order to foster social inclusion.
5. Vocational education and training (VET) policies should support research and development of new pedagogical approaches, drawing on theories of situated learning and social participation in communities of practice, in order to create better quality and more inclusive forms of VET. Collaboration between VET pedagogues and the youth sector should be encouraged, so that youth-work

expertise in informal and non-formal learning can contribute to these developments.

6. Policies to improve VET provision will not engage young people or ensure their social inclusion unless there are sufficient, decent, adequately-paid jobs for them. This may require regulation of the labour market.
7. Social inclusion policies should address the fact that many young Europeans in poverty are not "non-participants", but are already in some form of education, training or employment. Measures should be taken to ensure that young people engaged in learning and work are not socially excluded through poverty or other factors.
8. Policies for social inclusion should include specific attention to the needs of young people, since they are one of the groups most vulnerable to poverty and exclusion. This should form part of a co-ordinated and integrated youth strategy that responds to the de-standardisation and non-linearity of youth transitions.
9. Policies for social inclusion must also address the systemic and structural causes of social exclusion. In respect of the crucial issue of ensuring greater and more equitable access to the labour market, attention should be paid to activation measures directed at the demand side (employers) as well as to the supply side (young people). More effective measures are needed to ensure the co-operation of employers in reducing social exclusion.
10. Welfare systems should be reformed to provide adequate social protection for young people, recognising their particular vulnerability to poverty.
11. Policy initiation and development should involve the democratic participation of young people affected by social exclusion, and should aim to empower these groups. Policy makers should engage in dialogue with independent movements of young people campaigning against aspects of social exclusion as a means to develop policy, and provide funding for constructive measures they initiate.
12. Policy makers should consider longer-term, holistic initiatives rather than simplistic "quick fixes" of limited benefit. They should avoid piecemeal or short-term funding that results in the loss of successful initiatives and good practice. Multi-agency strategies should be funded adequately to resource the inter-professional learning and networking necessary to their effective and ethical functioning. While attention to "soft" outcomes from these strategies, such as increased social capital, is to be welcomed, policies should not treat this as a reason to reduce state funding in support of disadvantaged groups or communities.
13. There is a need for more open and productive dialogue between researchers, policy makers and practitioners. Policy makers and practitioners need to take account of the full range of evidence in planning and implementing initiatives. Research training for Ph.D. students should include developing the knowledge of policy-making institutions and processes and the skills of engaging effectively with policy. Researchers should also develop parallel skills and knowledge to engage with practitioner communities. Policies in higher education, especially quality reviews of research, should ensure that recognition is given to academics' engagement with policy and practice development on a par with the publication of academic papers.

List of contributors

Daniel Blanch is director of research at CIDEFA Research Center on Youth in Santiago de Compostela, Spain. He has participated in various political science, sociology and interdisciplinary conferences, focusing on current tendencies among youth in Europe. Within the framework of the Youth Research Partnership, he recently published "Between the traditional and the postmodern: political disaffection and youth participation in Galicia" in *Revisiting youth political participation*, edited by J. Forbrig, and published by the Council of Europe. He has also published on nationalism and federalism. His current interests span issues relating to youth transitions and attitudes, particularly as Europe moves towards an integrated political and economic system.

Philipp Boetzelen holds a Masters degree in Political Science and Hispanistics. He is currently co-ordinating the European Knowledge Centre for Youth Policy (www.youth-knowledge.net) within the Partnership on Youth between the Council of Europe and the European Commission. Previously he worked as a lecturer on German language and civilization in Brazil and France. His areas of interest include youth policy as well as economical transformations, indigenous people and social movements in Latin America. His publication on the conflict between Mapuche Indians and the state in Chile is forthcoming.

Helen Colley, Ph.D., is Senior Research Fellow at the Education and Social Research Institute at Manchester Metropolitan University, England. Her doctoral study, published by RoutledgeFalmer as *Mentoring for social inclusion: a critical approach to mentoring relationships*, is a groundbreaking study of engagement mentoring that questions prescriptive policy approaches to working with disadvantaged young people. Helen won the British Educational Research Association Award for Best Doctoral Dissertation in 2002 for this work. Her main research interests focus on the intersection of class and gender in post-compulsory education and transitions for young people, and in lifelong learning, and she has published widely on these topics. Her research has also explored the inter-relationship of formal, non-formal and informal learning (*Informality and formality in learning*, with P. Hodkinson and J.Malcolm, published by the Learning and Skills Development Agency). She has contributed to the Youth Research Partnership of the Council of Europe and the European Commission since 2004, and convened its seminar on social inclusion.

Eldin Fahmy, Ph.D., is a Research Fellow in the School for Policy Studies, University of Bristol, England, working on the analysis of poverty, citizenship and exclusion. His specific research interests include: youth, participation and social justice; rural poverty; youth, poverty and the life course; poverty, place and area-based initiatives; fuel poverty; and anti-poverty strategies. He convenes undergraduate

courses in "Demography, the life course and social policy" and postgraduate courses in "Quantitative analysis" and "Census and spatial analysis".

Rachel Gorman, Ph.D., is a Postdoctoral Fellow of the Women and Gender Studies Institute of the University of Toronto, Canada, where she is currently completing a two-year project funded by the Social Sciences and Humanities Research Council of Canada. Her current research deals with gender, disability and transnationality. Rachel has created the first two courses for a new "Disability Studies" stream of the Equity Studies programme at the University of Toronto: "Disability culture and social change" and "Theoretical approaches to disability and work". Rachel also teaches courses on violence against women, gender and disability, and feminist research methods, and supervises upper-year students doing independent research courses. As an activist, she has at various times worked on disability rights, anti-psychiatry, trade unionist, anti-war and anti-violence campaigns. Rachel is a choreographer and a member of the Canadian Alliance of Dance Artists.

Bryony Hoskins is currently working for the European Commission DG JRC Centre for Research on Lifelong Learning (CRELL) on the research topics of active citizenship and learning to learn. She is currently leading a research project, Active citizenship for democracy, with the purpose of creating indicators on active citizenship and education and training for active citizenship. Before arriving at CRELL she was employed by the Council of Europe as the Research Officer responsible for co-ordinating youth research in the framework of the Partnership between the European Commission and the Council of Europe on Youth. Thus she was responsible for organising research seminars, publications and a European research network. She was also the creator of the knowledge management system the European Knowledge Centre for Youth Policy (www.youth-knowledge.net). Previous to this she worked as evaluator for youth non-formal training programmes including the Council of Europe and European Commission Advanced Training of Trainers in Europe and for the European Commission SALTO training courses. Bryony completed her Ph.D. at Brunel University, UK, in Sociology and Social Psychology.

Amineh Kakabaveh is a social welfare worker in the Botkyrka community of Stockholm, Sweden. She works mainly with families, children and young people in vulnerable situations. She is also involved in various voluntary organisations in Sweden who work towards equality and integration for newcomers. She is a broadcaster for a community-based radio programme, in Kurdish, called Dengi Zhinan (Voice of Women Radio); she leads a project against "honour crimes" among youth; and she is the Swedish president of the anti-sexist, anti-racist movement "Neither Whores Nor Submissive". She has an MSc in Social Work from the University of Stockholm, and her dissertation focused on these issues.

Anna Kende, Ph.D., is a research fellow at the Department of Social Psychology of the Institute of Psychology, Hungarian Academy of Sciences. She received an MA in Psychology from the Eötvös University, Budapest, and an MA in Gender Studies from the Central European University. She completed her Ph.D. in Psychology at the University of Pécs. Most of her research projects focus on the social inclusion of Roma in Hungary, especially in connection to educational integration. She teaches social psychology courses for students of psychology, and is involved in educational policy projects of the Ministry of Education in Hungary.

Siyka Kovacheva, Ph.D., is a lecturer in sociology at the University of Plovdiv and Head of the New Europe Centre for Regional Studies in Bulgaria. Her areas of expertise are youth transitions to adulthood, civic participation, unemployment and self-employment, family life, including gender and intergenerational relations and youth policy. Her publications include *Exploring the European youth mosaic: the social situation of young people in Europe* (with L. Chisholm), Strasbourg: Council of Europe, 2002; *Keys to youth participation in eastern Europe*, Strasbourg: Council of Europe, 2000; and *Youth in society: the construction and deconstruction of youth in east and west Europe* (with C. Wallace), Macmillan, 1998.

Beatrix Niemeyer, Ph.D., is a senior researcher at the Institute for Technical Vocational Education at the University of Flensburg, Germany. The focus of her research and teaching is on school-to-VET-transition as a troubled process and its crucial implications for social inclusion, which she has studied from a comparative European perspective as well as at national level. She has co-ordinated a series of EU and national projects which aimed at generating new ways of thinking about the situation of young people who are at risk of (or experiencing) social exclusion by applying the perspective of situated learning. The results are published in Evans and Niemeyer (eds., 2004), *Reconnection – Countering social exclusion through situated learning* and in Niemeyer (2004) "Transcultural recommendations for the improvement of the quality of re-integration programmes" (www.biat.uniflensburg.de/biat.www/index_projekte.htm). In *Neue Lernkulturen in Europa* (Niemeyer, ed., 2005) she engages in a critical discussion of the current VET reforms in Europe.

Teodora Parveva is a research analyst at the European Unit of Eurydice, the network for education policies in Europe. Previously she worked on studies and reports on increasing access to education for under-represented groups (Organisation for Economic Co-operation and Development (OECD), Directorate for Education), and on patterns of participation in lifelong learning across Europe (European Commission, Joint Research Centre-Ispra). Teodora studied social sciences and history at the Central European University in Budapest from where she holds an MA and a Ph.D. degree.

Kate Philip, Ph.D., is a Senior Research Fellow in the School of Education at the University of Aberdeen, Scotland, and an associate of the Centre for Research on Families and Relationships. Her professional background is in community development and health promotion, and she has been involved in the development of health strategy and participatory approaches to studying health needs. Her doctoral study was an examination of informal mentoring which explored the perspectives of young people and adults. Her current research interests lie in the fields of young people, families, health and well-being, and youth mentoring. She was awarded a user fellowship by the UK Economic and Social Research Council (ESRC) Health Variations programme and, with co-authors, the 2004 Douglas Leather Award by the board of the international journal, *Health Education Research*. She is currently co-ordinating a collaborative seminar series, funded by the ESRC on "Researching Youth Mentoring – Building theory and building evidence".

Axel Pohl, educationalist, is working as a senior researcher at the Institute for regional Innovation and Social Research (IRIS) in Tübingen, Germany. His research interests consist of young people's transitions to work, especially those from an immigrant or ethnic minority background, and the evaluation of transition policies from a youth perspective. He has recently published "Learning biographies. Case studies into dimensions and prerequisites of competence development", in: Walther, A., du Bois-Reymond, M. and Biggart, A. (eds.); *Participation in transition*; and a thematic study on policy measures concerning disadvantaged youth, together with Andreas Walther.

Lorna Roberts, Ph.D., is a Research Fellow in the Education and Social Research Institute at Manchester Metropolitan University, England. Her main research interests revolve around issues of social justice, race ethnicity and education. Research projects have focused on the recruitment and retention of minority ethnic trainee teachers, and evaluation of race equality policies in schools within a Local Education Authority in the North of England. Currently, she is involved in a project, Inside Exclusion, funded by the Joseph Rowntree Foundation, which explores the impact of poverty on education and seeks to learn lessons from agencies and learning mentors who work with young people excluded from mainstream education. She also teaches research methodology to postgraduate and undergraduate students. Her most recent publications include: (2006) *Discourse, resistance and identity formation*, Trentham Books, edited with Jerome Sattherthwaite and Wendy Martin; (2006) "Did they Jump or were they pushed? Reasons why minority ethnic trainees withdraw from initial teacher training courses", *British Educational Research Journal*, 32(3), pp. 387-410, with Tehmina Basit et al.; and (2005) "Critical theories of race and their use in social science research: stories from the field," with Laurence Parker in Bridget Somekh and Cathy Lewin (eds.), *Research methods in the social sciences*, Sage Publications.

Janet Shucksmith is Professor in Public Health at the University of Teesside, England. She is also an Associate Director of the Centre for Research on Families and Relationships. Her current work is on the negotiation of responsibility for children's and young people's health and well-being between families and the state, particularly around issues of sexual health and mental well-being. Earlier longitudinal studies gave rise to a book, *Young people's leisure and lifestyles*, and a series of articles examining the variations in young people's health behaviours and the relationship of these to family patterns and parenting styles. Subsequent qualitative studies have sought to enable young people to find a voice in discussing their own health and health education needs. She has undertaken projects for the Scottish Executive, the Health Education Board for Scotland and the Joseph Rowntree Foundation.

Janet Tucker, Ph.D., is Senior Research Fellow at the Dugald Baird Centre for Research on Women's Health within the University of Aberdeen's Department of Obstetrics and Gynaecology, Scotland. She undertakes people-based research focusing on the health of women as individuals and as populations. Her recent research projects include a focus on sustainable maternity service provision in remote and rural areas in Scotland.

Edwin van Teijlingen, Ph.D., is Reader in the Department of Public Health at the University of Aberdeen, Scotland. His research interests include the social and cultural aspects of health, health care and health promotion, particularly: (1) disability; (2) children and smoking; and (3) sociology of midwifery. He has been co-ordinator of the MSc in Health Services and Public Health Research course, and has been involved in the design and implementation of Phases I and II of the Community Group's contribution to the new medical curriculum at the University of Aberdeen.

Andreas Walther, Ph.D., is a Senior Researcher at the Institute for Regional Innovation and Social Research (IRIS) and works as a part-time Lecturer for Social Pedagogy at the University of Tübingen, Germany. In addition, he has been co-ordinating the European Group for Integrated Social Research (EGRIS). In this context he has been conducting comparative research on the changed transitions of young people towards work and adulthood. Issues have been the traps of exclusion in so-called integration policies (*Misleading trajectories – Integration policies for young adults in Europe*, edited with Barbara Stauber et al., published by Leske & Budrich, 2002); young people's experiences with transition policies (*Young people and contradictions of inclusion*, edited with Andreu López Blasco and Wallace McNeish, published by Policy Press, 2003); and the potentials of participation and informal learning in young people's transitions into the labour market (*Participation in transition*, edited with Manuela du Bois-Reymond and Andy Biggart, published by Peter Lang, 2006). He has also co-ordinated a thematic study on policies for disadvantaged youth for the European Commission and participated in the Council of Europe's international review of the youth policy of the Slovak Republic.

Christiane Weis, MA ULB (Brussels), has worked at the CESIJE – Centre d'études sur la situation des jeunes en Europe (Luxembourg) – as a sociologist and youth researcher since 2002, conducting projects on youth leisure time and language education policies. Her main research interests are: social inclusion, sociology of language and language education, migration and gender equality. Major works include: Weis, C. (2001), "La discrimination des femmes au travail: le cas de la Commission européenne. Mémoire présenté en vue de l'obtention du grade de Licenciée en Sciences sociales, orientation sociologie". Bruxelles: ULB – Université libre de Bruxelles; Weis, C., Milmeister, M. and Willems, H. (2004), *Aspekte jugendlicher Freizeitwelten in der Stadt Luxemburg. Eine qualitative Analyse auf der Basis von Gruppendiskussionen*. Luxemburg: CESIJE; and Berg, C. and Weis, C. (2005), *Sociologie de l'enseignement des langues dans un environnement multilingue. Rapport national en vue de l'élaboration du profil des politiques linguistiques éducatives luxembourgeoises*. Luxembourg: MENFP/CESIJE.

Howard Williamson is Professor of European Youth Policy in the School of Humanities, Law and Social Sciences at the University of Glamorgan, Wales. He previously worked at the universities of Oxford, Cardiff and Copenhagen, as well as being a practising youth worker for over twenty years. He has contributed to youth policy development in Wales, the UK and across the countries of the European Union and the Council of Europe. He is currently a member of the Youth Justice Board. He has published extensively on a range of youth questions, especially concerning social exclusion, including *The Milltown Boys revisited* (Berg, 2004), a follow-up study of a group of men he first met twenty-five years earlier when they were young offenders in the mid-1970s. He was awarded a CBE in the New Year's Honours List 2002 for services to young people.

Sales agents for publications of the Council of Europe
Agents de vente des publications du Conseil de l'Europe

BELGIUM/BELGIQUE
La Librairie Européenne -
The European Bookshop
Rue de l'Orme, 1
B-1040 BRUXELLES
Tel.: +32 (0)2 231 04 35
Fax: +32 (0)2 735 08 60
E-mail: order@libeurop.be
http://www.libeurop.be

Jean De Lannoy
Avenue du Roi 202 Koningslaan
B-1190 BRUXELLES
Tel.: +32 (0)2 538 43 08
Fax: +32 (0)2 538 08 41
E-mail: jean.de.lannoy@dl-servi.com
http://www.jean-de-lannoy.be

CANADA
Renouf Publishing Co. Ltd.
1-5369 Canotek Road
OTTAWA, Ontario K1J 9J3, Canada
Tel.: +1 613 745 2665
Fax: +1 613 745 7660
Toll-Free Tel.: (866) 767-6766
E-mail: order.dept@renoufbooks.com
http://www.renoufbooks.com

CZECH REPUBLIC/ RÉPUBLIQUE TCHÈQUE
Suweco CZ, s.r.o.
Klecakova 347
CZ-180 21 PRAHA 9
Tel.: +420 2 424 59 204
Fax: +420 2 848 21 646
E-mail: import@suweco.cz
http://www.suweco.cz

DENMARK/DANEMARK
GAD
Vimmelskaftet 32
DK-1161 KØBENHAVN K
Tel.: +45 77 66 60 00
Fax: +45 77 66 60 01
E-mail: gad@gad.dk
http://www.gad.dk

FINLAND/FINLANDE
Akateeminen Kirjakauppa
PO Box 128
Keskuskatu 1
FIN-00100 HELSINKI
Tel.: +358 (0)9 121 4430
Fax: +358 (0)9 121 4242
E-mail: akatilaus@akateeminen.com
http://www.akateeminen.com

FRANCE
La Documentation française
(diffusion/distribution France entière)
124, rue Henri Barbusse
F-93308 AUBERVILLIERS CEDEX
Tél.: +33 (0)1 40 15 70 00
Fax: +33 (0)1 40 15 68 00
E-mail: commande@ladocumentationfrancaise.fr
http://www.ladocumentationfrancaise.fr

Librairie Kléber
1 rue des Francs Bourgeois
F-67000 STRASBOURG
Tel.: +33 (0)3 88 15 78 88
Fax: +33 (0)3 88 15 78 80
E-mail: francois.wolfermann@librairie-kleber.fr
http://www.librairie-kleber.com

GERMANY/ALLEMAGNE AUSTRIA/AUTRICHE
UNO Verlag GmbH
August-Bebel-Allee 6
D-53175 BONN
Tel.: +49 (0)228 94 90 20
Fax: +49 (0)228 94 90 222
E-mail: bestellung@uno-verlag.de
http://www.uno-verlag.de

GREECE/GRÈCE
Librairie Kauffmann s.a.
Stadiou 28
GR-105 64 ATHINAI
Tel.: +30 210 32 55 321
Fax.: +30 210 32 30 320
E-mail: ord@otenet.gr
http://www.kauffmann.gr

HUNGARY/HONGRIE
Euro Info Service kft.
1137 Bp. Szent István krt. 12.
H-1137 BUDAPEST
Tel.: +36 (06)1 329 2170
Fax: +36 (06)1 349 2053
E-mail: euroinfo@euroinfo.hu
http://www.euroinfo.hu

ITALY/ITALIE
Licosa SpA
Via Duca di Calabria, 1/1
I-50125 FIRENZE
Tel.: +39 0556 483215
Fax: +39 0556 41257
E-mail: licosa@licosa.com
http://www.licosa.com

MEXICO/MEXIQUE
Mundi-Prensa México, S.A. De C.V.
Río Pánuco, 141 Delegacíon Cuauhtémoc
06500 MÉXICO, D.F.
Tel.: +52 (01)55 55 33 56 58
Fax: +52 (01)55 55 14 67 99
E-mail: mundiprensa@mundiprensa.com.mx
http://www.mundiprensa.com.mx

NETHERLANDS/PAYS-BAS
De Lindeboom Internationale Publicaties b.v.
M.A. de Ruyterstraat 20 A
NL-7482 BZ HAAKSBERGEN
Tel.: +31 (0)53 5740004
Fax: +31 (0)53 5729296
E-mail: books@delindeboom.com
http://www.delindeboom.com

NORWAY/NORVÈGE
Akademika
Postboks 84 Blindern
N-0314 OSLO
Tel.: +47 2 218 8100
Fax: +47 2 218 8103
E-mail: support@akademika.no
http://www.akademika.no

POLAND/POLOGNE
Ars Polona JSC
25 Obroncow Street
PL-03-933 WARSZAWA
Tel.: +48 (0)22 509 86 00
Fax: +48 (0)22 509 86 10
E-mail: arspolona@arspolona.com.pl
http://www.arspolona.com.pl

PORTUGAL
Livraria Portugal
(Dias & Andrade, Lda.)
Rua do Carmo, 70
P-1200-094 LISBOA
Tel.: +351 21 347 42 82 / 85
Fax: +351 21 347 02 64
E-mail: info@livrariaportugal.pt
http://www.livrariaportugal.pt

RUSSIAN FEDERATION/ FÉDÉRATION DE RUSSIE
Ves Mir
9a, Kolpacnhyi per.
RU-101000 MOSCOW
Tel.: +7 (8)495 623 6839
Fax: +7 (8)495 625 4269
E-mail: orders@vesmirbooks.ru
http://www.vesmirbooks.ru

SPAIN/ESPAGNE
Mundi-Prensa Libros, s.a.
Castelló, 37
E-28001 MADRID
Tel.: +34 914 36 37 00
Fax: +34 915 75 39 98
E-mail: libreria@mundiprensa.es
http://www.mundiprensa.com

SWITZERLAND/SUISSE
Van Diermen Editions – ADECO
Chemin du Lacuez 41
CH-1807 BLONAY
Tel.: +41 (0)21 943 26 73
Fax: +41 (0)21 943 36 05
E-mail: info@adeco.org
http://www.adeco.org

UNITED KINGDOM/ROYAUME-UNI
The Stationery Office Ltd
PO Box 29
GB-NORWICH NR3 1GN
Tel.: +44 (0)870 600 5522
Fax: +44 (0)870 600 5533
E-mail: book.enquiries@tso.co.uk
http://www.tsoshop.co.uk

UNITED STATES and CANADA/ ÉTATS-UNIS et CANADA
Manhattan Publishing Company
468 Albany Post Road
CROTTON-ON-HUDSON, NY 10520, USA
Tel.: +1 914 271 5194
Fax: +1 914 271 5856
E-mail: Info@manhattanpublishing.com
http://www.manhattanpublishing.com

Council of Europe Publishing/Editions du Conseil de l'Europe
F-67075 Strasbourg Cedex
Tel.: +33 (0)3 88 41 25 81 – Fax: +33 (0)3 88 41 39 10 – E-mail: publishing@coe.int – Website: http://book.coe.int